MW00655356

HITLER'S SECRET COMMANDOS
OPERATIONS OF THE K-VERBAND

HITLER'S SECRET COMMANDOS

OPERATIONS OF THE K-VERBAND

by
Helmut Blocksdorf

Translation by
Geoffrey Brooks

Pen & Sword
MILITARY

First published in Great Britain in 2008 by
Pen & Sword Military
an imprint of
Pen & Sword Books Ltd
47 Church Street
Barnsley
South Yorkshire
S70 2AS

ISBN 978-1-84415-783-9

A CIP catalogue record for this book is
available from the British Library.

Typeset in 11/13pt Times by
Concept, Huddersfield, West Yorkshire

Printed and bound in England by
CPI UK

For a complete list of Pen & Sword titles please contact
PEN & SWORD BOOKS LIMITED
47 Church Street, Barnsley, South Yorkshire, S70 2AS, England
E-mail: enquiries@pen-and-sword.co.uk
Website: www.pen-and-sword.co.uk

Contents

List of Illustrations

One of the volunteers for one-man torpedo training was Oberfähnrich (Senior Midshipman) Helmut Bierbrauer. He made available many photos for this book.

A pilot climbs into the carrier-torpedo, the *Neger*.

The one-man torpedo *Neger* under way. The aiming prong is clearly seen ahead of the pilot's cupola. The photograph gives an idea of how limited was his vision, having to orient himself from a frog's perspective. No periscope, compass or radio was fitted.

Torpedo mechanics of K-Flotilla 361.

Men of K-Flotilla 361 about to entrain for Anzio.

A half-track towing vehicle with two *Negers* under tarpaulin in a pine wood near Anzio.

ObltzS Johann-Otto Krieg, awarded Knight's Cross on 12 August 1944 as Kapitänleutnant and Chief of K-Flotilla 361. Training leader and Staff duty, K-Verband.

Oberfernschreibmeister (Senior Warrant Officer – Telex) Herbert Berrer, recipient of the Knight's Cross, 5 August 1944.

US soldiers inspecting a stranded *Neger* at Anzio.

Neger pilot Walter Gerhold after the award of the Knight's Cross for sinking a frigate on 6 July 1944. Comrades bear him aloft on their shoulders. Despite heavy losses, the will to fight and *esprit dè corps* remained firm amongst K-Verband volunteers to the end.

17-year-old Matrose Horst Berger was a volunteer attached to K-Flotilla 361. He piloted a *Neger* one-man torpedo at Anzio and on the Normandy invasion coast. He is seen here in the uniform of Bootsmannsmaat wearing the Iron Cross First and Second Class and on the right pocket the German Cross in Gold, the highest decoration for bravery in the Third Reich.

The wreckage of a *Marder* destroyed by explosives.

Linse-pilot Oberbootsmann Herbert Berrer (left) with *Neger*-pilot Walter Gerhold (right) on the occasion of their award of the Knight's Cross. Between them is ObltzS Leopold Koch, chief of K-Flotilla 361.

Grossadmiral Dönitz awards decorations to members of K-Flotilla 361. Far left is Korvettenkapitän Frauenheim.

More than 50 years later: former Kriegsmarine one-man torpedo pilots before a *Marder* in the Bundesmarine Weapons School at Eckernförde. Amongst them are Horst Berger (4th from left),

Helmut Bierbrauer (5th from left) and Walter Gerhold (6th from left).

Korvettenkapitän Hans Bartels.

Midget German submarine Type XXVIIA *Hecht.*

The *Molch* cabin. Above it projects the steel cylinder in which were located the periscope and magnetic compass. The rectangular glass panel below the tower is a modern addition to afford museum visitors a view into the cabin interior.

A finished *Seehund* on trestles either at the shipyard or in the Konrad bunker, Kiel, May 1945.

Seehund on sea trials.

Kptlt Hermann Rasch.

Fregattenkapitän Albrecht Brandi.

Midget submarine *Delphin* in towing trials or seawater tests, 1944/ 1945.

Profiles of *Schwertwal* I.

Key: P = pilot room; Pk = plexiglass cupola; Z = engineer's control room; R = regulating tank; T = Ingolin tanks; B = Fuel tanks; M = Walter machinery room; H = stern section; K = master compass; vT = forward trim tank; hT = aft trim tank; SR = rudder; SF = stabilizers; VT = forward hydroplanes; To = Walter torpedoes (K-Butt)

Schwertwal II with improved streamlining.

Key: P = pilot's cabin; Z = engineer's control room; R = regulating tank; T = 1 to 10 Ingolin fuel tanks (10 tonnes); B = fuel tanks, 1 tonne Deakalin; M = engine room (Walter turbine drive); H = stern section; K = master compass; vT = forward trim tank; hT = stern trim tank

A model of the *Manta.*

The amphibious craft *Seeteufel* with caterpillar track/propeller drive.

Key: BM = gasoline motor; Z = control room (2 men); R = regulating tank; Bk = battery room; H = stern section; EM = electric motor; RA = caterpillar tracks; WB = breakwater; Pk = plexiglass cupola; SM = snorkel mast; S = periscope; A = Ultra short wave antenna; SR = rudder; SF = stabilizers; VT = forward hydroplanes; To = 2 torpedoes

Profile of the Deep-Sea submersible *Grundhai* designed for salvage work down to 1,000 metres.

Key: 1 = pressure hull for divers; 2 = casing and dive tanks; 3 = access
hatch with cupola for all-round vision; 4 = electro-magnetic grab;
5 = three searchlights; 6 = stabilizers; 7 = active hydroplanes;
8 = caterpillar tracks; 9 = lifting hooks.

Rittmeister Konrad von Leipzig, chief of the Brandenburg *Küstenjäger*.

Kptlt Helmut Bastian, awarded the Knight's Cross on 3 November
1944 as head of a *Linse*-flotilla.

LtzS Alfred Vetter, Group Leader, K-Flotilla 211, was decorated
with the Knight's Cross on 12 August 1944 for his *Linse* attack
of 8 August. He was also mentioned in the Wehrmacht report of
15 September 1944.

A *Linse* unit before an operation.

Kapitän zur See Werner Hartmann (photo dates from when
Korvettenkapitän).

An Italian MTSMA explosive boat being lowered into the water.

Proven K-Verband *Linsen* operators with Grossadmiral Dönitz, here
seen greeting LtzS Alfred Vetter.

MTSM boats on exercise.

A heavy assault boat of the Brandenburg *Küstenjäger* unit in the
harbour at Santa Lucia.

Frogmen at a display for Grossadmiral Dönitz (second right) showing
an interested admiral – possibly Heye – his watertight Junghans
diver's watch/compass.

This photograph of German frogmen was taken on 16 November
1944, probably during training at List on Sylt. Notice the Junghans
watches.

A frogman demonstrating the swimming position. Notice the veil
camouflaging the face.

German frogmen wearing full-face mask.

The Dräger compact oxygen rebreathing apparatus.

Key A = airbag; B = mouthpiece; C = tap; D = flexible hose;
E = demand valve; F = potash cartridge; G = nose clip; I = spiral
wire; J = oxygen bottle; K = hand-wheel; L = opening; M = spring
clip; N,O = belt; P = protective goggles; Q = excess pressure
release valve

German frogmen in captivity at Remagen respond to questions. Other
sources state that these are *Linse* pilots.

Foreword

The Kriegsmarine was the last Second World War European naval power to introduce ultra-light naval forces. Not until a year before the German capitulation was the *Kommando der Kleinkampfverbände* (Small Naval Units Command – for the purposes of simplicity referred to as K-Verband Command in this book) formed. It was a fighting force of which little is known to the present day. The reason for its creation was the superiority of the Allied surface navies, the falling success rate of the S-boat Arm as the principal Kriegsmarine coastal weapon of attack* and the increasing build-up of powerful enemy seaborne groups in areas close inshore.

Within a brief period a multitude of different systems, ranging from one-man torpedoes to midget U-boats, assault boats and explosive boats was designed, built and made operational. Frogmen and naval assault troops completed the new Arm of service. The K-Verband, consisting mainly of volunteers, had a standing force of 16,000 men of all ranks by the war's end. These volunteers were by no means the

---

*The author does not mention the S-boat Arm anywhere. The S-boat Arm was the coastal equivalent of the U-boat Arm. In 1944 some North Sea areas were restricted for S-boats to allow the K-Verband to operate freely there. By 1944 and early 1945 U-boats were rarely to be found in the North Sea or English Channel, and were not there very often beforehand. At Anzio, S-boats were warned off the operational area so as not to 'queer the pitch' of the K-Verband. Accordingly, where appropriate, I have translated 'U-boat' either as 'S-boat' or to include it.

'Last Gasp Fanatics' which they were so often accused of being, but in the main young men who saw no opportunity of advancement for themselves in their original units and who wanted to defend the Reich on its foremost front line. Thirst for adventure also played its part. These lone warriors were neither kamikazes nor suicide bombers. The Kriegsmarine was opposed to human sacrifice. It was a maxim of the K-Verband that every front-fighter should be guaranteed the high probability of surviving an attack. Each vessel would be so constructed and each operation so planned that the participants had a good chance of returning to their own lines afterwards. If discovered by the enemy defences, were pursued and saw no possibility of escape, they were to surrender. Despite their valour, the men of the K-Verband were unable to bring about change in Germany's fortunes. The enemy superiority in personnel and materials was too great.

Various individual accounts of the German K-Verband have been published, but a comprehensive history has not been prepared until now. In this volume the author has attempted to cover the entire spectrum, but is aware that despite his thorough research, and interviews with former serving K-men, more clarification is needed in some cases.

His thanks are due to everybody who has supported him in this work. Especial thanks are due to Herr Döringhoff and Frau Notzke of the Bundesarchiv/Militärarchiv Freiburg, who made files available to him: to Frau Pyrus at the Library of the Marineschule Mürwik, for her rapid and unbureaucratic support in the lending out of specialist literature, and to former K-men Walther Gerhold, Helmut Bierbrauer, Horst Berger and Manfred Lau, who provided valuable information.

Helmut Blocksdorf,
Berlin, summer 2003

Chapter One

The Development of Maritime Ultra-Light Forces in Italy and Great Britain

Italy

The Royal Italian Navy was the first to develop ultra-light forces and created an arm of service which achieved great success. In the First World War the Italians built fast, midget torpedo boats for anti-submarine work. These were the so-called MAS boats (*Motoscafi anti sommergibili*) which were spectacularly successful in the late stages of the war.

On the night of 9 December 1917, MAS 9 and MAS 13 were towed by coastal torpedo boats from Venice to Trieste and then proceeded alone on their mission. After passing through a minefield, MAS 9 entered the Bay of Muggia to sink the Austrian coastal armoured ship *Wien*.

On 14 May 1918 an Italian wood-built motor torpedo boat, *Grillo*, entered the main Austro-Hungarian naval base at Pola. *Grillo* had a very shallow draught, a U-shaped cross-section and a very long bow. Caterpillar chains were fitted to the sides of the vessel to enable beam and net barriers to be dragged aside. *Grillo* was towed from Venice to just off Pola by MAS 95 and MAS 96, passed an obstruction of beams and two net boxes to penetrate the harbour, but was discovered and shelled. The crew was captured. In another attack on 11 June 1918

1

in the Strait of Otranto, the midget torpedo boats MAS 15 and MAS 21 obtained two hits on the flagship *Szent Istvan*, which sank two hours later.

Cdr Rafaele Rosetti, an engineer, and Lt Dr Rafaele Paolucci, a Medical Corps surgeon, developed the first operational manned torpedo *Mignatta* (Leech), a torpedo-shaped vessel crewed by two pilots in divers' suits seated one behind the other. Propulsion was provided by a B57 torpedo motor regulated by a cranked valve and supplied from a 205-atm. compressed air tank. A four-blade propellor gave a speed of three to four knots. Range was eight to ten kilometres.

The operational concept was to make surprise night attacks unseen on warships in harbour or at anchor. The *Mignatta* had to be towed to the operational area, only the last leg of the approach being under its own power. In place of the usual warhead two limpet mines of a total 170 kgs trotyl were to be attached to the hull of the target. The crew wore diving gear. After months of training, on the night of 1 November 1918 a *Mignatta* penetrated the harbour at Pola and sank one of the most modern ships of the Austro-Hungarian Fleet, the 21,370-tonne battleship *Viribus Unitis*.

Between the World Wars the Italians worked to improve their ultra-light units and Rosetti's ideas were revived. At La Spezia Naval College, Lt Tilo Tertiosi and colleague Elviro Tianosi used Rosetti's experience to design a new submersible version of *Mignatta*. Under the tightest secrecy two prototypes were constructed in the submarine weapons factory at San Bartolomeo. This led to the series production of the so-called SLC (*Siluro a Lenta Corsa* = slow running torpedo). Improved breathing apparatus allowed the divers a stay of six hours under water. The SLC was nicknamed *Maiale* (pig) by its riders because of the difficulty in steering it. The SLC was a development of the 6.7 metre long, 53.3 cm diameter standard torpedo. Drive was provided by a silent running 60-volt, 30-element accumulator battery, the electric motor had automatic transmission switching for four speeds. Range was ten sea miles at 2.5 knots. The designed diving depth of 30 metres was not easy to trim and deeper dives often occurred on operations involuntarily or by intention. The warhead was an explosive charge of 300 kgs easily released from a bayonet lock. The seating for the crew was similar to *Mignatta*. Crew dress was a light Belloni diving suit of rubberized linen, hood and diver's mask. The breathing apparatus used a compressed air/potash cartridge combination giving a diving depth of 40 metres.

On either side of *Maiale* were located two quick-dive tanks and a small pump for diving and surfacing. The pilot operated a control stick controlling the rudders and dive-planes. The instrument board contained the magnetic compass, a voltage-ampère meter, depth and pressure gauges and a spirit level. The two crew had the following respective tasks. The pilot sat forward behind a protective torpedo and steered. At his back and serving as a rest was the main ballast tank with discharge vent and flap. This tank deflected water away from the co-pilot. His back rest was the container for tools and the compressed air bottle. The co-pilot trimmed the torpedo, operated the rapid-dive tank and at the target was responsible for detaching the explosive, fixing it on the hull of the target ship and setting the timer.

Because of their very short range, SLCs were towed to the immediate vicinity of a target. In 1940, three SLCs were carried openly on the submarine *Ametista* commanded by Prince Julio Borghese, later chief of the Italian K-force. The future carrier-submarines had two transport and pressure containers fitted, one each fore and aft of the conning tower so as not to prejudice dive-readiness. Each cylinder had space for one SLC. Later boats had four such containers, two on the saddle-tanks either side.

During the war the Italians developed two more types of SLC carriers. In April 1941 there appeared Motoscafi Turismo Lento (MTL), a one-man torpedo boat 9.5 metres in length, 2.85 metres in the beam and displacing 7.3 tonnes. This boat could carry two SLCs and crews. A winch was provided for lowering and raising the SLC. The MTL had a total range of 100 sea miles.

In 1943 the large speedboats MS 74 and MS 75 *Canguri* (kangaroo) transporters entered service. They had a built-in launching ramp from which two SLCs, two MTLs or a squad of frogmen armed with explosives and equipment could be brought to an operational area and disembarked. An improved design appearing at the end of the war, SSB, with greater operational depth and speed did not enter service.

The Italians also led the field in the development of explosive boats. The idea originated with Air Force General Armadeo, Duke of Aosta, who wanted a fast motor boat armed with an explosive charge capable of being carried between the floats of a seaplane. Approaching the target the boat-pilot would jump clear to be picked up by another boat. This bold technique was never tried out in practice.

Last on the scene came *Moscafo Turismo Modificato* (MTM), an explosive boat 5.2 metres long and 1.9 metres in the beam. Its 2,500 cc Alfa Romeo motor provided the flat-bottomed, keel-less craft with a top speed of 36 knots. 300 kgs of TNT with hydrostatic contact fuse was located at the bow. The backrests astern served as the pilot's life raft.

Pilots and frogmen received training in special camps such as the camp on the estate of Count Solverino by the river Serchio for torpedo charioteers. Other locations included the Naval Divers' School at La Spezia, the Frogman School at Valdagno/Vicenza and the Naval Swimmers' School at Termoli.

First chief of the Italian K-force was Captain Muriano (1940). He was succeeded to head the 10th MAS (*Decima Flottiglia Motoscafo d'Assalto* = explosive boat) flotilla by Prince Julio Valerio Borghese, former commander of the carrier-submarine *Scire*. Borghese, married to a Russian princess, a granddaughter of the Czar, hated the British and French and dreamed of a Mediterranean dominated by Italy.

After Italy entered the war on Hitler's side on 10 June 1940, the Italian K-force stepped up its preparations for a maritime offensive against Britain in the Mediterranean, but months passed before it was ready.

On the night of 25 March 1941 off Crete, six MTM explosive boats were transported by the destroyers *Francesco Crispi* and *Quintino* from the Greek island of Leros to Suda Bay, an important supply harbour for the British. Their purpose was to attack British warships and merchant vessels at anchor. The MTMs penetrated the bay unobserved and evaded the three barriers of nets and beams. Once inside they sank the large tanker *Pericles*, a large freighter, and damaged the heavy cruiser HMS *York* so severely that she had to be run aground.

A few months later 10-MAS Flotilla attacked Malta. On the night of 25 July 1941 eight explosive boats and two SCLs (torpedo charioteers) entered Valletta harbour and although spotted by radar one SCL and two MTMs blew up the harbour barrier. The blast collapsed the St Elmo bridge and blocked the path of the boats in the inner basin. The coastal batteries then opened fire, and all craft were lost, MAS 451

4

and 452 falling victim to fighter bombers next day. Casualties were fifteen dead and eighteen taken prisoner.

On the night of 20 September three SCLs achieved a spectacular success at Gibraltar where they sank the tanker *Fiona Shell*, 2,444 gross tons, the large freighter *Durham*, 13,052 gross tons and the naval oiler *Danby Dale*, 15,893 gross tons. Two freighters, *Forrest* and *Aberdeen* were damaged. The total bag of sunk or damaged was 50,000 gross tons.

Decima Flottiglia was successful again on 18 December 1941 when Borghese set down three SCLs from a carrier submarine off the Egyptian port of Alexandria. The torpedo riders penetrated the heavily-guarded main naval base of the British Mediterranean Fleet and attached explosive charges to the hulls of three warships and a tanker. The battleships *Queen Elizabeth* and *Valiant* sank but remained upright on an even keel in the harbour shallows. The destroyer *Jervis* and the Norwegian tanker *Sagona*, 7,554 gross tons, also suffered serious damage.

In July 1942 Italian frogmen struck at Gibraltar again. Operating from neutral territory at Villa Carmela near Algeciras they entered the naval harbour to sink the freighters *Meta*, 1,575 gross tons, *Sama*, 1,799 gross tons, *Empire Snipe*, 2,497 gross tons and *Baron Douglas*, 899 gross tons. This success was followed by further spectacular commando operations by frogmen and torpedo riders against Allied shipping in Algiers harbour on 12 December 1942 when a mixed group sailed from La Spezia on 5 December aboard the carrier submarine *Ambra* and were disembarked 800 metres off the port. The frogmen left the boat first through a diving chamber located below the foredeck and, using a swimming float, headed for the target with pencil detonators and hollow charge limpet mines. The three 'human torpedoes' were then lifted from their pressure-resistant containers and placed on the water. The operation was led by Lt Luigi Bercoli, pilot of the leading SCL. The frogmen's target was the shipping anchored on either side of the harbour basin. The SCLs were to attack large transports and tankers if they could not get past the net barrier into the warship harbour. The attack was very successful, the tankers *Pennsylvania* and *Bristol*, the freighters *Ocean Vanquisher*, *Berto*, *Empire Centaur* and *Madan* all being claimed sunk, while the freighters *Harmattan* and the tanker *Indian* were seriously damaged. 56,000

5

tons of shipping was thus claimed sunk or damaged. Only eleven of the special force of fifty-four returned. Sixteen were lost and twenty-seven captured.[1]

Decima MAS Flottiglia undertook two further operations against Gibraltar. On 8 May 1943 three SCLs sank the merchant vessels *Pat Harrison*, 7,053 gross tons, *Mahsud*, 7,540 gross tons and *Camerata*, 4,875 gross tons in the roadstead: in the attack of 2 August 1943 three SCLs sank or damaged the tanker *Thorshovdi*, 9,944 gross tons and the freighters *Harrison Gray Otis* and *Standridge*, a total of 13,151 gross tons.

The last operation of importance also took place in August 1943 when frogman Lt Ferraro, posing as a staff member at the Italian consulate in Alexandrette, used explosive charges to sink the ships *Orion*, *Kaituna* and *Fernplant*, a total of 15,000 gross tons.

Decima Mas Flottiglia was responsible for sinking or damaging seriously at least four major warships and twenty-seven merchant vessels of 225,298 gross tons. Of these the torpedo riders or charioteers (SCL) struck at thirteen ships of 142,771 gross tons, the frogmen ten ships of 38,411 gross tons. Working in concert, frogmen and SCLs sank or damaged three ships of 13,092 gross tons, while MTM explosive boats accounted for four ships of 31,024 gross tons.[2]

Great Britain

Shortly after World War I, in the course of their support for the 'Whites' against the Bolshevists in Russia, the British attacked the Red Fleet in an operation which can be classified as a naval commando raid, although there was no official structure behind it.

In the summer of 1919, the Royal Navy Light Cruiser Squadron and Destroyer Flotilla blockaded the Red Fleet at Kronstadt. The numerous shallows and strong shore defences prevented the British entering the bay. They decided instead to enter the harbour using seven Type CM1B-4 coastal motor torpedo boats and destroy there the anchored battleships, a cruiser and a submarine depot ship. On the night of 17 August, four boats got into the harbour. One was disabled by defensive fire, the other three sank the depot ship *Pamiat Asov* and seriously damaged the old battleships *Andrei Pervosvani* (18,900 tons displacement) and *Petropavlovsk* (23,606 tons).

6

From then, and well into the Second World War, the Royal Navy, possessing the world's most powerful Fleet, relied on its conventional superiority and showed disdain for the idea of developing ultra-light forces. Not until the successful attack by Italian SCLs at Alexandria was the British Admiralty prepared to revive the concept. On the initiative of Prime Minister Winston Churchill, the *Service for Special and Hazardous Operations* was formed. Responsible for overall control and expansion of the service was Admiral Sir Max Horton, C-in-C Submarines.

In 1940 the British had begun work on the Type X midget submarine. Some 15 metres long and 1.65 metres in the beam, it carried an armament of two 2-ton explosive devices in a half-nutshell shape carried on the hull. The lack of offensive capability for the open sea identifies the purpose of the boat as an inshore raider. It had a crew of four: commander, first officer, mechanic and diver.

A second design, the Mark I or 'chariot', was a copy of the Italian SCL, several of which had been captured by the Royal Navy. The British version differed from the original only in its method of propulsion and additional diving and trim planes. The Mark III improved version dating from February 1944 had a speed of 4.5 knots, a range of 30 sea miles and carried one ton of explosives.

A development halted in 1943 was the trouble-plagued *Welman* craft. It saw action just once, in November 1943 when after entering the Kriegsmarine harbour at Bergen it was captured by the Germans. Some British coastal MTBs were based on Italian MAS boats.

In April 1942 the British set up a special naval operations unit at Fort Blockhouse, Portsmouth, the first volunteers being mainly divers and submariners. The training was harsh, resulting in many dropouts and numerous fatal accidents. Only 25% of applicants completed the course to be distributed to units at the beginning of July 1942. By September the men stood at readiness for frontline operations.

In contrast to the Italians, the British concentrated into their commando raids assault troops of regiment strength. This proved very costly in men and equipment, but it was 1943 before their midget submarines idea found favour.

The first maritime commando operation, *Claymare*, targeted the German-held Lofoten Islands off Norway. On 1 March 1941, two cross-Channel ferries carrying 600 men left British ports with an escort of five destroyers. Two cruisers ran distant escort. The main aim of the expedition was to capture an Enigma coding machine and so read German naval signals, in particular those to and from U-boats. Surprise landings occurred on 3 March when the fish factory was destroyed and the factory ship *Hamburg* (2,800 gross tons) and several coasters sunk as a diversionary measure. After a hectic battle 213 prisoners were taken but no Enigma machine, the captain of the armed trawler *Krebs*, Hans Karpinger, having thrown the equipment overboard. He was killed before he could destroy the secret documentation, however. The latter included two rotor-wheels, the code for the day, code tables, ring settings and the 1941 plugging connections. It was a capture of inestimable worth, for with this material within a week the cryptanalysts at Bletchley Park were able to read all German Enigma radio traffic for the month of February for the region 'Home Waters'. They had not solved the principle of the Enigma coding machine, but it gave them insight into the Kriegsmarine organisation and its encoding procedures. Contrary to the claims made for them, British mathematicians did not 'crack' the radio code, it was the capture of Enigma machines and coding materials which provided the 'code breakers' with their success.

British air reconnaissance had confirmed a network of *Freya* radar installations along the French coast, and on 27 February 1942 a commando raid was arranged to capture the technology. A 120-man parachute unit led by Major John D. Frost headed for Le Havre in twelve old Whitley bombers and parachuted into deep snow near the village of Bruneval, about 19 kilometres north of Le Havre. After a firefight the occupants of the German radar station were captured and parts of a Luftwaffe *Würzburg* radar seized. Taking two prisoners, the commandos made for a bay in which six landing craft awaited. British casualties were two dead, six captured, but they learned a great deal about the stage reached by German radar technology.

Another commando raid followed on 26 March 1942 aimed at destroying the naval drydock at St Nazaire on the Biscay coast principally to dissuade the Germans from sending the battleship *Tirpitz* into the Atlantic. A total of 268 commandos and 353 Royal Navy personnel left Falmouth aboard the condemned destroyer *Campbeltown*, an MTB and 16 landing craft, escorted by two destroyers. The German ensign was flown as a ruse. A British submarine acted as a radio beacon to draw the squadron to the Loire Estuary. At 0130 hrs on 28 March the British force was discovered and an hour-long battle ensued during the course of which the *Campbeltown*, loaded with 3 tons of TNT, rammed the lock gates to the dry dock. The detonator for the explosive charge failed, but finally blew up eight hours later, achieving the purpose. In the land fighting the Germans gained the upper hand. Their losses were 67 dead, 62 seriously and 74 lightly wounded. Some 171 of the 353 naval personnel and all but five of the 268 commandos were killed. Four small landing craft returned to England.

The next major commando operation was Dieppe. Operation Jubilee ended in a catastrophe with very high casualties. On 19 August 1942, two Canadian brigades, an armoured regiment with 55 tanks, about 5,000 men, 1,000 British marines and an American reconnaissance and diversion unit of fifty Rangers landed with the alleged objective of destroying German coastal batteries and D/F stations, to bring back prisoners for interrogation and – in preparation for a later invasion – to plumb the depths of the German defences[3]. The landing force consisted of eight destroyers, nine infantry landing ships, 39 coastal defence vessels and 179 other landing craft. The operation was covered by fighters from RAF 2-Group. The brainchild of Vice-Admiral Lord Louis Earl Mountbatten, the raid was a miserable failure.

The destroyer *Berkeley* and 33 landing craft were sunk and 106 fighters shot down. Inf. Regt 571/302 Inf. Div. estimated that 4,350 Allied soldiers were killed or taken prisoner. Large quantities of weapons and equipment were seized together with secret files on the structure of the British commando force. This was later used as the basis for the German K-Verband. German losses were 600 dead or taken prisoner and 48 aircaft lost.

In November 1942, the British began a different approach with Operation *Frankton*, an attack on Bordeaux, one of the largest French harbours and the principal docks for the import by German blockade-runners of important raw materials from Japan and the Far East. Bordeaux is about fifty miles inland from the Bay of Biscay along the Gironde estuary. In preparation for this operation, in July 1942 the *Royal Marine Boom Patrol Detachment* was set up at Southsea under Major H.G. Hasler. The unit was to paddle Cockle Mark II canoes, folding boats with rubber-reinforced linen sides and a flat wooden bottom, into the harbour at Bordeaux, and attack merchant shipping there using limpet mines with time-fuses. The canoeists wore water-proof clothing and were armed with .45 Colt revolvers and commando knives. For communication amongst themselves they were equipped with whistles which imitated the cry of a gull.

On 30 November 1942 Major Hasler and his team of eleven canoeists shipped aboard the submarine *Tuna* with their canoes and were set down in the water five miles off the Gironde on the night of 6 December. The first canoe broke up, leaving only ten men to make the attack. At high tide on the coast two other canoes were damaged beyond repair, leaving only three to continue. It was planned to reach the harbour in three days, paddling by night, hiding up and sleeping in the reeds along the river bank by day. No arrangements existed to retrieve the commandos on the completion of the mission, afterwards they were to make their own way to neutral Spain and from there to Gibraltar.

Only the leader's canoe containing Major Hasler and Private Sparks reached the operational area. They attached limpet mines to six ships, of which four flooded and a mine destructor vessel was seriously damaged. While Hasler and Sparks were helped to cross the Pyrennees into Spain by the French Resistance and reached Gibraltar, the other four men were captured by the Germans and later shot as spies.

After several unsuccessful attempts, on the night of 2 January 1943 several British 'chariots' entered the Sicilian harbour of Palermo and sank the reconnaissance cruiser *Ulpio Trajano* and damaged the merchant ship *Viniuale*.

In the highly secret Operation *Source* on 11 September 1943, six Midget-Class submarines, X-5 to X-10, each with a crew of four, were towed by submarine to the Norwegian coast. X-6 and X-7 entered Asewn Fjord, an arm of Trondheim Fjord where the battleship *Tirpitz* was anchored. The mere presence of *Tirpitz* represented such a threat to British interests that they were detemined to sink her.

On 22 September towards 0700 hrs the two midget submarines tangled in the box of anti-torpedo netting protecting the battleship. This caused great difficulties because the X-crew were not fully trained in operating the craft. X-6 was difficult to steer and trim, struck an underwater obstruction, broke surface and was spotted. The boat dived and the crew succeeded in attaching two 2-ton mines to *Tirpitz'* hull. After that X-6 shot to the surface and had to be abandoned. The crew was taken prisoner and brought aboard *Tirpitz*.

Meanwhile X-7 had also reached the target and mines were placed on the battleship's hull. On leaving this submarine became entangled again in the nets. While attempting to free the boat, the X-6 mines exploded, setting off the X-7 mines at the same time. The powerful shock wave tossed X-7 to the surface where the submarine was subjected to MG fire. One man escaped to be taken prisoner. *Tirpitz* survived the detonation of 8 tons of explosives but the damage put her out of commission for a considerable period. The attack on the battleship by midget submarines demonstrated to the Kriegsmarine for the first time the effectiveness of ultra-light naval forces.

The British were becoming increasingly aware of the usefulness of these operations, and in the autumn of 1943 the Admiralty devised Operation *Barbara* in which, as originally conceived, *Welman Craft*-Type midget submarines were to disrupt German shipping in the Nowegian coastal skerries.

On 20 November 1943 MTBs towed four *Welman* boats[4] numbered W-45 to W-48 with Norwegian crews from Lunna Voe on the Shetlands to the small uninhabited island of Hjelteholmen. W-47 and W-48 were to destroy the Labsevaag floating dock at Bergen, the other two boats had orders to attack shipping in Pudde Fjord and the Dokkeskjär Quay. The attack was planned for the night of 21 November. W-46 entangled in a net barrier in Westby Fjord, was forced to surface and was seen by German guard boat NB59, compromising the entire operation. Lt Pedersen attempted to scuttle W-46 but both he and the craft were captured. W-46, now a German prize, became the subject of thorough research by the Kriegsmarine. The British persevered with midget submarine operations and in April 1944 X-24 finally destroyed the large floating dock at Bergen, the German freighter *Bärenfels* (7,569 gross tons) going down with it.

In 1943/1944 the number of commando operations in the Mediterranean theatre spiralled. Various British units, amongst them commandos, SAS and SBS, played a role in operations where the sinking of shipping was less important than striking at enemy morale. Accordingly in March 1944, Major Leigh-Fermor received orders to kidnap the Commandant of Crete, General Friedrich Wilhelm Müller, and bring him to Cairo. On 4 February 1944 a Wellington bomber left

11

Barid in Egypt with Major Fermor and two Greeks, Paterakis and Tyrakin, aboard. For reasons unknown only the major parachuted down to land on the Lazithi plain. The two Greeks followed a fortnight later aboard a motor boat.

It was soon discovered that General Müller was no longer in Crete and the orders were changed to kidnap his successor, General Heinrich Kreipe, CO 79 Inf. Div. With the help of the Crete Resistance, the general's daily schedule was established. His quarters were at the Villa Ariadne at Knossos. On 26 April the kidnappers, disguised as German feld-gendarmes, stopped the general's car and spirited him over the mountains to an MTB waiting on the coast. From Mersa Matruh in Libya he was flown to Cairo. Although the commando operation was well-planned it failed in its objective in that Kreipe was not liked by the German occupying army and his disappearance was greeted with relief.

In the early summer of 1944 the British transferred their midget submarine activities to the Far East. Using the further development XE types which had been taken to Australia, at Singapore they sank the Japanese heavy cruisers *Takao* and *Nachi*. The charge opened a hole 18×9 metres in the hull of *Takao*. Amongst other successes in the Far East was the sinking by a 'chariot' in October 1944 of the Dutch steamers *Sumatra* and *Volpi*, prizes taken by the Japanese.

Notes

1 An extensive portrayal of this and other Mediterranean operations appears in Manfred Lau's outstanding work *Schiffssterben vor Algier, Kampfschwimmer, Torpedo-reiter und Marine-Einsatz-Kommandos im Mittelmeer, 1942–1945*, Motorbuch Verlag, Stuttgart, 2001.

2 At the end of the 1940s, based on the Italian model, the Israeli Navy formed an explosive-boat unit attached to 13th Flotilla. A former member of *Decima MAS Flottiglia* served as instructor. Amongst the operational successes of the Israeli explosive boats was the sinking of the Egyptian flagship *Amir El Farouk*, 1,440 tons, in October 1948. Eldar, M: *Israels geheime Marinekommandos – Geschichte, Einsatz, Hintergründe der Flotilla 13*, Motorbuch Verlag, Stuttgart 2000.

3 It would appear that the purpose of the Dieppe Raid was to assess if it would be possible to capture a German-held port on the French coast when the invasion took place. When Dieppe proved this virtually impossible, the artificial *Mulberry* harbours were designed for the purpose.

4 The *Welman-Craft* was a one-man submarine displacing two tons. Length 6.1 metres with charge, beam 1.06 metres. Propulsion: 2.5 hp electric motor, 40 volt 220 amp/hr battery. Speed (submerged): 3 knots. Range (surfaced): 36 sea miles at 4 knots. Armament: 1×540 kg explosive charge. Tested safe depth: 35 metres. Builder: Morris Car Plant, Oxford.

Chapter Two

Development and Structure
of the K-Verband

The bottling-up of Germany's remaining battleworthy surface ships, the general turn of the tide against the U-boats and S-boats from about May 1943, led to the appointment of Vizeadmiral Weichold, Admiralty Staff Officer at Fleet Staff, as Special Naval Chargé d'Affaires to investigate within the SKL ways of intensifying the naval war and to make proposals relevant thereto.

The further construction of major warships had long been abandoned, and it was from the conviction that sooner or later the Allies would launch an amphibious landing on one of the German-occupied coasts that the plan to develop ultra-light forces emerged. The successes of the Italians and British had provided evidence of what might be achieved. The basic idea was to set up a small force of outstandingly well-trained and absolutely dependable commandos to carry out numerous one-off operations. Variations each using the element of surprise were to so disconcert the enemy as to force him either to tie down or disperse his forces so that they would not then be available at the decisive location.

The Fleet instructions introduced the following avenues of pursuit:

1. To design and develop a viable midget U-boat for single operations.
2. To develop a small torpedo-carrier for such purposes as those for which the Italians had built one-man torpedoes and explosive boats.

15

3. To form a naval assault corps on the lines of the British marine commandos to strike ashore against strategically or tactically important targets in the enemy area after disembarking from naval vessels.

Many apparently viable projects could not be realized because of the difficulties in production. A large number of the new craft thus tended to be of an improvised nature. Despite lack of experience and incomplete trials, the war situation forced the introduction of such machines as could be made available.

The K-Verband was not structured in the manner originally envisaged. German industry was still able to turn out a few weapons in large numbers but small runs of a multitude of different designs was beyond it. Admiral Weichold concentrated too deeply on the theoretical side at the expense of the practical and was soon relieved of office by Dönitz to be replaced by KptzS Hellmuth Heye as K-Verband chief on 20 April 1944.

Heye was a very capable naval officer. As a Kapitänleutnant in 1932 he had commanded the four boats of the Torpedo Boat Half-Flotilla. In the autumn of 1939 he took command of the heavy cruiser *Admiral Hipper* and, besides minor Fleet operations, from the bridge of his flagship led Warship Group 2 (*Admiral Hipper* and four destroyers) from Cuxhaven to Trondheim during Operation *Weserübung*, the invasion of Norway. Later he served as Chief of Staff to C-in-C Baltic and in the West. From 1942 he was attached to Naval Group Command South and for a period was deputy to Admiral, Black Sea and Chief of Staff Group North. He remained head of the K-Verband from his appointment until the capitulation.

Heye looked for experienced naval officers with sea-time for his Command Staff and the developing K-Staffs. His Chief of Staff was Knight's Cross holder FKpt Fritz Frauenheim.

Frauenheim had been a U-boat commander since 1936. Immediately before his appointment to K-Verband he had been Senior Officer, 29 U-Flotilla at La Spezia. His personal tally was 23 ships of 113,133 gross tons sunk, he damaged the cruiser *Belfast*, a destroyer and a netlayer. Another Staff Officer and former U-boat commander was FKpt Albrecht Brandi, holder of the Knight's Cross with Oak-leaves, Swords and Diamonds (together with Wolfgang Lüth the only holder

16

of this high award in the Kriegsmarine). Brandi was later to command the *Seehund*-type pocket U-boats. Knight's Cross holder KKpt Hans Bartels was appointed to lead the *Biber* midget submarine flotillas, in the development of which he had participated personally. As commander of the minesweeper *M1* during the Norwegian campaign he had captured a Norwegian destroyer and an entire torpedo boat flotilla. Chiefs of the tactical K-Staffs for individual operational areas were KptzS Böhme (West) later also succeeding Hartmann (Levico/ Italy and then Pola/Adriatic), Beck (Nord-Oslo), Musenberg (Holland) and Düwel (Skagerrak).

K-Verband Command was officially constituted on Hitler's birthday, 20 April 1944. Heye adopted an unconventional approach and had his men trained in an atmosphere reminiscent of a secret society. There was very little formal indoctrination, insignia of rank were not worn and ranks not observed. For the production and testing of the new weapons speed was of the essence. For this purpose Heye had received special plenipotentiary powers from Dönitz and had direct contact to industry.

The K-Verband was divided into various Commands according to necessity and was composed of the Command Staff, Quartermaster Staff, K-Verband Court, Personnel Bureau and the scientific and technical branches. Below this umbrella came:

- Recruitment, formative and training divisions together with training and completion camps and K-bases
- Training branches
- Testing branches
- Naval Operations Commands
- K-Regiment (mot)
- K-Verband vehicles
- Naval meteorological office and the Kriegsmarine meteorological-oceanographic work group.

K-Staffs were set up as tactical Staffs for individual areas. The Staff HQ of Admiral, K-Verband and all other headquarters and camps received a codename ending in the suffix *koppel* (meadow). The most important of these were:

Strandkoppel:	K-Verband HQ and Staff, Timmendorfer Strand, Hotel/Pension *Zur Kammer*, finally at Plön
Blaukoppel:	Lübeck-Schlutup
Gelbkoppel:	Mommark/Denmark
Graukoppel:	Wilhelmshaven
Grünkoppel:	Priesterbeck/Waren, Speck/Müritzsee, Kolding/Denmark
Schwarzkoppel:	Bad Sülze/Rostock
Weisskoppel:	List/Sylt
Fischkoppel:	Cuxhaven/Oxstedt
Dorfkoppel:	Surendorf/Eckernförde
Netzkoppel:	Plön
Neukoppel:	Neustadt/Heligoland
Raumkoppel:	Schönberg/Mecklenburg
Steinkoppel:	Lübeck
Frogmen:	Lehrkommando 700 Venice/Italy
	Lehrkommando 702 Bad Tölz
	Lehrkommando Valdagno/Italy

K-Verband Command operated various ships and boats as auxiliaries, target vessels and for training purposes. Four security groups of Security Division 12 were part of K-Verband. Special squads were formed according to the exigencies of the service. In the framework of the wartime K-Organisation, the following types of craft were either operational or in the testing stage:

Battery propelled
Neger and *Marder* one-man torpedoes, SCL 'chariot' torpedoes, midget U-boats of the types *Hai*, *Molch* and *Hecht*.

Petrol engine/battery drive
Midget U-boats of types *Biber I, Biber II, Seehund, Seehund II, Schwertwal, Kleiner Delphin* and *Grosser Delphin*.

Surface Craft
Explosive boat *Linse*, small MTBs *Wal III, Schlitten, Seedrache* and *Tornado*.

Amphibious Craft
Amphibien-Panzer, Margel and *Seeteufel*.

Admiral K-Verband, Staff
(German officer ranks are abbreviated hereinafter as follows: Lt (or LtzS) = Leutnant (zur See), Oblt = Oberleutnant, Kptlt = Kapitän-leutnant, KKpt = Korvettenkapitän, FKpt = Fregattenkapitän, KptzS = Kapitän zur See. (The commonest indications of branch which occur following rank are: (MA) = naval artillery, (V) = Administration, (Ing) = Engineer, (S) = Sonderführer, temporary honorary equivalent rank accorded to non-naval personnel co-opted into the Kriegsmarine.)

Admiral, K-Verband – Vizeadmiral Hellmuth Heye (4.44–End)

Chief of Staff – FKpt Fritz Frauenheim (4.44–End)

Command Staff:
Kptlt Klaus Thomsen (7.44–End), Kptlt Wache, (8.44–End), Kptlt(S) Michael Opladen (4.44–End), Kptlt (Ing) Rüdiger Burchards, (7.44–End), Kptlt Friedrich-Wilhelm Schmidt, Kptlt Erich Habelt, Oblt Herberst Mohrstedt, Oblt Hans Gregor, Oblt Wolf Gericke, Oblt Friedrich Wendel, Oblt Kurt Scheifhaken, Lt (Ing) Horst Haug, Lt (Ing) Otto Wolf.

Consultant, Welfare and Wills – Kptlt Hans-Konrad Perkuhn

NSFO (National Socialist Leadership Officer) – KKpt Friedrich von Holzhusen

Command Centre – Oblt Felix Leffin

Press Officer – Oblt Dr Wolfgang Frank

Courier Officer – Oblt Filibert von Du Fresne von Hohenesche

QM-Staff
QM – FKpt Dahle (2.45–End)

K-Verband Engineer – Kptlt (Ing) Kattau (7.44–End)

K-Verband Medical Officers – all rank of Marinestabsarzt: Dr Weyrich (2.44), Dr Armin Wandel (2.44–4.44), Dr Hans-Joachim Richert (4.44–End)

Medical Officer at Staff: Kptlt Dr Gerhard Kowalzig

Lehrkommando 350 – Marinestabsarzt Dr Kundt

Lehrkommandos Blau- and Steinkoppel – Marine-Oberassistenzarzt Dr Maschewski

Lehrkommando 250 – Marineassistenzarzt Dr Tobias Brocher

Lehrkommando Weisskoppel – Dr Friedrich Jung

Mine Defences Officer – Kptlt Moosmann (6.44–End)

Adminstration Officers – KKpt (V) Lüdke (5.44–1.45), KKpt (V) Wicke (1.45–End)

Manager – Marineoberstabsintendant Bleese (4.44–End) and Dr von Harling (1.45–End)

Technical section – KKpt Herbert Burckhardt (4.44–End), Kptlt (Ing) von Rakowski (8.44–End)

Development and Testing Section – Director, Oblt Friedrich Wendel

Scientific Office – Kptlt Mohrstedt (5.44–End)

Personnel Office
Head – Kptlt Rudolf Koehler

Consultant – Oblt Franz Tegtmeyer (2.44–End)

Asst to Director – Lt Karl-August Hoffmann

Personnel Staff – Oblt Friedrich Schätzel, Oblt Hermann Kampe

Court Judge – Marineoberstabsrichter Wiegand

K-STAFFS and DIVISIONS

K-Staff West (HQ Sengwarden)
Senior Officer – KptzS Friedrich Böhme (6.44–10.44)

K-Staff North (HQ Oslo)
Senior Officer – KptzS Wilhelm Beck (10.44–End) (later 1 K-Div. Narvik)

Operations Leader – Kptlt Graf Viktor von Reventlow-Crimine

Senior Officer, K-base Stavanger – Kptlt Bosümer

Senior Officer, sub-office Sengwarden – Kptlt Wilfried Karsten

Officer at Staff – Kptlt Bernhard Hinst

Naval Signals Officers – Oblt Waldemar Heinemann, Oblt Graf Horst von Korthus

Navigation Officer – Lt Götz Hunger

Officer at Staff – Lt Fritz Barthel

K-Staff Skagerrak (HQ Aarhus/Denmark) also K-Staff (Special Purposes)
Senior Officer – KptzS Düwel (11.44–End)

Adjutant – Oblt Konrad Wenzel

Head, Heligoland Base – Kptlt Dr Karl-Heinz Kinscher

K-Staff Holland (HQ Rotterdam, depots at Groningen and Utrecht). Later 5 K-Div. at Ijmuiden
Senior Officer – KptzS Musenberg (8.44–3.45)

K-Staff South (HQ Levico/Italy). Later 6 K-Div at Pola
Senior Officers – KptzS Werner Hartmann (8.44–10.44), KptzS Friedrich Böhme (10.44–End)

Naval Admin Officers – KKpt Hugo Gerdts, Kptlt Günther Thiersch, Oblt Günther Hering

Interpreter – Lt Ritter Emil von Thierry

Supply Officer – Oberfähnrich Wilhelm Gehrke

4 K-Division (Holland)
Senior Officer – Kptlt Helmut Bastian (3.45–End) also Senior Officer, Lehrkommando 200

5 K-Division (Holland)
Senior Officer – FKpt Albrecht Brandi (1.45–End)

Marine-Einstellungsabteilung (Lübeck)
Naval recruitment section.

Commander – Kptlt Heinz Schomburg – (1.44–10.44)

Aufstellungs- und Ausbildungsabteilung
This unit was set up in May 1944, and the *Bereitstellungsabteilung* (Readiness Section) was formed from it in October 1944. The section was split into two parts in November 1944, one part at Kappeln, the other MEK unit at Sonderburg (see below).

Commanders – Kptlt (MA) Buschkämper (5.44–7.44), KKpt (MA) Hans-Hinrich Damm (8.44–11.44)

Ausbildungsabteilung Kappeln
Training section formed in November 1944 by splitting of *Aufstellungs- und Ausbildungsabteilung*.

MEK-Ausbildungsabteilung (Sonderborg, later Silkeborg)
Training section formed November 1944 by splitting of *Aufstellungs- und Ausbildungsabteilung*.

Commanders – KKpt (MA) Hans-Hinrich Damm (11.44–End), KKpt (MA) Buschkämper (4.45–End)

Bereitstellungsabteilung (Readiness Section) Waren/Müritz
Assembled on 1.10.1944 from elements of *Aufstellung- und Ausbildungsabt.* One company of the Readiness Section was transferred from Waren to Flensburg in March 1945. From the remaining parts of the section, Naval Rifle Batallion 979 was formed on 16.4.1945 and fought in Mecklenburg.

Commander – Kptlt (MA) Heinrich Schlüter

K-Regiment (mot)
In the spring of 1944, 3 Vehicle Operations Section was attached to Adm. K-Verband. When 5 Vehicle Operations Section was formed in July 1944, this was also attached to K-Verband.

3 Vehicle Operations Section (Kraftwageneinsatzabteilung)
Commander – KKpt (Ing) Banditt (8.42–10.44)

5 Vehicle Operations Section
Commander – FKpt (Ing) Sandel (7.44–10.44)

In the conference of 12 July 1944, Grossadmiral Dönitz ordered the supply of the following vehicles for the K-Verband: 52 motor-cycles,

75 motor-cycle combinations, 60 saloon cars, 244 3-tonne lorries, 126 5-tonne lorries, 20 commando vehicles, 23 ambulances, 12 fuel tankers, 23 water tankers, 10 workshop vehicles, 23 field kitchen vehicles, 61 radio vehicles, 3 road tugs, 30 MG vehicles, 10 flak vehicles, 60 wheeled towing vehicles, 19 8-tonne road locomotives, 5 18-tonne road locomotives, 54 3-tonne trailers, 52 5-tonne trailers and twelve fuel-tank trailers. In October 1944 3 and 5 Vehicle Operations Sections were merged to form the four sections of K-Regiment (motorized).

K-Regiment (mot)
Commander – FKpt (Ing) Wert (10.44–End) also FI, Staff KdK

Staff Officers at Staff: All KKpt (Ing) – Dipl-Ing. Bräkow, Helmut Eddicks, Grathoff, Heinrich Hartwig, Liebing, Friedrich-Karl Schwarz

The regiment also had a naval signals section and motorized flak unit. In March 1945 4 Vehicle Operations Section was subordinated to K-Verband Command and then renamed Naval Vehicles Section (Special Purposes) OKM.

Vehicle Operations Section
Commander – FKpt (Ing) Banditt (11.44–4.45)

Naval Vehicles Section (Special Purposes) OKM
Commander – FKpt (Ing) Banditt (5.45–End)

LEHRKOMMANDOS (Training Units) AND K-FLOTILLAS

Lehrkommando 200 (Priesterbeck/Waren, later Plön/Holstein)
Training unit for *Linsen* boats formed July 1944

Senior Officers – Kptlt Ulrich Kolbe (7.44), Kptlt Helmut Bastian (7.44–End), from 3.45 also Senior Officer, 4 K-Div.

Flotillas: 211 (7.44), 212 (7.44–End), 213 (7.44–End), 214 (11.44), 215 (11.44–End), 216 (8.44), 217 (10.44), 218 (11.44–End), 219 (1.45–End), 220 (no details)

Lehrkommando 250 (Lübeck-Schlutup)
Training Unit for *Biber* formed August 1944

Senior Officer – KKpt Hans Bartels (8.44–End)

Flotillas: K-Flot. 261 (1.45–End), 262 (1.45–End), 263 (9.44–End), 264 (no details), 265 (2.45–End), 266 (10.44–3.45), 267 (12.44–End), 268 (1945–End), 269 (1945), 270 (1945)

Lehrkommando 300 (Neustadt/Holstein)
Training unit for *Seehund*

Senior Officers – Lt Kiep (6.44), Kptlt Hermann Rasch (7.44–2.45), FKpt Albrecht Brandi (2.45–End) also Senior Officer 5 K-Division.

Flotillas: K-Flot.311 (*Hecht*), 312–316 incl. (*Seehund*)

Lehrkommando 350 (Surendorf)
Training unit for *Neger* and *Marder* formed July 1944

Senior Officers – Kptlt Franke (7.44–3.45), Kptlt Horst Kessler (3.45–End)

Flotillas: K-Flot. 361 (*Neger*: 3.44–End), 362 (*Neger*, 1944–4.45), 363 (*Neger*, 9.44–End), 364 (no details, 7.44–End), 365 (*Marder*, 7.44–End) and 366 (*Marder*, 12.44–End)

Lehrkommando 400 (Surendorf)
Training unit for *Molch*, formed July 1944

Senior Officers: Kptlt Heinz Franke (7.44–3.45), Kptlt Horst Kessler (3.45–End)

Flotillas: K-Flot. 411 (7.44), K-Flot. 412 – this flotilla was divided into K-Flots. 412/1 and 412/2 in November 1944: K-Flot. 412/1 (11.44–End), K-Flot. 412/2 (11.44–4.45), 413 (7.44–End), 414 (no period known), 415 (7.44–End), 416 (11.44–End), 417 (4.45–End)

Lehrkommando 600
Training unit for Assault boats, formed October 1944

Senior Officer – Kptlt Heinz Schomberg (10.44–End)

Flotillas: K-Flot. 611 (7.44–4.45), K-Flots. 611, 612, 613, 614 (period unknown) and K-Flot. 615 (3.45–End)

Lehrkommando 700
Training unit for frogmen, formed June 1944

LK 700, Venice/Italy. From 11.44 List/Sylt

Senior Officers – Marinestabsarzt (Naval-Staff Medical Officer) Dr Wandel (6.44–1.45), KKpt (V) Hermann Lüdke (1.45–End)

LK 702 Bad Tölz (SS), LK 704 Valdagno/Italy

Lehrkommando 800
Training unit for ground staffs and liaison commands

The following officers were trained for various flotillas:

Oblts – Raimund Babinsky, Werner Hollmann, Otto Kansog, Jacon Kaub, Kurt Lössl, Heinrich Müller, Walter Paysan, Friedrich Strehle, Heinrich Wenzke.

Lts: Arnold Aruno, Clemens Hilger, August Jaeger, Berhhard Nadolny, Bruno Schawaller, Heilmut Wessel.

Naval Commandos (Marine-Einsatzkommandos) – MEK
MEK MAREI (Abwehr) Senior Officer – Kptlt (S) Michael Opladen

MEK Black Sea (Abwehr) Senior Officer – KKpt Dr Arnim Roth (6.41–7.43)

MEK MARKO (Abwehr) Senior Officers Kptlt (S) Michael Opladen, Oblt (MA) Broecker

MEK 20 (formed April 1944 renamed from MEK MARKO) Senior Officer – Oblt (MA) Broecker (4.44–End)

MEK 30 Senior Officer – Kptlt (MA) Gegner (1944–End)

MEK 35 Senior Officers – Kptlt Breusch (11.44–3.45), Kptlt Wolfgang Woerdemann (3.45–End)

MEK 40 Senior Officers – Kptlt (MA) Buschkämper (8.44–3.45), Oblt (MA) Schulz (3.45–End)

MEK 60 Senior Officer – Oblt (MA) Prinzhorn

MEK 65 Senior Officer – ObltzS Richert (5.44–End)

MEK 71 Senior Officer – Oblt (MA) Wolters (Operational at latest by 1.45–End)

MEK 80 Senior Officer – Kptlt (MA) Dr Krumhaar (3.44–End)

MEK 85 Senior Officer – Oblt (MA) Wadenpfuhl (1.45–End)

MEK 90 Senior Officer – Oblt (MA) Heinz-Joachim Wilke

MEK zbV (special purposes) – nothing known

Chapter Three

The One-Man Torpedoes
Neger and *Marder*

Design and Construction

In 1943, warship designer Richard Mohr of the Torpedo Testing Institute (TVA) at Eckernförde began work on the development of the first weapons system for the proposed German K-Verband. His idea was to use two standard G 7e torpedoes, almost silent running, electrically-driven torpedoes which left no bubble trail, converting one into a carrier to transport the attack torpedo to the battle zone. The carrier torpedo was fitted with a tiny enclosed cockpit from which it was steered manually. The device was named *Neger* (negro), this being a play on the designer's name (German: *Mohr* = English *blackamoor,* origin: North African person of Moorish ancestry).

The Carrier and Attack Torpedoes

The carrier was simple and primitive in the extreme being basically a G 7e torpedo from which the warhead had been removed and replaced by a small cockpit for the pilot. The position was covered by a plexiglass dome, a cupola manufactured by the Dornier aircraft company at Frederickshafen on Lake Constance.

The carrier displaced 2.7 tonnes. Propulsion was an AEF 12 hp electric-torpedo motor Type AV 76 with 110-volt battery and a drive shaft. Speed was around 4 knots, therefore relatively slow, range 30 sea miles.

The 53.34-cm calibre attack torpedo was slung about 7 cms below the carrier. It weighed 1.608 tonnes, length 7.17 metres. Its top speed was 40 knots, and it could run 31 sea miles. Warhead was 279 kgs. Two small electric batteries provided the drive. The propulsion system of the carrier was sufficient to propel both torpedoes to the target area. The carrier was not submersible.

The pilot had three instruments: a control stick for the rudder, a lever to work the propulsion system and another lever to discharge the attack torpedo which then ran its course at a pre-set depth. The pilot's vantage point was very low in the water, which afforded poor vision. Only his head would be in the plexiglass dome. During the voyage the seas would wash over the cupola, which was usually soon smeared with an oil film. The only aid for aiming the torpedo was a scale etched along the inner rim of the cupola and a thin upright metal prong projecting above the surface at the nose. Navigation was by the stars.

Marinestabsarzt Dr Arnim Wandel, the first medical officer of the K-Verband, who had himself piloted a *Neger*, criticized the builder's ignorance of the CO_2 danger. At his intervention pilots were eventually supplied with a Dräger breathing set used by the Luftwaffe (the so-called 'fighter-pilot's mask' = *Jägermaske*) fitted with two potash cartridges to absorb the CO_2 exhalations and so protect against possible poisoning.

The major drawbacks of the *Neger* were its inability to dive, which represented a grave danger to the pilot, its slow speed, making escape from pursuing forces impossible, and the lack of a compass. The *Neger* was no tried and tested coastal craft, as experience would soon prove. Occasionally the attack torpedo would not release when the lever was pulled, creating an immediate disaster for the pilot and mechanical assembly.

About 200 *Negers* were built, 140 of which were lost to enemy action or accident. Their high losses on the coast of Normandy and in the Mediterranean, principally to aircraft and fast enemy warships, led quickly to the development of an improved version able to submerge.

Along with other types still in the design stage or under development, necessity forced urgent consideration to be given to the question of making the *Neger* submersible, if only in the first instance and to a limited extent. The new design was named *Marder* (marten). The men of the Eckernförde Institute worked at a feverish pace, and by August 1944 the *Marder* was ready.

The new carrier-torpedo, virtually identical outwardly to the *Neger*, was fitted with a dive-tank forward of the cockpit. This increased the length from 7.65 metres to 8.93 metres, and the displacement from 2.7 to 3 tonnes. The craft was pressure-safe to 40 metres, but more importantly could dive to 10 metres. The time submerged was very brief and did not improve efficiency much but ability to operate while dived was of great importance for success and the survival of the pilot. 300 *Marder I* and the slightly improved *Marder II* were completed, deployed equally between northern and western Europe and the Mediterranean.

Theoretically, and especially in the eyes of the planners ashore, the vision of a great number of one-man torpedoes built primarily to fight the invasion fleet was an attractive proposition. The reality was rather different, however. The low silhouette of a floating torpedo gave the pilot a very limited field of vision, particularly since the plexiglass dome was constantly washed by the sea and covered by an oil film. If the pilot opened the cover to see better he risked flooding the device and thus sinking it. In action the one-man torpedoes had an appalling loss rate of 60%–80%.

Pilot Selection and Training

Within a relatively short time, in March 1944, the first German one-man torpedoes were ready and naval architect Mohr began the initial testing in Eckernförde Bay. From the outset a number of men with sea-going experience were recruited for these trials and later operations, amongst them midshipmen Pettke and Potthast, previously with 3 S-boat Flotilla, and ObltzS Johann-Otto Krieg, a submariner. In 1941 Krieg had served as watchkeeping officer aboard U-891, a Type VIIC boat attached to 298 U-Flotilla. U-891 (ObltzS Guggenberger) had taken part in many convoy battles and Krieg was aboard on 13 November 1941 when U-81 sank the aircraft carrier HMS *Ark Royal* near Gibraltar. At age 24, Krieg had taken over U-81 from Guggenberger and remained her commander until 4 January 1944 when the boat was bombed and sunk at Pola in the Adriatic.

Krieg, on leave, was surprised to be summoned before Grossadmiral Dönitz in Berlin to attend a conference at which Vizeadmiral Heye,

KKpt Frauenheim, designer Mohr and about twenty admirals and 'top brass' were present. Dönitz made Krieg familiar with the designs for *Neger* personally, explaining how the device worked and was to be used operationally. After that he was ordered to the TVA at Eckernförde to try out a *Neger* for himself. Under Mohr's guidance, Krieg, Pettke, Potthast and the designer now put *Neger* through its paces.

Krieg was appointed the first chief of K-Flotilla 361 in March 1944. Shortly after acceptance of the one-man torpedo by the Kriegsmarine, the first forty potential *Neger* pilots arrived at the base. They were predominantly volunteers of all ranks from the three Wehrmacht arms of service and most lacked sea experience. The assertion of some British military historians that these men had been given the opportunity to serve in order to expunge some crime or military offence is not justified. Certainly it cannot be denied that there were a few such cases, but the majority of these brave men volunteered from whatever personal motives.

Great value was placed on mental and physical fitness, and the guiding principle behind the training was physical education. Enormous efforts were demanded of pilots in 24 to 60-hour periods. They had to run 10 kilometres before breakfast. They were taught hand-to-hand fighting by veteran infantry instructors. Cutter-rowing, canoeing and 30-kilometre night marches were also on the programme. There were tests of personal courage, for example jumping off a steep cliff into the darkness without knowing what was below.

After the would-be pilots had passed through Kptlt(S) Michael Opladen's tough school, the training turned to instruction in operating and navigating the carrier-torpedo and firing the attack-torpedo. The pilots were also required to pass an endurance test simply sitting in the *Neger*. It was no place for claustrophobics. Since in practice it might be necessary in an extreme case to pass lengthy periods in the torpedo, unbroken periods of 20 hours had to be spent in the cockpit. The pilot had to discipline himself to overcome drowsiness and resist sleep, as failure to operate the oxygen unit at a timely stage could lead to CO_2 poisoning and death.

One of the first technical problems to solve was how to introduce fresh air into the tiny enclosed cockpit. The pilots suffered constantly from CO_2 poisoning which caused nausea, vomiting and headaches.

Equipment to purify the cabin environment of exhaled CO_2 had not yet been completed, and in test voyages of more than three hours' duration the CO_2 level caused toxic reactions. Readings showed that the level was much higher in the cockpit than elsewhere in the torpedo. The installation of air-change equipment by Dräger-Werke delayed *Neger* operations by one week to 30 March 1944.

Despite these drawbacks and the extremely short training period for pilots, preparations were now taken in hand for operations at Anzio where the Allies had made landings and set up a bridgehead. A total of 30 one-man torpedoes had by now been completed.

Later, in July 1944, *Lehrkommando 350* set up a unit for *Neger* and *Marder* training at Surendorf, a village about 25 kilometres east of Eckernförde codenamed *Dorfkoppel* (village-meadow). Head of training was Kptlt Heinz Franke and from March 1945 to the war's end Kptlt Horst Kessler. In all, six of these K-Flotillas were set up. (The exact posts cannot be determined exactly since they changed frequently due to the death or incapacitation of the incumbents).

K-Flotilla 361 (formed March 1944)
Flotilla Chief – Obltz Heinrich Frank

Torpedo Officer – Lt Hermann Oertel

Group Leaders: Oblt Ulrich Seibicke, Lt Friedrich-Konrad Jürgensen, Lt Alfred Riess, Lt Joachim Stork, Lt Karl Welz

K-Flotilla 362 (formed April 1944)
Flotilla Chief – Oblt Leopold Koch

Torpedo Officer – Lt Ernst Müller

Group Leaders: Lt Heinrich Beierlein, Lt Gerhard Gotthardt, Lt Bernd von Oertzen

K-Flotilla 363 (formed September 1944)
Flotilla Chief – Oblt Siegfried Wetterich

Torpedo Officer – Oblt Karl-Heinz Fiedier

Group Leaders – Lt Kurt Basler, Lt Rolf Dittmar, Lt Otto Hentling

K-Flotilla 364 (formed July 1944)
Flotilla Chief – Oblt Peter Berger

Torpedo Officer – Oblt Franz Worm

Group Leaders – Lt Wilhelm Lehmbruck, Lt Kurt Müller, Lt Oskar Schmitz

K-Flotilla 365 (formed July 1944)
Flotilla Chief – Oblt Hans-Georg Barop

Torpedo Officer – Oblt Erich Strecker

Group Leaders – Lt Hermann Rossner, Lt Felix Ewerhart, Lt Hermann Messmer, Lt Alfons Stecher, Lt Herbert Resch

K-Flotilla 366 (formed December 1944)
Flotilla Chief – Oblt Paul Heinsius.

Nothing further is known of this flotilla

The First One-Man Torpedo Operations at Anzio
At 0200 on Saturday 22 January 1944, four divisions of VI Corps, US 5th Army (Lt-Gen Clark) made surprise landings on the west coast of Italy. At Anzio, fifty kilometres south of Rome, they set up a bridgehead. The operation presented them with more problems than first thought and a long delay resulted before the bridgehead could be enlarged or left. It was the responsibility of the Kriegsmarine to cut off supplies to the bridgehead from the sea and prevent the sending of reinforcements. Neither the few U-boats operating in the Mediterranean, nor 3 and 7 S-boat Flotillas were able to disrupt Allied shipping effectively.

To support German naval forces, OKM decided to use *Neger*-type one-man torpedoes. In all haste in February 1944 K-Verband set up Naval Operations Unit 75 (MEK 75) under KptzS Böhme, former commander of the destroyer Z-22 *Anton Schmitt*, (torpedoed and sunk in the First Battle of Narvik, 10 April 1940) and currently without an active post while his new command, destroyer Z-23, was under repair at La Pallice.

The *Negers* were subject to delays for modifications after Dr Wandel, later K-Verband medical officer, identified dangerous defects leading to serious health problems amongst pilots during trials at Eckernförde. The unit had no practical experience to fall back on, and it was not even certain that it would be possible to carry out operations with the device.

In a conference at Kiel on 16 March 1944 between Konteradmiral Heye, then Chief of Staff, Group North and Fleet Command, Professor Orzechowski, pharmacologist of the naval medical service at Naval Command Baltic and Dr Wandel, divisional surgeon, Naval Reserve Division, Heye made an urgent request for medication aimed at keeping lone operators physically alert for long periods and mobilizing their reserves of energy. Orzechowski drew up various tablet preparations and asked the apothecary at the Kiel-Wik naval hospital to supply them the next day. Tests on fifty men at the Schlutup training camp *Blaukoppel* resulted as follows: 'guinea-pigs' who took the combination of drugs following a good night's sleep suffered no side-effects, those taking the pills the evening before night duty reacted without significant negative side effects and displayed an enhanced alertness especially with preparations which included Pervitin. The most effective was a combination of 5 mg Eukodal, 5 mg Cocaine-5 and 3 mg Pervitin, and accordingly 500 tablets of this preparation 'D IX' were ordered for *Neger* pilots. The actual dosages are not known.

At the beginning of April 1944, after only two weeks' training, ObltzS Krieg took K-Flotilla 361 to Rigano near Florence by train with 40 *Negers*, arriving on 6 April. The carrier-torpedos were then trans-shipped to heavy vehicles for the road journey to Practica di Mare near Anzio. Thirty-seven arrived safely on 13 April, three having been written off due to damage on the way. The machines were brought to a pine wood about three miles behind the front line, 18 sea miles from the Allied anchorages, camouflaged against aerial reconnaissance and concealed amongst beach bathing huts.

The attack was set for the dark night of the new moon, 20 April when the *Negers* were to be floated off near the ruined Vajanica tower. Here unforeseen difficulties were encountered. The beach was too flat to get the heavy double torpedoes afloat and 500 Luftwaffe para-troopers were called upon to drag the thirty-seven 5-tonne machines to deeper water. During these manoeuvres the first fatal accident occurred. A *Neger* laid correctly on its side for launching was pushed out but failed to reach water deep enough to float it. The breakers swirled the submerged device around on the sandy bottom, the helpless pilot was unable to get free and his body was retrieved next morning. A second fatal accident occurred later on the way to the operational area. A seaman-pilot who had failed to operate the oxygen equipment correctly died of CO_2 poisoning. The torpedo was lifted from the water by an Allied ship and thus the enemy learned the secret of the new weapon.

The operation began at 2200 hrs once the torpedoes had been relocated to deeper water. Special amphibious vehicles needed to get the *Neger* devices afloat safely were not yet available, and were never ready until the last days of the war. The result at Anzio was that on the first night, fourteen *Neger* one-man torpedoes finished up on the sandbanks or stuck in the shallows and had to be blown up next day.

Group 1 (ObltzS Leopold Koch, see photo p. 00) was to round Cape Anzio to attack shipping in Nettuno Bay. Group 2 (Lt Seibicke) was to attack vessels in the Anzio roadstead. Group 3 (Oberfähnrich Potthast) was to attack the port.

Oberfähnrich Hermann Voigt of Group 2 discharged his torpedo at an anchored ship. There was a loud explosion and Voigt watched the target, a patrol vessel, break up.

In Anzio harbour, Karl-Heinz Potthast torpedoed a steamer which blew up with a deafening explosion. Oberfernschreibmeister Herbert Berrer claimed a troopship. Schreiberobergefreiter (Leading seaman, clerk) Walther Gerhold, formerly aboard torpedo boat T-20, fired his torpedo at a gun on the mole and exploded its ready-ammunition magazine. Oberfähnrich Pettke and other pilots turned for home without sighting the enemy although one pilot torpedoed a patrol vessel on the journey back to shore.

Seventeen-year-old Matrose (ordinary seaman) Horst Berger wrote of his adventure later:

> Start just before midnight. I was a bit worried about our mine-fields. After five minutes or so I was through them. I glanced at my watch: 0020. The orders read: 'Put to sea. Navigate by the pole star.' I was making three to four knots. Beyond the minefield by some miracle the overcast began to disperse. I looked astern and now I saw the pole star.
>
> Glanced at my watch. 0200. The flak was supposed to give us covering fire. Why weren't they shooting?

34

0300. Only water to see in all directions. Even the sky was a monotone. I have always loved the sea, but here it was soulless, oppressive! The wave-height was increasing constantly. I tried to parry each violent slap by rudder movements, but it didn't work. The pole star was now hidden by cloud. It was still very dark. My head was getting heavy. I felt a strong pressure at the temples. Suddenly a sickening feeling, rising from the stomach. I vomited. The control stick was now wet and slippery. I tried to dry my hand on my battle combinations but the vomit was everywhere. For God's sake! Where was the oxygen thing? It was so crammed in the cupola. I was sick as a pig. The pressure in my head was getting worse. My pulse was hammering wildly. Suddenly I realized what was wrong. I was sitting on the oxygen tube. Doing that had cut off my supply. With a tug I freed the tube and held it under my nose, breathed and breathed and felt much better. I'm saved, I thought. But only from suffocation. Now I had to consider – where is Anzio-Nettuno. Where are my comrades?

I looked at my watch. It was just before 0500. In a few minutes we had permission to fire. Suddenly the heavens were lit by star shell. It had started! The Luftwaffe flew its scheduled feint air attack. The target was illuminated light as day. All hell must have been let loose at Anzio. The enemy was thinking it was only an air attack. The flak was tremendous. To my right a great fire had broken out in the harbour. I was still far from a shooting position. My comrades had been busy. By now they would certainly be heading for home. Should I launch a lone attack after taking so long to arrive?

It was well after 0500 when I took the decision to attack. I tried to estimate my distance from the harbour. Suddenly all doubts disappeared. I knew what I had to do. Aiming my torpedo at the harbour installations, which I could see clearly, I pulled the release lever. A jolt! Under its own power my attack torpedo headed for the target. Soon it would hit. Faster, much faster! I urged it. I trembled in expectation, anxious to turn for home. An explosion, a great cloud of smoke rising slowly. 'A hit!' I cried.

Now I had to leave. I thought there was another explosion. I had to get back to Mum or at least my comrades. Yes, but what was the quickest way? Probably quickest right under the coast. But that is suicide, I told myself. I wouldn't let Tommy get me. Out to sea again. For hours I navigated my torpedo as if in a dream. The sun baked me through my glass cupola. My eyes kept closing. Suddenly I fell asleep.

When I awoke it was 1000. Land ahead. I headed for shore. The indicator on my oxygen connection was almost at zero. Wonderful white sand. Tack, tack ... rish! A torrent of water cascaded against the plexiglass hood at both sides. The water kicked up – MG fire! Another burst! I released the cupola and dived out. The inflated life-vest kept me afloat. I didn't realize I was breathing the yearned-for fresh air at last.

Two soldiers came across the sand towards me. Americans? Both were naked from the waist up and wore no headgear. Their weapons were drawn. Pidgin English: 'You American? Where you come here from?'

'You won't believe I came here from Berlin!' I responded. The younger soldier chuckled, the other pulled a long face and said dismissively, 'Don't laugh, can't you see how boiled up he is? Don't let him out of your sight!' I could hardly believe my ears when I heard them speaking German. I found the whole situation distinctly odd. They refused to talk and escorted me towards their captain. A third soldier appeared, also naked from the waist up but wearing a cap. And this cap – I could scarcely believe my eyes – had the Wehrmacht eagle, swastika and cockade. In the Luftwaffe style. In jubilation I challenged them: 'You are Germans?' I had never seen such blank looks in ages. 'What else are we supposed to be then?'

I explained to them I had been on a secret mission. More than that I was not at liberty to say. When I saw their disappointment at not having captured an American I told them how happy I was to have finished up with them. I was really at the end of my reserve. Their joy was great. They brought me to their Hauptmann, who was also a Berliner. I requested that he should call my unit. I spoke with my superior and reported my torpedo fired at the harbour installations. Shortly afterwards they came to fetch me. All my comrades who had returned safely were invited to be received at HQ by Generalfeldmarschall Kesselring. I was awarded the Iron Cross Second Class and promoted to Gefreiter (able-bodied seaman).

The Generalfeldmarschall invited us to dine. As the youngest of our group of sixteen who had returned safely, during the meal I sat at Kesselring's side. He made me tell him everything about the operation. Everybody laughed a lot, and so I hardly ate a mouthful. Finally I received 21 days' special leave. My mother was very pleased.

On the day following the operation the men of K-Flotilla 361 destroyed the remaining *Negers*. The Allies had captured an intact model and now knew what the Kriegsmarine was up to. The element of surprise had been lost. K-Flotilla 361 returned to the Baltic without its torpedo-carriers. K-Verband analyzed the operation and identified the reason for its failure as being the lack of adequate reconnaissance and knowledge of the terrain. To avoid these problems in the future it was decided to create a Scientific Staff to thoroughly prepare beforehand for all impending operations.

The K-Verband Command Scientific Staff
The Scientific Staff began work on 15 May 1944 in a school building at Schönberg in Mecklenburg, camouflage name *Raumkoppel*. Dr Konrad Voppel, curator at the Museum of Anthropology, Leipzig, was appointed leader. The team consisted of geographers, geologists, oceanographers, meteorologists and mathematicians, cartographers, printers and book-binders. An efficient technical photographic laboratory was also at their disposal together with a comprehensive technical library of almost 30,000 volumes containing over a quarter of a million maps and charts, 50,000 photos and a huge collection of geographic and similar journals from all parts of the world. The source of knowledge covered almost every square metre of the world's surface and all coasts of Europe.

As a rule the Scientific Staff could produce all appropriate material relevant to a question working 20 hours non-stop. The types of enquiry which might need an answer were:

1. What are the geographic/oceanic conditions in the operational zone?
2. What is the best place on the coast for our purpose?

3. What sea currents do we have to reckon with?
4. Are there prominent points for orientation purposes?
5. Where are the most favourable areas for landings?
6. How is the land or island laid out?
7. Is there sufficient cover?
8. What peculiarities must be observed?

The *Raumkoppel* team supplied all K-Flotillas and Naval Operations Commands (MEKs) to the end of the war with all necessary information for the required operational purposes.

The Allied Invasion of Normandy

After months of preparations the long expected Allied invasion of France began in the first hours of 6 June 1944. It took place in Normandy and not, as many German senior commanders had thought probable, in the area of the Channel Narrows. Troopships carrying 287,000 men of the various arms of service sailed from embarkation ports in the early hours of 5 June in order to assemble that night *en masse* in the control area 30 to 40 sea miles off the English coast south-east of the Isle of Wight. The armada then headed down ten swept channels towards the Bay of the Seine while strong Allied air attacks were mounted against the German coastal defences and supply lines. The ten main coastal artillery batteries were attacked by 1,140 British bombers dropping 5,000 tons of bombs. At dawn a second wave of 1,100 USAF aircraft repeated the air offensive.

Shortly after midnight into 6 June, airborne forces were dropped or landed from 2,400 British and American aircraft and 850 troop-carrying gliders. Early that morning, in poor weather, the first invasion forces reached the coast. These were followed by 6,500 Allied vessels, 4,500 of them carrying troops, tanks and landing craft crammed with armoured vehicles. There were 75 convoys, each five sea miles long. By the evening the Allies had penetrated the 'Atlantic Wall' along thirty miles of its length and established three bridgeheads from two to nine kilometres deep.

OKW had been reckoning on landings on the southern shore of the Channel Narrows. The correct assessment of the situation by the C-in-C Army Group B, Generalfeldmarschall Rommel, that the landings would stretch from the mouth of the Somme up to and including the Cotentin Peninsula was ignored.[1]

At the time of the invasion there were 58 German divisions in France, Belgium and the Netherlands. These troops were not really battleworthy. Thirty-three divisions were classified as 'static' or 'on the ethnic basis', i.e. *Volksdeutsche* conscripts from occupied countries, and, having no vehicles, were relatively immobile. About 18 divisions were either newly raised or re-grouping. Most of the nine panzer-divisions had only between 90 and 130 tanks each. Luftflotte 3 stationed in the West had only 160 battleworthy aircraft. Sections of the Luftwaffe had been transferred away to southern France and Czechoslovakia on 17 May.

The anti-invasion strategy on the coasts of northern France was a system of strongpoints, most of which being independent of each other as regards fire control. Beach sectors where landings were thought most probable had been mined or protected by wire fencing, barbed wire hedges, explosive traps and so forth, but good bunkers existed only in individual locations. Rommel's request to the Kriegs-marine to lay ground mines with magnetic and acoustic detonators seaward of the Army's foreshore obstructions in the stretch between Vire and Orne, and to sow anchored mines in deeper water, had not been complied with because Group West considered the area to be safe by reason of the sandbanks and reefs off the Calvados coastline.

The operational plan for the invasion and the further offensive by the Allied Expeditionary Force in France provided for troops to be put ashore along an 80-kilometre long reach of coast around the Bay of the Seine. By the twentieth day the bridgehead was to have expanded to 100 kilometres in length and 110 kilometres deep inland.

Operation Overlord was under the supreme command of US General Eisenhower. Field Marshal Montgomery was Commanding-General, Army invasion troops and C-in-C 21st Army Group: General Omar Bradley led 1 US Army. The landings took place along the Normandy coast between Le Havre and Cherbourg in the jurisdiction of the German 7th and 15th Armies. The focal points of the landings were beaches on the east coast of the Cotentin Peninsula (*Utah* section), between Vierville and Colleville sur Mer (*Omaha* section), at Arromanches (*Gold*), Ouistrehan (*Juno*) and Lyon sur Mer (*Sword*).

The Allied naval forces were divided into the *Eastern Naval Task Force* (Rear Admiral Vian) consisting of two battleships, one monitor, 13 light cruisers, two gunboats, 34 destroyers, four sloops, 19 frigates,

129 minesweepers, 17 corvettes, 116 miscellaneous craft and 2,426 landing craft. The *Western Naval Task Force* (US Rear Admiral Kirk) was composed of three battleships, three heavy cruisers, six light cruisers, two light French cruisers, one British monitor, one Dutch gunboat, 35 destroyers, 12 frigates, 118 minesweepers, four corvettes, 140 small fighting craft and 1,700 landing craft. This enormous armada was reinforced during the next few days by seven more battleships, two monitors, 23 cruisers, three gunboats, 105 destroyers and 1,073 small warships.

The Allied air forces had air supremacy with their 10,860 fighting aircraft and 2,300 transport aeroplanes. The Luftwaffe and Kriegsmarine had little available to oppose this powerful superiority at sea and in the air.

What did the Kriegsmarine possess to take on 1,210 Allied warships, 4,120 landing craft and 1,600 auxiliary and merchant ships? The C-in-C Group West, Vizeadmiral Krancke had three torpedo boats, 38 S-boats (MTBs), 160 minesweepers, 57 patrol boats and 42 artillery lighters in the area of the landings on 6 June 1944. That same day Grossadmiral Dönitz ordered 17 of the 36 U-boats lying in submarine pens in bunkers at Brest to head for the Channel. This took six to nine hours. On the way six of the boats were sunk by air attack. Over the next few weeks the losses rose significantly. Despite great resolve and valour on the part of the German Navy, their successes were a mere drop in the ocean and had hardly any effect on the Allied landings.

The *Mulberry* Harbours

It had been clear to Allied planners from the outset that for a considerable time they would have no port available in the zone of their intended landings through which they could channel the huge quantities of supplies necessary. Therefore in August 1943 SHAEF (*Supreme Headquarters Allied Expeditionary Force*) had begun designing two artificial harbours. Each would have the capacity of Dover harbour and be ready a few days after the invasion. *Mulberry* Harbour 'A' would be set up off the French fishing village of Vierville sur Mer by the Americans, *Mulberry* Harbour 'B' at Arromanches by the British and Canadians. Rear Admiral W.G. Tennant was given the job of arranging for the construction material to be towed cross-

Channel and for its subsequent erection. For this purpose he had a workforce of 500 officers and 10,000 men. The most important parts, the foundations, were the 5,000-ton *Phoenix* reinforced concrete caissons, each 60 metres long. Inside their protection, floating roadways and piers supported by pontoons were the quaysides to which freighters, landing craft and other amphibious vessels would deliver. In the landing sector of each division five breakwaters were to be created to provide a protected anchorage. Known as *Gooseberries*, they were each 7.2 kilometres long and made by sinking 60 blockships.

Two days after the invasion began, on 8 June 1944 off Varreville, Saint Laurent, Arromanches, Courselles and Ouistrehan, artificial harbour moles were laid to provide a temporary sheltered anchorage enabling supplies to be landed on the beaches while the *Mulberries* were under construction. Amongst the blockships sunk as breakwaters were the old French battleship *Courbet*, the Dutch light cruiser *Sumatra*, the old British battleship *Centurion*, the AA-ship *Alynbank* and later the damaged light cruiser HMS *Durban*. On Sunday 11 June 1944 the moles for the two *Mulberry* harbours were laid and four small beach-ports within *Gooseberry* breakwaters were in business, the only delays to the latter being caused by German coastal artillery fire from Quinville adjacent to *Utah* beach. In all, more than 5,000 warships and merchant vessels were to use the artificial harbours, a collossal logistical and technical achievement by the Allied navies. What the Allied supreme command had not bargained for, however, was unforeseeable acts of nature.

On the morning of 19 June 1944 warning was given of hurricane force winds. The worst summer storms since 1900 pounded the Channel. Strong north-westerlies whipped up great rolling seas along the Normandy coast which soon overwhelmed the American *Mulberry* at Saint Laurent. Over 800 ships, landing craft, tugs and lighters were damaged or sunk.

By Wednesay 21 June a hurricane had set in and *Mulberry* B also began to break up. The floating breakwaters known as bombardons came adrift. Ships tore loose. The raging sea hurled troopships against the quays. The blockships prevented worse. As much tonnage was lost to this storm as on the first day of the invasion.

Besides the inclement weather, Allied shipping was threatened by German coastal batteries, the few Luftwaffe aircraft and Kreigsmarine

41

warships. The plan to defend the anchorages of the invasion fleet was based on clearing away German minefields and holding off German naval attacks. The principal threat to the anchorages lay in the eastern sector where strong German forces were at hand east of the Orne and at Le Havre. Therefore Anglo-American High Command formed the *East Flank* support squadron. Led by the AA-ship HMS *Locust*, 71 boats, mainly armed landing craft and motor launches staffed by 240 officers and 3,000 men were to provide the security.

The security line to seaward consisted of minesweepers supported by destroyers, each anchored five cables (925 metres) apart. This line was parallel to the coast and six miles out. A double line of patrol vessels projected six miles to sea northwards from Ouistrehan and the Orne estuary, and then bent two sea miles to the north-west to the sea zone where the naval defence patrols operated. The first line consisted of landing craft at anchor 3.5 cables apart while the second line was made up of an armed motor launch (ML) for every two landing craft in the first line. When no alarm was in force, each ML covered one of two landing craft. If the alarm was raised, they broke the outer line and filled the gap between their two allotted landing craft. This system was called the *Trout-Line*.

The nightly setting-up of the *Trout-Line* was an event which needed very precise timing. If the lines formed too early, the boats would receive fire from the German coastal artillery. For the same reason it had to be dismantled before first light. The *Trout-Line* was first set up on 28 June 1944. This defensive system presented German surface forces and the K-Verband with a serious obstruction.

One-Man Torpedo Attacks in Normandy
It had been intended to deploy the K-Verband as soon as the invasion began but delays in production and training on the various seagoing devices resulted in no unit being operational before the end of June.

K-Flotilla 361 crossed Germany by road on 13 June 1944 with 60 *Negers*. The flotilla left Rudolstadt in Thuringia aboard 92 heavy lorries for Paris and then Normandy. The first group arrived at Trouville on 28 June and at Villers sur Mer found protected shelter in the Favrol Woods. The second group found its way there on 5 July from Pont l'Eveque. Operational leader was KptzS Fritz Böhme.

Because of shortages in personnel the pilots had been brought up to strength by the addition of 12 Waffen-SS volunteers detached to SS-Sturmbannführer Otto Skorzeny's SS-*Jagdverbände* at Oranienburg. The men were convicts serving sentences of up to ten years' imprisonment and had now been offered the opportunity for rehabilitation and remission of their sentences.

This time the operation had been prepared more thoroughly. Böhme had requisitioned a farm and hidden the *Negers* out of sight in stables. The weather was good and two companies of engineers opened gaps in the beach defences and minefields to allow limited passage. Wooden launch ramps had been built so that the *Negers* could be trolleyed into water deep enough to float them. During the day the ramps were hidden under camouflage netting.

On 4 and 5 July the wireless observation service (*B-Dienst*) reported five different convoys which had disembarked 6,280 men, 5,336 tons of supplies and 1,291 vehicles. Böhme was opposed to a *Neger* operation since he thought it likely they would have to fight their way out and back. The start phase would last too long, and in the last third there was no guarantee of contact with the enemy. The carrier torpedoes could only be launched in darkness and on the ebb to carry them outwards to the attack zone. The pilots had to carry out their attacks and then catch the flood to get back. In each month there were only three or four days in which these conditions of tide prevailed. The first of these was the night of 5 July 1944.

ObltzS Krieg was in a military hospital after receiving a serious head injury in a lorry accident and ObltzS Leopold Koch took command of K-Flotilla 361. In the evening hours of 5 July, 26 *Negers* rumbled down the wooden slipway into the sea for their first operation against the *Trout-Line*, the advanced line of patrol craft protecting the Allies' *Mulberry* harbours. Two *Negers* suffered motor damage and were forced to return. The other 24 reached the target zone, attacking between 0300 and 0630 on 6 July.

At 0307 a pilot fired his torpedo at a landing craft. It ran under motor launch ML 151 and continued towards landing ship LCG 681. ML 151, which had seen the *Neger*, headed for it intending to ram but was forced to bear away when landing ships LCF 21 and LCG 681 opened fire. ML 151 sprayed the general area with 2.3 kg explosive rounds. The minesweeper HMS *Orestes* fired on another *Neger* with oerlikons and rifles. A pilot found in the water near the minesweeper was taken aboard and made prisoner.

After 0200 pilot Walter Gerhold had come across eight large merchant ships and 20 to 25 landing craft. At 0304 he fired his torpedo at a warship. After 40 seconds he saw the torpedo hit astern causing an enormous explosion, great tongues of flame stabbing into the night sky. The victim was the frigate HMS *Trollope*. The British began to fire wildly. HMS *Stevenson* took aboard the survivors of the sinking frigate while destroyers and corvettes combed the sea. Gerhold escaped his hunters and German soldiers lifted him out of the water at Honfleur. The British had no idea what they were supposed to be shooting at. Confusion reigned. Despite the capture of a *Neger* at Anzio, and the publication of a detailed description in the *Weekly Intelligence Report* of 9 June 1944, nobody in *East Flank Support Squadron* had digested the contents.

At 0353 the minesweeper HMS *Magic* was torpedoed and went down with 25 of her complement. HMS *Cato* had rescued many of her survivors before being torpedoed and sunk herself. Some 26 of her own crew were lost.

Neger-pilot Horst Berger remembered:

We started about 10 kilometres from the Bay of the Seine. They pushed us into the water down a ramp of beams. 14 pilots came back. Next day another 30 were sent out. None returned. Whether they were captured or drowned I never discovered. Our quarters were on the beach at Villers sur Mer. The day before, we saw the ships, our targets, from the shore. They stretched out like a great island. So many ships! Naturally everybody wanted to sink the biggest. Many of our support staff were very happy about not having to put to sea that night.

When I set out I was very keyed up for it despite it being my second operation. I steered for the invasion fleet for two or three hours without anything happening. The waves were high. My head in the cupola was under water half the time. The moon was bright. The worst thing was having no contact to the outside world. Everybody had to rely entirely on himself.

In the night I saw many ships pass at a great distance. No chance for me to reach them. I was making only 3 knots. During my journey I heard many explosions far off. It was like fireworks

44

night at Treptow. Slowly the hours passed. Then at 0545 I had a ship ahead of me. I began my attack approach. I was just about to release my torpedo when there was an explosion. Lightning flashed up aboard her, then she disintegrated. I turned away at once to look for another target. Later I found out that one of my comrades had sunk the ship. It was a 3,000-tonner.

My chance came 15 minutes later. I began my attack run-in and fired my torpedo. I thought at first I had missed. After about a minute I saw and heard an explosion. A hit! I must have got him astern. This tub was bigger than the other one.

Meanwhile it had got very light. I was anxious to get back as quickly as possible. I saw aircraft in the distance. I was shitting myself. About 0930 a fighter-bomber rattled off at me suddenly with his MGs. My *Neger* was hit and sank. I got out quickly and swam for two hours and a half before I got to the shore. I was totally exhausted and trembling when I reached land. While I was swimming no aircraft fired at me. I was happy to have survived. Later I was promoted to Bootsmannsmaat (boatswain's mate). Admiral Heye, our K-Verband chief, presented me with the German Cross in Gold.

Oberfähnrich Potthast on the other hand had bad luck when his attack torpedo began to flood. This caused the *Neger* to stand up almost vertical in the water. To avoid being dragged down Potthast fired the attack torpedo. It came free but the tail fin hit the *Neger* causing a leak. Water poured in. Potthast managed to abandon the vessel. An hour later he reached the Orne estuary by swimming. After getting through the static beach defences and walking four kilometres he found a German infantry unit.

During the morning the surviving pilots returned one by one to their barracks, a small Norman castle. Walter Gerhold reported sinking the Polish light cruiser *Dragon*. This was an error of identification, the *Dragon* would be sunk next day, his victim was the frigate HMS *Trollope*. Only 14 men came back from the operation, ten were lost due to navigational error, capture, MTB attack or defensive fire from landing craft.

The next *Neger* operation followed next day. At 2225 on 7 July, 21 *Negers* slid into the water and headed along the coast to landing sector *Sword*. The first sighting of a *Neger* by the British occurred at 0307. This heralded the beginning of much confusion, for by midday on 9 July 31 *Negers* had been sighted, more than the number which set out. The anti-aircraft guns fired wildly, depth charges exploded everywhere.

At 0430 Oberfähnrich Potthast fired his torpedo at a destroyer. He got a hit, and saw flames shooting upwards from the stricken vessel. The stern of the destroyer torn away, she burned, listed and then went down. Shortly afterwards Potthast's torpedo-carrier was spotted by the minesweeper HMS *Orestes* which opened fire with a burst from an MG. Potthast, severely wounded, got out. A British officer fished him out of the water. Another *Neger* pilot, a leading seaman, was also seriously hurt and saved by the British. After Potthast had sunk the Polish destroyer *Dragon*, at 0650 another *Neger* torpedoed the minesweeper HMS *Pylades*. The explosion forward was so powerful that the stern of the vessel stood upright in the water.

Despite these individual successes and the confusion which the *Negers* had sown amongst the Allied defences, K-Flotilla 361 losses were great. None of the craft returned. All were sunk by surface vessels, or RAF and Free French air force aircraft. Four pilots, including Fritz Poltz, an Austrian, were captured. As a result of these losses, K-Verband Command decided to abandon *Neger* operations.

What remained of K-Flotilla 361 was transferred back to the Reich. The surviving operators were listed for training for the newly delivered, improved *Marders* at *Dorfkoppel* (Eckernförde). As the men were 'burnt out' and the leadership thought there might be Allied landings to come in the Norwegian-Danish region, in late autumn 1944 they were relocated with 60 *Marders* to Skagen on the northern tip of Jutland, and then moved to Aasa at readiness. K-Flotilla 361 was never again operational, however.

Previously in October 1944, the men of K-Flotilla 361 had had to pass long hours in 'seated trials' in the *Marder* at Saalburg, the place of manufacture, the reason being that leaks were occurring in the fixed piping. The pressure in the air tanks dropped disproportionately fast, increasing the risk of fire. The K-Verband medical officer pointed out that oxygen had to be introduced into the air tanks first, and then the compressed air.

On the night of 2 August 1944 at Houlgate in Normandy a combined attack was launched against the *Mulberry* harbours by *Marders* of

K-Flotilla 362 and *Linse* explosive boats of K-Flotilla 211 supported by German bombers. K-Flotilla 362 had divided into two groups on leaving Germany. From the launch point, a small wood near the Orne estuary between Houlgate and Trouville, 58 *Marders* set out and headed for the *Mulberries*. The main attack was concentrated on the northern end of the *Trout-Line* so as to reduce the chance of contact with Allied patrol boats. During the night a violent battle ensued with heavy losses on both sides.

Everything started with the British landing craft LCG1 and the motor launch ML 131 engaging a *Marder* unsuccessfully. At 0310 a torpedo barely missed the destroyer HMS *Duff*. At 0325 the armed trawler HMS *Gairsay* was torpedoed and sunk. The armed landing craft LCT 764 was sunk by a *Marder* torpedo. The troopships *Fort de Lac* and *Samlong* were torpedoed and damaged, the Liberty ship *Samtucky*, 7,219 gross tons, sunk. The light cruiser HMS *Durban* was so badly damaged as to be written off and condemned as a blockship to reinforce the *Mulberry* breakwaters.

At 0610 a *Marder* was sunk by motor launch HDML 1049. The Fleet destroyer HMS *Blencathra* captured an intact specimen with its torpedo still attached, but as the device was being heaved inboard the torpedo exploded and caused extensive damage. The British had more luck with another captured *Marder* which they sent to Britain for examination. The *Marders* which survived the battle were hunted by Spitfire fighter-bombers of 132 Squadron RAF and at least six were destroyed. Of 58 *Marders* which had sailed, only 17 returned, an appalling casualty rate. Amongst the survivors of this operation were pilots ObltzS Winzer and Schiebel, Lt Haun, Oberfähnrich Pettke, Obersteuermann (coxswain) Reuschoff, Steuermannsmaat (coxswain's mate) Schroeger, Maschinenmaat (leading stoker) Gushi and Matrosen (ordinary seamen) Glaubrecht and Roth.

Linsen Explosive-boat Operations on the Invasion Front (see also Chapter 9)

K-Flotilla 211 (*Linsen*) was ordered to the Normandy coast for the end of July 1944. On 24 and 25 July the flotilla left Müritzsee by train for France via Holland and Belgium. The flotilla spent a few days lodging at the German occupation forces' radio station *Sendestelle West* in the former Rothschild Palace in Paris. The last leg of the journey, from St Germain to Houlgate, was made in four columns of fifteen vehicles, the craft being concealed under tarpaulin on special trailers. As Flotilla Chief Oblt Plikat had sustained a concussion, Kptlt Helmut Bastian, formerly *Linse* training instructor at Plön, took over command. On the first night, only the first three groups with twelve command boats and 20 explosive *Linsen* started, the earlier *Marder* launch having so delayed the fourth group under Lt Vetter that it stood down.

The *Linsen* used a small channel to exit the minefield at Houlgate. In order to protect against accidents, flotilla members in rubber dinghies holding red lanterns lined the path through the danger zone. At the outset there was light cloud and occasionally the moon was visible through breaks in the cover. The light swell afforded the boats no problems. After the *Rottenführer* (pair leader) had refuelled from the reserve drums, enemy ships were sighted: MTBs, frigates and destroyers.

At 0251 the *Rotte* of Frank Gorges decided to attack the escort destroyer HMS *Quorn*. *Linse* pilot Werner Thybben set the fuze and jumped overboard. The *Linse*, remote-controlled from the command boat, sped for the target. After a brief lapse of time a violent explosion followed – a hit starboard amidships. The destroyer assumed a 40° list, and then rolled on her side. After a pause she struggled upright but then broke in two halves and sank quickly. Before she vanished the stern projected 9 metres and the bow 4.5 metres above the surface. Four officers and 126 men lost their lives. Gorges fished Thybben out of the water. Suddenly receiving fire from astern, they raced for shore, finally impaling the command boat on German beach obstructions but walked away without injury.

Towards 0300 Oberfernschreibmeister Herbert Berrer aimed at a ship but was unable to determine the result. Returning to base his command boat was hit by aircraft fire and Berrer had to abandon. He spent six hours in the water before being washed ashore on the right bank of the Orne totally exhausted. Kptlt Bastian in his report on the *Linsen* operation stated that K-Flotilla 211 started from the Dives estuary. The target was shipping clustered around the Orne bridge-head near Courselle. Weather and visibility were favourable. Attacks were made in three groups from north, east and south. Despite fire from massed anti-aircraft weapons and ships' guns, all *Linsen* got through the defences to sink five freighters, a destroyer, a patrol boat and a landing craft. Four command boats failed to return, two being sunk by enemy fighters just off the Trouville access channel.

Marder Operations in August 1944

K-Verband Command reported to SKL on 12 August: '60 *Marders* operational in France. Next operation planned for 14 August. Further flotilla will be ready end of month. Decision requested whether operation, if required, will take place on coast of southern France, still has some days' time left.'

On the night of 13 August, K-Flotilla 363 had orders to sail an offensive from Villers sur Mer against Allied shipping. Because of an approaching storm front with heavy rain the operation was postponed.

Towards 1800 on 14 August, during an attack on K-Flotilla 363 by low-flying aircraft, Flotilla Chief Oblt Wettreich was killed and a Group leader wounded. Of the 53 *Marders* listed to sail that day only 11 did so, and two of these put back early. Five of the other nine were lost to the tempestuous conditions. Heavy explosions and a red glow of long duration were observed from the land. At 0515 an ammunition ship of 8,000 gross tons blew up. Other explosions, probably depth charges, continued until 0700.

A fresh operation was called for on the night of 16 August in which the *Mulberry* harbours were the target. Under the most difficult conditions 42 *Marders* set out. The destroyer HMS *Isis* was torpedoed and sunk, the barrage-balloon ship HMS *Fratton* (757 gross tons) torpedoed and damaged. At 0632 a landing ship at anchor was torpedoed, the explosion killing all seventy crew aboard. The Germans could not ascertain whether this had been LCF1, LCG 831 or LCG 1062. Another *Marder* torpedoed the hull of the freighter *Iddesleigh*, beached after receiving bottom damage caused by an underwater explosion on 9 August. Two *Marders* attacked the old French battleship *Courbet* which had been grounded upright as a blockship in *Gooseberry* breakwater 5.

Although the operation was a success, the casualties were disproportionately high. Twenty-five *Marders* were lost to shelling, depth charges and air attack. Seven pilots were captured. A damaged *Marder* with dead pilot was retrieved by the landing ship LCS 251 and taken to Portsmouth for examination. 17 *Marder* pilots returned to base, one having been rescued by a French fishing boat. As Villers sur Mer was being threatened by the advancing Allied front, the flotillas had to pull back to Le Havre.

KptzS Böhme, head of the operational commandos, drew the necessary conclusions. The enemy knew the method of the one-man torpedo, the element of surprise had gone. On 18 August the equipment was withdrawn from Normandy. Böhme and his Staff relocated to Amiens. The *Marders* of the K-flotilla were sent to St Armand-Tournai in Belgium and then to the Scheldt near the French-Belgian border. The last *Marder* transport to be evacuated crossed the Seine on 20 August.

That same day Oblt Peter Berger coming from Germany with K-Flotilla 364 arrived at Rheims via Tournai. On 19 August he drew back to Tournai and set up camp in a wood near St Armand since the *Marders* could not reach the landing area from Le Havre because of the Allied advance. Local reconnaissance had shown that the opportunity for *Marder* operations no longer existed along the stretch Le Havre–Fécamp. On the way there, there had been an exchange of fire with partisans in which a mechanic, Dienemann, had been fatally wounded. Even the flotilla medical officer Dr Jung, returning from the Army Medical Park at Brussels with medical supplies, Chinin and Pervitin, had encountered difficulties, his car tyres being punctured by the use of nailed strips and so-called *Wolfangeln*.

Because of the Allied advance through northern France there were no prospects of further missions for the *Marders*. The K-Verband Chief of Staff, KKpt Frauenheim, therefore suggested stationing viable torpedo-carriers at Jutland. Norway was also considered, even the idea of sending *Marders* to the Gulf of Finland, but Denmark seemed more favourable.

Operations in the Mediterranean
In August 1944 OKW believed further Allied landings likely in the Mediterranean, and these began on 26 August in southern France under the cover name *Dragon*. On 23 August OKM had decided to merge the support personnel of K-Flotillas 363 and 364 and transfer the flotillas in several groups by road or rail to the Mediterranean region, favourable sites for operations from Cannes on the Riviera

being sought. To head defensive operations at the end of August, K-Verband Command set up a command structure at St Remo designated K-Staff Italy.

The four *Marder* groups proceeded through the Brenner Pass and South Tyrol to southern Italy. *No. 1 Group* was forced to stop short of Bozen for a wrecked bridge. They continued by road to Mezzecorona and then entrained via Trient and Verona for Genoa, arriving on 1 September with 15 *Marders*, proceeding next to Mentone, a village a few kilometres east of Monte Carlo, near San Remo, where a forward base had been set up. Here the equipment and men arrived on 3 September and began working up immediately.

No. 2 Group reached San Remo on 6 September and the rail tunnel at Savona was requisitioned as a sheltered camp.

No. 3 Group reached Verona by rail. During a low level air attack the locomotive fell into a bomb crater. Four men received light injuries and a lorry was written off.

No. 4 Group reached Valle Lomellina via Monza, Milan and Montora by rail. Because the bridge over the river Po was down they were forced to continue by road. In low level air attacks on 5 September at Voghera, *3* and *4 Groups* suffered twenty men wounded.

In the course of time K-Flotilla 365 (Oblt Barop) and K-Flotilla 366 (Oblt Paul Heinsius) were also transferred to Italy.

In the early hours of 5 September, five *Marders* left Mentone for the first attacks on Allied supply ships. After a failed attempt to torpedo the large French destroyer *Contre Torpilleur*, at 0810 the *Marders* ran into the French destroyer *Le Malin* and the US destroyer *Tudlow* patrolling off Cap Ferrat. Four of the one-man torpedoes, semi-submerged, were destroyed by shelling or depth charges. Only one pilot returned to base.

On 7 September fifteen more *Marders* arrived to reinforce the ten surviving machines at Mentone. Another thirty went to Genova on the Italian west coast as reserves. On 10 September, fourteen *Marders* sailed from Ventimiglia near Monte Carlo to attack US warships in the Gulf of St Tropez. The destroyers USS *Madison*, USS *Hilary P Jones* and two MTBs including PT 20T sank ten *Marders,* the other four pilots returned to base. A lightly wounded pilot, injured by perspex splinters when his cupola was hit, was brought out under enemy fire and treated by flotilla medical officer Dr Jung. The operation claimed no successes. The same evening the US destroyers and the old French battleship *Lorraine* shelled the launching ramps at Ventimiglia and either damaged or destroyed all one-man torpedoes at the site.

Eleven *Marders* were held back at Savona to operate to the enemy's rear in the event of fresh landings. K-Flotilla 364 also pulled back to Padua. Not until the night of 18 November 1944 did fifteen *Marders* leave San Remo for an attack: it failed with heavy losses, seven pilots failed to return.

On the night of 19 December fifteen *Marders* of K-Flotilla 363 sailed to attack the enemy destroyer defences off San Remo. There were no successes. Nine pilots failed to return. Five torpedoes missed and one dud failed.

The last *Marder* operation of 1944 followed on 31 December against shipping near Ville Franche. Five *Marders* set out. After a sixth was lost in heavy surf, the later departures were cancelled. Four pilots returned next day, one remains missing. Of the four, one had found a patrol boat but could not fire the torpedo, another was forced away by the heavy escort. The others sighted no traffic. From the Bordighera signals station three heavy explosions were heard from the Ville Franche direction, but since no ship appears to have been sunk possibly they were depth charges.

The remaining *Marders* were transferred to the Adriatic, most to Verona, the crews being lodged in Saonara near Padua. Orders were received to transfer to Savona the machines stationed at Treviso, a town about 30 kilometres north of Venice, but this was countermanded and the torpedoes went for overhaul to Venice instead and finally to Trieste in the far north-east corner of the Adriatic near the Slovenian border.

The last *Marder* mission of the war was sailed on 24 April 1945. Seventeen pilots sailed from San Remo to attack shipping off Livorno. Fifteen were lost to Allied warships, coastal batteries and aircraft.

German one-man torpedoes carried out twelve operations in the 13 months from April 1944. A total of 264 machines were used of which 162 were lost, and about 150 brave pilots gave their lives. These lone warriors, dependent wholly upon themselves, defied the elements in their primitive craft and pitted themselves against a powerful, superior naval enemy while exposed and defenceless to his aircraft.

They were not *kamikazes*. Such a manner of conducting warfare was alien to their European mentality. Nevertheless each of these operations amounted to a suicide mission.

Notes

1 Initially it had been Hitler himself who suspected Normandy as a possible destination for invasion. In May 1944 radio specialists of 15 Army (Generaloberst von Salmuth) and, independently, a Luftwaffe signals company stationed on Guernsey, predicted that beyond a doubt the invasion would be at Normandy. Both passed their reports to Rommel's Army group Staff. 15 Army raised the alarm, but 7 Army (General Dollmann) and other coastal units which lay directly in the path of the invasion remained stood down. After the Allied landings began, battleworthy divisions such as 21 Pz. Div. and 12 SS-Pz. Div. *Hitler Jugend* received no orders for days. These delays, chaotic orders, constantly changing commanders and the abortive misdirection of whole groups created the conditions under which the invasion succeeded. The few 'ethnic mixed' infantry divisions in the most forward positions should have been sufficient to repulse the landings in the sensitive phase. (*Omaha* beach could not be taken from the sea because of a single machine-gun nest at Courville firing from a protected position 150 metres inshore.) Many military specialists agree that a single battleworthy German division would have decided the invasion in Germany's favour provided the division could have, *or was permitted to*, become involved in events immediately as they unfolded. If all this muddle was due solely to operational mismanagement or the failures of OKH is open to question. In his book *Der Verratene Sieg*, British historian H.H. Saunders assumed that only deliberate disinformation, linked to the suppression of communications and situation reports slanted in a particular manner, could have resulted in the invasion being resisted in the way it was.

Chapter Four

Midget Submarine Type
XXVIIA *Hecht*

The *Hecht* (pike) was the first midget submersible of the Kriegs-marine. The design originated in K-Amt, the main OKM architectural office for warships, and was based on technical details of the British Type X. On 23 September 1943 when midget submarines of this type had attacked the battleship *Tirpitz* in Kaa Fjord, one specimen fell into German hands.

K-Amt was given the task of building the German equivalent. Its role would be to approach enemy warships in roadsteads or harbours while submerged and attach limpet mines to the ships' hulls. Standard U-boats would tow the craft to the enemy coast and release it for independent operations. It would have a crew of two.

The design was classified Type XXVIIA, later the cover name *Hecht* was given. The boat was smaller than the British X-Class and would reach its objective always submerged. The radius of action was limited and it seemed the best idea to transport the *Hecht* to the vicinity of the operational zone on the surface.

On 18 January 1944 Grossadmiral Dönitz obtained Hitler's approval for the construction of 50 *Hecht*. On 9 March contracts were awarded to Germania Werft to build three prototypes. On 28 March the yard received orders for series production. Construction work began in April 1944. Fifty-three boats were completed, these were numbered U-2111 to U-2113 and U-2251 to U-2300 inclusive.

***Hecht* – technical details:**
Length: 10.4 m
Beam: 2.7 m
Displacement: 11.8 tonnes
Propulsion: 1 × 12 hp electric torpedo-motor
Speed: (submerged) 6 knots
Range: 69 sea miles
Armament: 1 × G 7e (battery driven) torpedo or 1 limpet mine
Crew: Two

The boat was propelled by a 12 hp AEG torpedo motor, its revolutions controlled by V-pulley. Drive was provided by five 17T 8 × 210 batteries, the plates of which were exchangeable for greater capacity at low output and to extend battery life. As operations were to be entirely submerged, dive-tanks were deemed unnnecessary. Regulating tanks were installed to provide enough freeboard for the crew to access the hatch. These tanks were then flooded with about 200 litres of water which would then be used to trim the boat during passage.

Since the boat had to be kept in trim when submerged, and further operations might require the boat to force a way through anti-submarine netting, diving planes were replaced by manually-moved weights on a spindle. In practice this idea proved hopeless because the weights could not be moved fast enough to restore the trim when the boat became nose- or tail-heavy suddenly. To remedy this, hydroplanes and stabilizing fins were then incorporated, an emergency measure which fell short of providing satisfactory control of the depth.

The *Hecht* was equipped with a standard U-boat gyro compass and transformer. This made the vessel larger by a third than had been originally intended and required a plumper outline amidships to house the gyro. The range had to be sacrificed to compensate for the additional demand on electric current.

Originally one large limpet mine was proposed as armament, but the development and accommodation of this mine caused great difficulties. The procedure of attaching it to the hull of an enemy vessel was very laborious and in practice rarely successful, and so even before the first *Hecht* was completed, the mine idea had been scrapped.

The designers then had the idea of replacing the mine with a battery head containing more accumulators with a view to extending the radius of action, and finally they wanted to build a cabin to carry frogmen. Last of all it was thought it might be possible to sling a torpedo below the *Hecht* for discharge from within the submarine. The chief difficulty here was that a submarine of only 947 cubic metres could not carry a standard torpedo weighing several hundred kilos and the alternative types of torpedo of suitable weight did not have the battery capacity for a worthwhile range and speed.

The crew consisted of the commander, who was responsible for conning the boat and firing the torpedo, and the engineer. Admiral Heye said later of *Hecht*: 'Germany's first small U-boat, the *Hecht*, was built only in a small series. Mass production was not considered. The *Hecht* was only used as a training boat with the accumulator head. Its advantage lay in enabling the naval architects to familiarize themselves with that kind of project for the first time. From the development much experience was gained which was useful for the later types (particularly the two-man *Seehund*).'

If the *Hecht* really was a submarine, it makes its successors look like classic little submersibles. It was a fat, insufficiently manoeuvrable boat with poor diving capability only ever used for training purposes with K-Flotilla 311 at *Lehrkommando 300* Neustadt (*Neukoppel*). At the beginning of November 1944 it is reported that twelve *Hecht* were stationed at Asaa in Denmark for anti-invasion duty.

K-Flotilla was formed of *inter alios* the following officers:

Flotilla Chief: Oblt Felix Schaefer

Adjutant: Oblt Walter Ploke

(All of rank of Leutnant): Eberhardt Nehes, Horst Reindorf, Rolf Rendtdorf, Hans Rettberg, Tielko Tillmann, Gerhard Pankow, Magnus Radtke, Eugen Stahlhacke.

This flotilla was used mainly to train crews for the pocket U-boat *Seehund*. In December 1944 a series of accidents occurred in which the following eleven submariners lost their lives:

Oblt (Ing) Gerhard Hempel, LtzS Konrad Gieseking, LtzS Hans-Georg Krüger, LtzS Georg-Wilhelm Burmeister, LtzS Karl-Heinz

Riethmüller, LtzS Günter Bernhardt, LtzS Stefan Andersch, Maschinen-maat Johann Meyer, Maschinenmaat Werner Hardt, Maschinenmaat Friedrich Springemann, Maschinenmaat Martin Strobel.

These men were buried with full military honours in Neustadt Cemetery.

Chapter Five

The Midget Submersible
Biber

Development, Construction, Trials

In contrast to *Hecht*, the *Biber* (beaver) was a new idea originated by KKpt Hans Bartels (FKpt from 1 December 1944), a K-Verband Staff officer. Bartels based his design on the British *Welman* type midget submarine W-46, captured at Bergen on 22 November 1943. The *Welman* was technically unfinished and a dangerous little boat, but Bartels believed it could be improved substantially.

On 4 February 1944 together with Kptlt (S) Michael Opladen, an Abwehr officer from an industrial family, Bartels negotiated with Director Bunte of the Flenderwerft at Lübeck to build his concept of a midget submarine. By 23 February the provisional design designated *Adam* and *Bunte-boat* was on the table, and by 15 March the *Biber* prototype, as it was known officially, was completed by the Flender yard.

The initial trials, in which Bartels participated personally, were held on the River Trave. During one of the early dives the boat sank with Bartels aboard. He survived, the craft was raised and quickly restored. On 27 March Dönitz accepted the boat into the Kriegsmarine personally. Doubts expressed by the naval construction board (*Hauptausschuss Schiffbau der Kriegsmarine*) regarding the use of a petrol engine were dismissed by Director Bunte with the observation that it gave unlimited capacity and ran silently. OKM ordered four

59

prototypes followed with a series order for twenty training and 300 operational boats.

The hulls and fittings were manufactured by Flenderwerft Lübeck and the Italian Ansaldo yard at Genoa. The latter shipped the hulls for completion to the Klöckner-Humboldt-Deutz works at Ulm. In May 1944 three, in June ten, in July nineteen, in August fifty, in September 117, in October seventy-three, in November fifty-six boats were completed and delivered to the K-Verband.

The *Biber* consisted of three sections bolted together. The bow section, and part of the section aft held the main dive tanks. The control room lay between the two bulkheads and accommodated the pilot seated with his head in the 0.71 metre-diameter conning tower, the upper part of which projected only 0.51 metres above the surface in a flat calm. Viewing ports were fitted in this tower and a periscope for use when submerged. The pilot faced the instrument panel, economic on space and limited to essentials. To dive he had to perform sixteen hand movements. The control room contained compressed air tanks for blowing the dive tanks, oxygen bottle and breathing gear, the batteries, the gasoline tanks and fuel leads to the motor. The pilot had no personal facilities. For nutriment he had a ration of chocolate laced with a pep pill to ward off sleep on lengthy operations (see *Insert*).

The surface drive was the controversial 2.5 Otto motor of 32 hp, originally designed for the Opel Blitz lorry, which gave the *Biber* a range of 100 sea miles and a top speed of 6.5 knots. The exhaust gases contained carbon monoxide and thus the pilot created a lethal atmosphere for himself if he kept the engine running longer than 45 minutes with the hatch shut. The build-up of poison gas would then overwhelm him, he would fall asleep and succumb to the poisoned environment. A number of pilots died of carbon monoxide poisoning on operational missions. The pilot's breathing apparatus was sufficient for twenty hours. This was a nose-mouth mask with a tube leading to three potash cartridges to purify his exhalations of carbon dioxide.

In an attempt to reduce fatalities from posioning Bartels set up a unit composed of naval officers, technicians, engineers and a medical officer to investigate the effects of inhaling petrol exhaust gases. Symptoms were dizziness, torpor and tinnitus. After subsequently breathing fresh air intensive headaches would develop behind the forehead with later vomiting. It was hammered into *Biber* pilots that they had to ensure that

Opiates and Pep Pills

Medications of the type described previously were marketed by Temmler GmbH as early as 1938, the leading drug being *Pervitin* (1-Phenyl 2-Methylaminopan). The firm Knoll brought out an identical preparation, *Isophan*, somewhat later. The preparations met lively interest for their ability to overcome fatigue, depression and hunger, and revive those suffering from exhaustion. Tested on ninety midshipmen and Army cadets at the Military-Medical Academy in Berlin it was found that a 9 or 12 mg *Pervitin* removed the need for sleep that night and the following day without side effects and imbued in the taker an enhanced feeling of confidence. In 1944 the effects were examined on sportsmen, and concentration camp inmates at Sachsenhausen. The correct dose greatly increased efficiency in healthy people.

In order to master problems of fatigue in the K-Verband, *Biber*-pilots were used as guinea pigs in trials. In one trial involving five officer volunteers, unpleasant effects occurred an hour after taking one or two D IX tablets. Those officers who were fresh and well rested found their hands trembling. Those who had been fatigued before ingesting now complained of weakness at the knees and muscular contractions. With a large enough dose D IX would cause a gradual paralysis of the central nervous system. Euphoria would evaporate suddenly, the ability to make decisions and intellect would become limited. This opiate did not bestow alertness but was a pronounced narcotic. The medical fraternity was outspoken in its opposition to the drug.

Further tests on *Biber*-pilots proved that normal chocolate containing cola and other extracts from the cola nut had a reviving effect. To combat fatigue, because of its purine and caffeine content, only a small *Pervitin* dose was allowed.

the exhaust piping valve was closed; if left open the carbon monoxide concentration in the control room would rise to lethal proportions (1.2VO%).

Three racks, of four 13T 210 type batteries each, provided the power for a 13 hp electric motor. Range was 8.6 sea miles at 5.3 knots at 20 metres depth. The pressure hull was of 3 mm sheet steel guaranteed to a depth of 20 metres. The hull was pressure-resistant to 40 metres and various *Biber* pilots found on operations that this could be exceeded easily. The inner bulkheads and three longitudinal ribs reinforced the hull plating.

The *Biber* had no compensating or trim tanks, only dive tanks in the fore and aft compartments to get her under in an emergency. Therefore the boat hardly merited being called a 'submarine'. She handled well on the surface, but submerged was almost impossible to steer in any axis mainly because she could not be trimmed. Accordingly only surface attacks could be made, submergence was to avoid attack and to escape. The boat had to be adjusted with fixed ballast before each sailing. When under way changes in displacement or trim could only be equalized by partially flooding the dive tanks. This was a tricky job for the pilot, adding to his problems when he submerged the boat.

The armament was two torpedoes each slung on a rail and fitting into a moulded cavity either side of the keel. The torpedoes were of limited battery power to save weight. To fire them the piston in a compressed air cylinder jerked back to release a pressure screw and force open a release lever on the torpedo. This started the torpedo motor. The missile, held clear of the hull by two bridles on the retaining rail, would then set off under its own power. This firing mechanism was primitive and resulted in serious accidents. Inattention when releasing the torpedo caused the destruction of a number of boats and the death of the occupants. As an alternative to torpedoes the *Biber* could carry two ground mines activated by magnetic/acoustic or magnetic/water pressure detonators.

Further developments of the *Biber* which ultimately remained in the planning stage were the two-seater *Biber* II and III projects. Abandonment of the design resulted after an OKM instruction at the beginning of 1945 put paid to all work on projects not yet in series production. This directive was not obeyed universally. The fact that Admiral Heye had a fairly independent position ensured that work on favoured designs continued until the war's end. *Biber* III was designed for a 60 hp diesel (40 hp closed circuit circulation) instead of the Otto motor, providing a range of 1,100 sea miles at 8 knots. The project was scrapped in favour of the *Seehund* and the need at that time for a modern 'pocket U-boat'.

The *Biber*-Flotillas

In August 1944 at Lübeck-Schlutup, KKpt Hans Bartels established *Lehrkommando 250*, cover name *Blaukoppel*, for *Biber* crews. After evaluating earlier experiences, the pilots were men with training as U-boat watchkeeping officers. *Lehrkommando 250* was staffed as follows:

Chief: KKpt Hans Bartels

Adjutant: Oblt Alexander Mitbauer

1. Consultant: Oblt Wilhelm Dietermann

Camp Commandant: Oblt Bernhard Dettloff

Camp Physician: Kptlt Rudolf Püschel

Training Leaders: Kptlt Friedrich Braasch, Oblt Ernst Grassrick, Lt Willi Preussner

Lehrkommando 250 trained personnel for the following K-Flotillas:

K-Flotilla 261 (formed August 1944)
Flotilla Chief: Kptlt Friedmar Wolters

Staffel (Overall-group)-Leader: Kptlt Richard Sommer

Torpedo Officer: Hans Dobat

K-Flotilla 262 (formed January 1945)
Flotilla Chief: Kptlt Schmidt

Torpedo Officer: Lt Julius Schmidt

Group Leaders: Oblt Frans Bullmann, Lt Wolfgang Isenbart, Lt Hans Heller, Lt Leo Steinmeier

K-Flotilla 263 (formed September 1944)
Flotilla Chief: Oblt Dieter Erdmann

Torpedo Officer: Lt Werner Seidel

Group Leaders: Lt Friedrich Schmeling, Lt Friedrich Homrich, Lt Lothar Bading, Lt Wolfgang Jung, Lt Gerhard Wanzer

63

K-Flotilla 264
Flotilla Chief: Kptlt Siegfried Timper

Torpedo Officer: Lt Heinz Neumann

Group Leaders: Lt Karl Schechtner, Lt Lothar Steuer

K-Flotilla 265 (formed February 1945)
Flotilla Chief: Oblt Walter Fahje

Staffel Leader: Lt Horst Pukownik

Torpedo Officer: Lt Rolf Biedermann

Group Leaders: Oblt Wolfgang Kirschner, Oblt Gustav Dose, Lt Karl-August Woldmann, Lt Rudolf Breske, Lt Joachim Lemhöfer, Lt Kurt Merz, Lt Karl-Albert Reitz, Lt Gerhardt Sporns

K-Flotilla 266 (formed October 1944)
Flotilla Chief: Oblt Udo Heckmann

Group Leaders: Lt Franz Kreusche, Lt Joachim-Georg Krämer

K-Flotilla 267 (formed December 1944)
Flotilla Chief: Kptlt Herbert Wagner

Group Leaders: Lt Heinz Andresen, Lt Rudolf Breuer, Lt Werner Jahn, Lt Martin Freudenreich

K-Flotilla 268 (formed 1945)
Flotilla Chief: Kptlt Joachim Stetzer

Torpedo Officer: Oblt Erhard Burghardt

Group Leaders: Oblt Rudolf Schmidt, Lt Wolfgang Zinsser, Lt Heinz-Jürgen Mentler

K-Flotilla 269 (formed 1945)
Flotilla Chief: Kptlt Kurt Halledt-Holzapfel

Group Leaders: Lt Walter Schmidt, Lt Peter-Claus Rehbehn, Lt Rüdiger Ott

K-Flotilla 270 (formed 1945)
Oblt Kurt Warnke, Lt Horst-Hermann Bunte

It is not known if K-Flotillas 269 and 270 were fully staffed. Changes in personnel amongst the officers in individual flotillas by reason of casualties or administrative reshuffling not reported to the Naval Personnel Office is possible.

The Failed Operation at Fécamp
On 21 August 1944 the first *Bibers* attached to K-Flotilla 261 (KKpt Hans Bartels) left Lübeck for Normandy to replace the depleted ranks of the one-man torpedoes. It was intended originally that the flotilla would operate from Le Havre against the invasion fleet, but on 20 August Allied armoured formations broke out of the landing heads and began to fight their way east. Houlgate, a former *Marder* base, was overrun by the Dutch brigade *Princes Irene* on 21 August.

Bartels, pausing at the Scheldt after reaching Tournai in Belgium with a motorized column transporting 25 *Bibers*, found that he could not reach his intended destination Le Havre, since Admiral Channel Coast had advised him that the town was to be abandoned by German occupying forces within a few days. The evacuation began on 23 August, the last German units leaving on the 31st of the month.

This important naval base had been severely damaged in June 1944 when the Kriegsmarine sustained heavy losses. On the night of 14 June RAF bombers attacked Le Havre. After Mosquitos dropped marker flares on the concrete bunkers, 22 Lancaster bombers unloaded 5-ton Tallboy bombs on the harbour. The second and third waves of 209 and 116 Lancaster bombers respectively, dropped 1,230 tons of bombs on Le Havre, destroying the harbour installations. The Kriegsmarine lost the torpedo boats *Falke*, *Jaguar* and *Möwe*, 14 S-boats including all of 4 S-boat Flotilla, 20 minesweepers and patrol boats, 19 tugs and 7 other small vessels. Only one S-boat survived. The wrecks blocked the harbour exit for the ships still navigable inside.

The same evening Boulogne was attacked by 12 Mosquitos, 130 Halifax and 155 Lancaster bombers. A depot ship and 24 light craft including 7 R-boats were sunk. The Kriegsmarine, which had only minor warships in the Normandy area, was seriously weakened by these losses. Only 10 S-boats remained in the area of the landings. To replace the losses, 6 S-boat Flotilla was ordered to the Channel from the Gulf of Finland. The offensive fighting forces were now principally the few U-boats and the K-Verband.

It was decided that K-Flotilla 261 should set up camp in the village of Fécamp in the department of Seine-Maritime, 30 kilometres north-east of Le Havre. As an operational base it was particularly unfavourable, being too far east of the landings zone in the Bay of the Seine. The flotilla arrived on 28 August at Fécamp just as the German occupation forces were pulling out. Bartels was ordered to be operational within 20 hours. He set the shore crew to work at a feverish pace in the fish dock.

On the way to Fécamp the flotilla had been attacked by low-flying aircraft and bombers resulting in nine dead, three *Biber* and six heavy lorries lost. For the night of 29 August, 22 *Biber* were listed to start but the damage to the harbour installations permitted only 14 boats to be lowered to the water by crane. Strong winds and rough seas forced 12 of the boats to put back prematurely: the pilots of the other two submersibles, Lt Dose and Funkmaat Bösch, who reached the Bay of the Seine, claimed on their return to have sunk a 7,000-ton Liberty ship and a minesweeper or landing craft, but these losses were not confirmed by the Allies.

On 31 August Fécamp was given up, the 15th Army falling back on Dieppe. The British 1 Corps (Lt-Gen. Crocker) entered Le Havre. A number of *Biber* had had to be destroyed. K-Flotilla 261 retired behind the Somme with 14 boats, and from there headed for Mönchen-Gladbach. The chief of MEK forces Normandy, KptzS Böhme, also left with his Staff.

During the road and rail transport, and in a skirmish by night with an American armoured column there were losses in personnel and boats. The remainder of the flotilla reached Lübeck. On 24 September, K-Flotilla 261 was re-formed at Hurup, east Jutland. The quarters supplied were poor hovels and many personnel suffered severely from the cold. A number of shore personnel who spent long periods working inside the boats were diagnosed with gasoline-benzol poisoning. On 31 October 1944 the flotilla relocated to Groningen in Holland for fresh operations.

Biber-Flotilla Operations in Holland

Most operational *Biber* flotillas transferred into the Netherlands between September and November 1944, from where it was intended that they should attack Allied supply ships in the Scheldt. The main base was Rotterdam, advanced bases being at Poortershavn and Hellevoetsluis, and also Groningen. On 26 November 1944 there were two K-Flotillas plus one reserve in the region with a total of 30 *Biber*. In the course of time operations were sailed from the Hook of Holland, and shipping destined for Antwerp was attacked.

On 3 September 1944 there occurred an armed uprising at Antwerp, and next day the British 11th Armoured Division (Major-Gen. Roberts) advanced on the city. By early afternoon his leading tanks had met up with an armed group of the Belgian 'armée sécrète' which had control of the large sluice gates and the harbour. They took the docks intact but the British neglected the Albert Canal bridges on the northern outskirts of the city. The attack ground to a halt and the Germans kept the connection to the island of Walcheren. They also remained in possession of both banks of the Scheldt estuary, through which traffic passed to Antwerp from the North Sea, and for the next three months the Scheldt was unnavigable for the Allies.

The operational area for K-Verband craft was more complicated than the French Channel coast. Every day the *B-Dienst* at Zieriksee on the island of Schouwen reported convoys leaving the Thames, but a *Biber* could only sail when wind and sea state did not exceed Force 4. The procedure then was to leave Rotterdam on the ebb during the day and cover the 40 sea miles to the western Scheldt near Flushing, availing themselves of the strong south-west current off the coast. The ebb carried the *Biber* to the enemy so that they arrived in the combat zone in the evening, allowing a night attack. It must be remembered that the *Biber* was no submarine, but a surface torpedo-carrier which could dive if things got too hot. Navigation through the numerous sandbanks caused *Biber* pilots many difficulties. The major risk was from the regular fighter-bomber attacks which caused many losses.

K-Verband Command was quick to recognize that the chance of a *Biber* torpedoing a ship under way involved very long odds against. Therefore on 25 November thirty GS mines – 20 with magnetic/acoustic and 10 with magnetic/water pressure detonators – were sent from Lübeck to Groningen. Trials were scheduled for completion by 3 December. Meanwhile three VP-boats and an R-boat flotilla was made ready to tow the *Bibers* to the operational zone. On 25 November all K-Verband missions in the Scheldt area were suspended so as to avoid compromising a planned operation by Army High Command (AOK 15).

To seal off the Scheldt, the river between Flushing and Antwerp was sown with about 300 ground mines, amongst them the difficult to sweep MA2 and DM1 types. Off Flushing were numerous fields of mixed mines. Other mines were laid in the Wieling Channel between Knocke and Kadzand, between Osterschelde and Steendeep and in the western Scheldt. Channels were kept mine-free for S-boats and K-Verband vessels.

In mid-1944, K-Verband Command devised a comprehensive plan for the deployment of its forces in the western area. A telex from SKL to Admiral, Führer-HQ read: 'Flotillas are spread from the Meuse Estuary to Den Helder. Transfers at short notice to departure points possible.' The first *Biber* operation began on the night of 22 December. Eight boats were towed by R-boats from Poortershavn, ten by VP-boats from Hellevoetsluis. Off the Hook of Holland the first group ran into British MLs which sank four *Biber*, while the other boats cut their towlines and submerged. The second group entered a minefield off the West Schouwen Bank. One *Biber* sank, another was damaged. This left 12 boats armed with torpedoes and mines to fulfill the mission. Off Flushing a *Biber* sank the Panamanian munitions ship *Alan-a-Dale*, 4,702 gross tons, the only certain *Biber* success.

All 12 boats were lost. Nothing is known of the causes. Suffocation by gasoline fumes and unintentional swamping during surface travel with the hatch open were considered the most probable reasons after enemy action. The *B-Dienst* reported several explosions but what these signified is not known.

On the night of 23 December 1944 another 11 *Biber* left Hellevoetsluis for the Scheldt, being towed to a position north-west of Goerre. One boat sank on the outward voyage two sea miles off Hellevoetsluis, another stranded on the West Schouwen Bank west of Battede Hamstede. Nothing is known of the fate met by the other nine. On Christmas Eve three more *Biber* headed for the western Scheldt and these were also not heard from again.

At 2330 hrs on Christmas Day 1944 six *Biber* were towed by the Rhine-Flotilla from Hellevoetsluis to lay mines in the western Scheldt. On the morning of 26 December Typhoon fighter-bombers sank two of these boats off Flushing, the fate of the other four remains unknown. Causes of loss could have been rough sea conditions, poor visibility, navigational problems. Within a few days, thirty *Biber* had been lost.

Despite these appalling losses, on 27 December at Hellevoetsluis in daylight, but under cover of artificial fog, another 14 *Biber* prepared to sail. While manoeuvring in the lock a *Biber* pilot fired both his torpedoes accidentally. The cause was linked to icing-up of the firing mechanism. The torpedoes exploded, sinking eleven *Biber* and two harbour defence boats. The tidal locks were also damaged. K-Flotilla 262 and the Rhine-Flotilla reported several dead and injured. Three sunken *Biber* were written off, the others would require overhaul after being salved. Undeterred the three undamaged boats put to sea. On 29 December the minesweeper HMS *Ready* found a *Biber* with the recognition number '90' adrift off North Foreland. Its dead pilot was aboard. While under tow the line broke and the *Biber* sank, but the British salvaged the craft ten days later. An autopsy established the cause of death of the pilot as carbon monoxide posioning. This *Biber* can be inspected today at the Imperial War Museum in London.

Between 22 and 27 December 1944, about fifty *Biber* were lost. The extraordinary courage and morale of the men in carrying out missions like these having a high probability of non-survival cannot be overstated. The word 'impossible' was not to be found in their vocabulary. They did not rush blindly into the unknown, or volunteer for death as did the *kamikazes*. For these highly motivated volunteers, the missions seemed to offer the chance to inflict losses on an enemy vastly superior in numbers, and to obstruct and delay his advance into Germany, so making a vital contribution to the defence of the homeland. It was a tragic fact that no machines properly tried and tested for the job were available for this kind of operation. Because of the high casualty rate, Naval High Command West suggested the suspension of *Biber* operations, pointing to the wastage in men and material. Generaladmiral Dönitz rejected the suggestion. He had great hopes for the *Biber*, particularly as a minelayer. Before Christmas he had mentioned that for his *Sturmwikinger* (Assault Vikings) as the *Biber* crews described themselves, he was proposing to introduce

69

the term *Opferkämpfer* (Sacrificial Warriors). Admiral Heye found this undesirable.

At New Year 1945, K-Verband in the West had the 20 *Biber* of K-Flotilla 261, another 30 boats of K-Flotilla 262 at Groningen, and 60 more expected soon to boost the numbers. By 7 January 1945, of the eleven sunken *Biber* six had been raised and would be operational in three days. On the night of 29 January 15 *Biber* were towed to the coast from Poortershavn and set off for the Hook of Holland. The conditions at sea were bitter cold with drifting ice. The pilots steered from the open hatch. Only when they reached the open sea, a point between the islands of Goerre and Voorne, or the signal station on the mole at the Hook of Holland, did they enter the boat and seal the hatch.

This time the *Biber* escaped enemy air reconnaissance but not the weather. Five boats put back with damage from ice, three sank after collisions with drifting ice floes. A *Biber* was stranded at Hellevoetsluis after its pilot spent 64(!) fruitless hours waiting for a target to appear. The other six boats were lost without trace.

In January 1945 ten of the fifteen boats used on operations were lost. No successes were reported. In wintry conditions in deceptive waters, poorly equipped for navigation, *Biber* pilots had to accept these serious losses.

On 3 February 19 Lancaster bombers attacked the *Biber* base at Poortershavn. Tallboy bombs (6.4 metres long, 5.4 tonnes, 2.43 tonnes HE) were dropped. These bombs had been devised originally to destroy the German U-boat bunkers on the Atlantic coast. Although none of the 20 *Biber* were harmed, great damage was caused to the harbour installations and the cranes used to lower the boats into the water, and in February no *Biber* operations were sailed. On 10 February the proposal of C-in-C West to abandon the island of Schouwen was turned down by Führer-HQ on the grounds of its importance for the protection of the seas around southern Holland and for K-Verband operations against shipping in the Scheldt. Three days later however the entire front was pulled back to Ijssel-Zee west of Arnhem, which meant that north-west Holland was given up.

On 6 March another disaster occurred. During overhaul work on the raised *Biber* at the Rotterdam Depot basin, another *Biber* pilot discharged a torpedo accidentally. 14 *Biber* were destroyed in the explosion and nine damaged. Despite this setback, the same day 11 undamaged boats were towed from Hellevoetsluis to the Scheldt. None returned. One was captured by a British ML off Breskens on 7 March. Four were found abandoned on the shore at Noord Beveland, Domberg, Knocke and Zeebrugge respectively. One boat was sunk on 8 March off West Kapelle by coastal artillery. Nothing is known of the fate of the other three.

On the night of 11 March a combined operation involving S-boats, *Linsen* and midget submersibles of the types *Biber* and *Molch* was sailed. The attack was aimed at supply ships in the western Scheldt bound for Antwerp. The 15 *Biber*, armed with torpedoes and mines, started out from Hellevoetsluis. Two boats were sunk by Swordfish aircraft of Coastal Command on the afternoon of 12 March near Schouwen island, four boats next morning by British MLs off West Kapelle and one boat that afternoon by a Spitfire. Four others were sunk around midday by land batteries at Flushing and Breskens. At 0325 on 13 March the escort destroyer HMS *Retallick* sank a *Biber* west of Walcheren. In this disaster, 13 *Biber*, 9 *Molch* and 16 *Linsen* were lost without a single enemy ship being sunk.

The last *Biber* operation of March 1945 was sailed on the night of the 23rd. 16 boats armed with mines and torpedoes left Poortershavn for the Scheldt. No enemy ships were sunk. HMS *Retallick* sank four *Biber*, a Beaufighter of 254 Squadron RAF a fifth. One boat washed up abandoned on Schouwen. Seven *Biber* returned to base. In March 1945, 42 of 56 *Biber* and *Molch* were lost for no successes, a macabre balance.

On 9 April *Biber* missions were resumed. Five left the Hook of Holland, two returned on 11 April with mechanical problems. One of these hit a mine while entering harbour and sank, the other three were sunk on 12 April west of the Hook of Holland by Beaufighter and Swordfish aircraft.

On 11 April two *Biber* left Zierikzee to lay mines in the channel between Noord and Zuid Beveland, one boat returned. In the next operation on 21 April six *Biber* sailed at night to lay mines in the Scheldt, four returned. The last *Biber* operation took place on 26 April 1945, nine days before the cessation of U-boat warfare in the West, when four *Biber* left to mine the Scheldt. One boat stranded on a sandbank on the outward journey, the other three were attacked by US

Thunderbolt aircraft off the Hook of Holland, two being sunk, one escaped.

By the beginning of May the Scheldt was almost completely surrounded by British forces, and K-Verband Command was no longer able to bring up reinforcement boats by road and rail.

When one analyzes the fearless operations of the K-Verband pilots, one is forced to conclude that the missions sailed by *Biber* flotillas in particular were cavalier and irresponsible because the boats were so primitive. The volunteers had little chance of returning from a mission, whatever it was, and were almost suicide pilots to compare with the Japanese *Kaiten* one-man torpedo riders.

Biber Flotillas in the Arctic

A lighter burden fell to K-Verband men stationed in the Far North. Even after the Normandy invasion in June 1944, OKW was not convinced that more landings might not be planned in Norway and Denmark. For this reason a part of the so-called Atlantic Wall remained monitored closely, and sections of the K-Verband were stationed in these two countries.

After KptzS Böhme transferred to Italy to take command of K-Operations Staff at Levico, KptzS Düwel headed the K-Operations Staff at Arhus, Denmark, KptzS Beck at Oslo, Norway. Because of the deteriorating situation on the Eastern Front, Düwel was appointed to command K-Operations Staff *Sonderaufgaben* (Special Tasks) at Kammer am Attersee, maintaining liaison with the Army during operations on the Danube, Drau and Oder. He was replaced at Arhus by Knights Cross-and-Diamonds holder FKpt Brandi.

In the autumn of 1944, *Biber* of K-Flotilla 264 were stationed at Arhus and Aalborg in Denmark to resist possible enemy landings in the Skagerrak. The initial plan to transfer K-Flotilla 263 from Kristiansand South to Bodö in northern Norway was shelved in favour of defending the Skagerrak from Kristiansand in liaison with its radar station.

On 22 November 1944 K-Flotilla 264 arrived at Andes Fjord near Harstad with 30 *Biber*. They had come up from Holland through Lübeck and the unit was allotted a base close to the heavy coastal battery at Trondeness. The same day SKL issued a directive to the effect that:

72

(1) In collaboration with K-Verband Command (Chief of K-Staff, Norway, KptzS Beck), the Führer of U-boats Arctic (FdU Arctic) is to prepare an operation against Kola Bay using *Biber* transported there by U-boats.
(2) FdU Arctic will draw up the operational orders. Preparations and instructions for the *Biber* mission in the Bay itself will originate from K-Verband Command.
(3) U-716 is intended for the operation. The tests ordered specially must be completed beforehand.
(4) FdU Arctic is to transmit the operational orders by telex to 2/SKL and Naval High Command, who will be kept informed constantly once the operation begins.

This operation was codenamed *Caesar*. By the end of 1944 K-Verband Command had drawn up its working plan. Six *Biber* of K-Flotilla 264 were to attack a battleship reported in Wayenga Bay, secondary target was the shipping at Kola. The *Biber* would be towed to Kildin, entering its estuary individually. The approach period allowed was three days. The latest attack day with adequate moonlight to pick out the target was 10 January, most favourable day was 8 January.

The *Biber* pilots familiarized themselves beforehand with photographs showing an eye-level silhouette of the coast taken 8 sea miles offshore. Courses and distances off, names and images of coastal promontories, the tides, risings of the moon and its direction, and the specified operational timings and return tracks were all provided.

From the 30 *Biber* of K-Flotilla 264 the eight pilots in best physical condition were transferred to a training base given the English name *Black Watch*. Here they carried out exercises and practice attacks in a fjord strange to them fitted out with net barriers. Two accidents occurred during this training period. During major demands on the boats, the gasoline supply lines loosened allowing gases to enter the interior. When the electric motor was activated for a dive a spark ignited the gas. The pilot was seriously injured while attempting to save his burning boat. In a second similar accident the pilot managed to escape but the *Biber* was lost.

The target of the operation was the Soviet battleship *Archangelsk*, the former HMS *Royal Sovereign* which the British had transferred to the Russians. Once the operation was completed or aborted, the *Biber* were to make for a rendezvous with the carrier U-boats. When the pilots were safely aboard, the *Biber* were to be scuttled. The alternative rendezvous was seawards of Syet Navolek off the Fisher Peninsula. If neither rendezvous could be reached, the pilots were to head for Pers Fjord and attempt to reach Sweden.

The operation began on 5 January 1945. Three Type VIIC U-boats from 13 U-Flotilla (U-295 Kptlt Wieboldt, U-318 Oblt Will and U-716 Oblt Thimme) left Harstad each with two *Biber* on deck. The voyage was made surfaced. It was soon reported that the vibrations of the U-boat diesels had caused leaks in the *Biber* gasoline piping. Although the damage was repaired by U-boat personnel and the voyage continued, a later inspection east of North Cape revealed a recurrence of the problem and additionally leaks through the stuffing box covers allowing the ingress of water into the engine rooms of several *Biber*. Operation *Caesar* was abandoned.

On 8 March 1945 in Norway there were ten *Biber* at Narvik and a K-Flotilla at Kristiansand South. On 29 March, twenty *Biber* of K-Flotilla 265 were transferred to southern Norway, but no more operations ensued.

Chapter Six

The Midget Submersible
Molch

The *Molch* Technology

The operations at Anzio and Normandy had shown that the element of surprise of the *Neger* and *Marder* one-man torpedoes had been lost and the machines were too primitive. The Allied defences had quickly adjusted so as to deal with them. TVA Eckernförde had now come up with a new midget submarine design with a greater radius of action and higher speed. It could also dive and so approach the enemy unseen. But even this project, *Molch* (salamander), was born of necessity and in practice showed that it was again a mere interim development. Although Deschimag Bremen built 390 of them, only a few saw action.

The *Molch* was only battleworthy to a limited extent, but proved useful for training purposes. This successor to the manned torpedoes was basically an enlarged torpedo 10.78 metres long and able to carry two Type G 7e torpedoes slung on retaining rails either side of the keel. The hull shape was cylindrical, therefore built as a pressure hull, the bow rounded off, the stern tapering to a sharp point with fixed vertical and horizontal stabilizers. All control surfaces were at the rear, the hydroplane flap was an extension to the horizontal stabilizer, the propellor and relatively small rudder were located below it.

The small tower, placed just forward of where the hull began to taper, was fitted with small viewing ports. A plastic dome for all-round vision was fitted to the hatch cover. A fixed periscope projected

1.5 metres upwards and sat immediately before the dome, the metal mantle also accommodated the magnetic compass. Its gradations were projected by mirrors into the control room. Since the latter was too cramped for a chart table, the compass was the only means of orienting the boat.

Before each operation a refined yet primitive procedure of navigation came into effect once the timings were known. Feverish calculations would be made taking into account current, tide and wind, and the various courses to be followed would be noted on a small wooden board, for example: *'From 00 to 0120 hrs course 250, from 0120 to 0315 hrs course 330'* and so on. The pilot wore a watertight watch and compass on his wrist, and to avoid the danger of falling asleep he also carried an ordinary converted alarm clock.

The fixed, non-retractable periscope could be turned 30° either side so that a field of view of 60° left and right was possible. The boat was easily manoeuvred if a wider angle of vision was required. A night torpedo-aiming device was installed in the dome. The control room with tower and dome offered one cubic metre of space. The instruments, apart from the motor controls and the rudder (hand-wheel to steer, control stick for hydroplanes) consisted of the trim and regulating tank flooding valves, the compressed air pump and two foot pedals, one to adjust the speed, the other to fire the torpedoes. The pilot sat in this narrow space in an aft section located abaft the batteries and between twin tanks which equalized the battery weight. Their location and modest size ensured that they served no useful purpose.

In the cabin the pilot stowed his life-jacket, fighter-pilot mask with potash cartridges to purify the air of CO_2 exhalations and a box for his rations. An inflatable boat with two paddles served as his backrest.

The ballast tanks were a mixture of dive, regulatory and trim tanks. Therefore ballast and trim had to be just right before sailing. Any change in weight or trim during the voyage had to be compensated for dynamically or by partial flooding of the tanks.

The forward section of the *Molch* had twelve racks each holding eight batteries with 26 Type 13 T210 cells, each of which could drive a 13 hp torpedo motor. This battery size shows that the *Molch* was a relatively large vessel of 8.4 tonnes (displacement without torpedoes) and had considerable underwater range.

The battery sets were so wired that the boat could run for nine hours at slow speed (3 knots) and 18 hours at full ahead (5 knots). There was no reverse. The oxygen was contained in three steel tanks at the stern and was good for 50 hours. A reduction valve located in the cabin permitted a limited flow of oxygen to enter the cabin continuously. The pilot wore the *Jägermaske* to purify the air of his exhalations.

The *Molch* Flotillas

Only fragmentary knowledge exists regarding the *Molch* flotillas and the fate of their men. The flotilla war diaries have been lost and very few of the lone warriors addressed the public on their experiences post-war. The author's research has provided the following flotillas:

K-Flotilla 411 (formed July 1944)

Flotilla Chief: Oblt Heinrich Hille

Group Leaders: Oblt Johann Fischer, Oblt Ernst Jahn, Lt Karl-Heinz Herrlich

Flotilla Medical Officer: Oblt Dr Ulrich von der Leyen

K-Flotilla 412 (formed August 1944)

Flotilla Chief: Oblt Kuno Arens

K-Flotilla 1/412 (formed November 1944)

Flotilla Chief: Oblt Kuno Arens

K-Flotilla 2/412 (formed November 1944)

Flotilla Chief: Kptlt Wolfgang Martin

To these two half-flotillas belonged:

Staffel Leader: Oblt Hans-Joachim Huelsebeck

Torpedo Officers: Oblt Horst Gale, Lt Max Eitel

Group Leaders: Kptlt Bruno Boxhorn, Oblt Rudolf Gross, Oblt Günter Prechel, Oblt Helmut Volkstädt, Oblt Wilhelm ter Glane, Oblt Walter Schlichtmann, Lt Hans Lüpkemann and Lt Karl-Heinz Buschhüter.

K-Flotilla 413

Flotilla Chief: Oblt Lothar Vieth

Torpedo Officer: Oblt Heinrich Sennewald

Group Leaders: Oblt Werner Schlegel, Lt Anton Schweiger, Lt Jürgen Kuthe, Lt Herbert Knop, Lt Frank Graupner, Lt Hans Braband, Lt Heinz Jähner, Lt Helmut Böhmer, Lt Herbert Haase

K-Flotilla 414

Flotilla Chief: Kptlt Fritz Heinz

Torpedo Officer: Kptlt Fritz Heufelder

Group Leaders: Lt Joachim-Christian von Robertus, Lt Hans Rieger, Lt Lothar Prenk, Lt Emil Neuscheler, Lt Friedrich-Günter Krebs, Lt Eckart Hermendahl, Lt Georg-Wolfgang Dralle, Lt Hans Danner, Lt Hermann-Josef Albers, Officer Applicant (Reserve) Hans Müller

K-Flotilla 415 (formed July 1944)

Flotilla Chiefs: Kptlt Graf Reventlow-Criminie, Oblt Werner Pülschen

Torpedo Officers: Oblt Werner Meineke, Lt Kernchen

Flotilla Engineer: Lt Kroll

Leader Ground Staff: Oblt Kaub

Group Leaders: Lt Wilhelm Ude, Lt Werner Beckemeier, Lt Hans-Ulrich Hark, Lt Manfred Hein, Lt Ewald Dzadeck, Lt Otto Hausner, Lt Adolf Hallmann, Lt Ernst Gonsior, Lt Dietrich Devermann, Lt Sieghard Deringer, Lt Heinz Bensch

K-Flotilla 416 (formed November 1944)

Flotilla Chief: Oblt Friedrich Breckwoldt

Half-flotilla Chiefs: Oblt Dähne, Oblt Joachim Peschke

Torpedo Officer: Lt Kurt Kerchen

Loading Officer: Lt Hans-Jürgen Heinicke

Group Leaders: Oblt Joachim Peschke, Oblt Günter Jülke, Lt Gerhard Schweden, Lt Helmut Maschke, Lt Helmut Kessler, Lt Karl-Heinz Hiob, Lt Herbert Dehm, Lt Volker Bergmann, Lt Volland, Fähnriche (midshipmen) Schenck and von Linde-Sudau

K-Flotilla 417 (probably never formed)
Flotilla Chief: Oblt Wilhelm ter Glane

The first working flotilla, K-Flotilla 411, had sixty boats and 350 personnel. During transportation to the first operational area attacks by Allied aircraft and Italian partisans against the endless columns of lorries resulted in heavy losses, the flotilla reaching its destination late and badly battered. K-Verband Command concluded that the next flotilla, K-Flotilla 412, should be split into two half-flotillas, and afterwards all *Molch* flotillas were limited to 30 boats and 200 men.

A *Molch* flotilla consisted of command staff such as the flotilla-chief, group leaders, torpedo and navigation officers, engineering personnel, torpedo mechanics, *Molch* pilots, shore personnel, lorry drivers, administration clerks and writers, flotilla medical and nursing staff, radio operators, cooks, craftsmen, etc.

The *Command Staff* was responsible for *Molch* training and operations.

The *Engineering Personnel* maintained the boats, cleaned the engines and ensured that the air tanks were topped up for operations.

The *Torpedo mechanics* set the torpedo running depths and detonation timers, and mounted the torpedoes on the *Molch*.

The *Shore Staff* arranged for harbour tugs and cranes to be at readiness for operations, supervised the lowering of the boats into the water from the special low-loaders, and also performed the infantry and flak role.

After the writers handed the pilots their substitute identity/pay books (*Soldbuch*), (paint on silk), the kitchen staff handed out rations for the operations, the navigation officers wrote out on the wooden tablets the courses to be followed and the flotilla-chief had read out the operational orders, the pilots carried out a test dive. Once all was ready for the operation, they climbed in and were towed to the departure point where lines were cast off and the pilots headed their submersibles towards the operational zone.

When a *Molch* flotilla was formed, its command staff, pilots, engineering and torpedo personnel were trained in the practice and theory at *Lehrkommando 400* Surendorf (*Dorfkoppel*). The head of *Lehrkommando 400* was also head of *Lehrkommando 350*, responsible for the training of one-man torpedo crews. Therefore there would be up to 2,000 men at *Dorfkoppel* including the training staffs. *Lehr-kommandos 350/400* were led by Kptlt Heinz Franke, and from March 1945 Kptlt Horst Kessler. Oblt Werner Simon was responsible for *Molch* training, his adjutant was Oblt Herbery Romiger.

The *Molch* Operations

The first *Molch* flotilla to be formed, at Surendorf, was K-Flotilla 411. Training was held in July and August 1944. Together with theoretical instruction on the midget submersible, emphasis was laid on training voyages and torpedo firing. For this purpose the boats were accompanied by torpedo recovery vessels. The men of the shore personnel trained at List on Sylt island (*Weisskoppel*) and the vehicle drivers trained at Lübeck (*Steinkoppel*) before joining the flotilla.

K-Flotilla 411 fell behind schedule because a number of pilots had shown symptoms of gas poisoning after the endurance tests and the addition of a protective bulkhead had become necessary. The flotilla was finally operational on 20 August 1944 at Gettdorf. Late that month, lacking any practical experience, the flotilla was ordered to Normandy. As a result of the Allied advance there, however, the operational orders were changed, and the new theatre of operations, as with the one-man torpedoes, was Italy.

Split into a number of groups, the *Molch* flotilla reached Verona, and from there the endlessly long convoy of heavy transports made for Genoa, arriving on 10 September. Attacked by Allied aircraft and partisans on the way, it arrived at San Remo on the Ligurian coast on 20 September, late and badly damaged. Trial voyages were begun at San Remo immediately. These resulted in several fatal accidents. On diving a number of boats descended too rapidly, could not be trimmed and were crushed by the water pressure. The difference in salt content between the Mediterranean and Baltic had not been taken into consideration. Once the forward tank filled with water to submerge, the *Molch* sank to 60 metres before blowing compressed air through the tank could have effect. At that depth it was already too late and the pilot had no chance.

As a result of these errors in trimming, the yards had to change the forward tanks and so reduce the space so that only a third was constantly flooded. Despite these misfortunes the first and last operation of K-Flotilla 411 was scheduled for the evening of 25 September. Led by KptzS Hartmann, K-Staff South, twelve *Molch* set out that night to attack Allied patrol vessels patrolling off Mentone and Nice. The operation was a disaster. Ten of the *Molch* failed to return. No successes were claimed. The two boats which got back were destroyed in the subsequent shelling of San Remo by Allied warships. The operations of the flotilla were suspended. On 11 November it was at Trieste in the Adriatic, and went from there to Sistiana. Of its activities thereafter nothing further is known.

K-Flotilla 412 was also formed in August 1944 and trained by *Lehrkommando 400* at Surendorf. Its first operational station was at Gettdorf near Kiel. Meanwhile K-Verband Command had learned its lesson following the K-Flotilla 411 disaster, and *Molch* flotillas would henceforth be smaller. In 1944 K-Flotilla 412 was split into K-Flotilla 1/412 (Flotilla Chief Oblt Arens) and 2/412 (Flotilla Chief Kptlt Wolfgang Martin). Both half-flotillas had 30 *Molch*.

The point was also taken to heart at the training school. The standards set to be a *Molch* pilot were insufficient. Accordingly the pilots had to be of higher rank. About 50% of the pilots would now be officers and midshipmen. Ranks below Bootsmannsmaat were not competent to operate the *Molch*. Training now lasted three months.

In mid-1944 K-Flotilla 1/412 moved to Rotterdam where it was subordinated to Staff Musenberg responsible for Holland. After working up to operational readiness, in favourable weather operations they were to be sailed in liaison with the Rhine-Flotilla. Nothing is known of any operations by the flotilla in the Netherlands. Later it was held at readiness near Skagen in Denmark. It never saw action and Kptlt Martin took over as flotilla leader from April 1945 to the capitulation.

After basic training in September, K-Flotilla 2/412 were transferred by rail to Emden. Command Staff were Flotilla Chief Kptlt Martin, adjutant Lt Buschhüter, who doubled as flotilla welfare officer, Oblt (Fortifications Engineer) Hülsebeck, head of shore personnel, group leaders Pechel and Gross, navigation experts Kptlt Boxhorn, Oberfähnrich Welters and Maat Dey, Feldwebel (V) Mertens and two Leutnante who supervised the torpedo mechanics. In all, K-Flotilla 2/412 consisted of eight officers, one senior midshipman, seven warrant officers, 26 other NCOs and 148 men. Of these, 30 were *Molch* pilots and five reserves: 35 were machinery and torpedo mechanics, about 65 shore personnel, five were drivers and fifteen clerks.

It was discovered at Emden that not all available barges were suitable for shipping the *Molch* to Borkum Island, only those with loading hatches 14 metres in length could take a *Molch*. The submersibles were lifted off the rail waggons into the lighters. The destination was an abandoned naval aviation station on Borkum. The waters around the island were used for trials and practice voyages under simulated battle conditions. A KFK (naval trawler) played the leading role. In endurance tests *Molch* pilots were required to sit for 12 to 18 hours in the cabin in freezing temperatures with the engine running as a preparation for operations. It was found that the issue clothing was inadequate for winter, and thick sweaters, socks and fur boots were indented for.

After the defects in the boats had been rectified and the flotilla was finally operational, it moved from Borkum to Delfzijl and then to Amersfoort in Holland at Christmas 1944. The Musenberg Staff considered that the *Molch* flotilla offered the opportunity to disrupt enemy shipping, and had them brought to Schiedam. The boats were allocated a large shed and crane facilities in the Rotterdam repair yard. The flotilla men were found quarters at Schiedam. On 20 January 1945 there were 30 *Molch* at Rotterdam, 60 at Amersfoort and another 60 at Zeist.

There were still problems initially because the boat's radius of action was so short that they had to be towed from Rotterdam to the starting point in the Scheldt estuary, the direct route from Rotterdam to the Hook of Holland and into the open sea being too far to sail. Finally it was decided to send them through the small Kanal der Voorne which leads from Rotterdam to Hellevoetsluis and is used by inland shipping traffic. For operational purposes small harbour tugs would tow the *Molch* to Hellevoetsluis and release them to reach the main channel between Goerre and Walcheren island for the estuary.

The first operation of K-Flotilla 2/412 with 12 *Molch* to attack Thames-Antwerp shipping in the Scheldt was planned for 10 January 1945. It was postponed for bad weather because the bitter cold would reduce battery efficiency to only 50 sea miles – not enough for operations in the western Scheldt. The *Molch* returned to Rotterdam and were put ashore to recharge batteries.

In January and February, the flotilla received orders on 15 occasions, and on 13 occasions the operation came to a halt at Hellevoetsluis.

Italian manned torpedo SLC *Maiale* (Photo Franz Kurowski).

SLC passing through a net barrier.

MTM boat in the Gulf of Tarent, 1942.

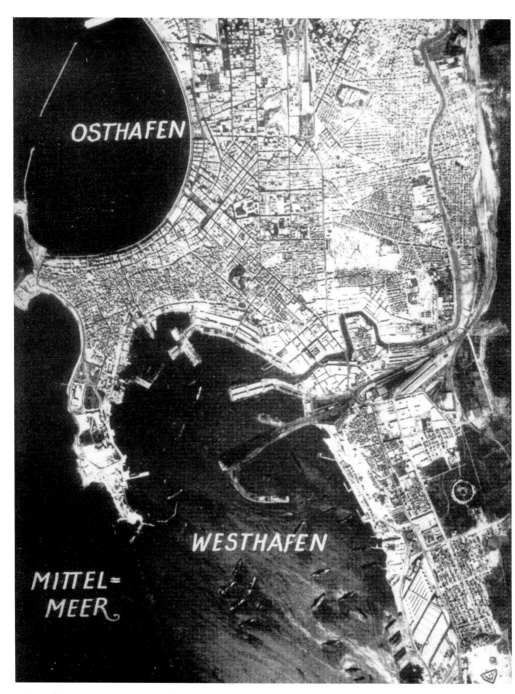

OSTHAFEN

WESTHAFEN

MITTEL=
MEER

Luftwaffe air reconnaissance photo of Alexandria, principal Royal Navy base in the Mediterranean.

Italian frogman.

Vizeadmiral Hellmuth Heye, Kriegsmarine K-Verband head, awards the Knight's Cross to one-man torpedo pilot Herbert Berrer. Formerly an Oberfernschriebmeister (Senior Warrant Officer – Telex) Berrer was regraded Oberbootsmann (Warrant Officer Boatswain) when serving in the K-Verband.

Fritz Frauenheim in the rank of Korvettenkapitän. From *Jäger der Sieben Meere*.

A *Neger* being lowered into the water. A good impression of the carrier- and attack-torpedo assembly.

Fitting the
plexiglass
dome.

The plexiglass dome
of the *Neger* with
scale gradations.

A *Marder* one-man torpedo preserved for the
Instuctional Collection, Bundeswehr Naval Weapons
School, Eckernförde. Before it stands Knight's Cross
holder Walter Gerhold, one of the most famous one-man
torpedo pilots of the war.

The spartan cockpit of the *Marder*. Control stick, above it the release lever for the torpedo, to the right the pressure gauges. The depth gauge is positioned left above the pilot's seat, below the seat is the *Jägermaske* breathing apparatus.

One of the volunteers for one-man torpedo training was Oberfähnrich (Senior Midshipman) Helmut Bierbrauer. He made available many photos for this book.

A pilot climbs into the carrier-torpedo, the *Neger*.

The one-man torpedo *Neger* under way. The aiming prong is clearly seen ahead of the pilot's cupola. The photograph gives an idea of how limited was his vision, having to orient himself from a frog's perspective. No periscope, compass or radio was fitted.

Torpedo mechanics of K-Flotilla 361.

Men of K-Flotilla 361 about to entrain for Anzio.

A half-track towing vehicle with two *Negers* under tarpaulin in a pine wood near Anzio.

ObltzS Johann-Otto Krieg, awarded Knight's Cross on 12 August 1944 as Kapitänleutnant and Chief of K-Flotilla 361. Training leader and Staff duty, K-Verband.

Oberfernschreibmeister (Senior Warrant Officer – Telex) Herbert Berrer, recipient of the Knight's Cross, 5 August 1944.

US soldiers inspecting a stranded *Neger* at Anzio.

Neger pilot Walter Gerhold after the award of the Knight's Cross for sinking a frigate on 6 July 1944. Comrades bear him aloft on their shoulders. Despite heavy losses, the will to fight and *esprit de corps* remained firm amongst K-Verband volunteers to the end.

17-year-old Matrose Horst Berger was a volunteer attached to K-Flotilla 361. He piloted a *Neger* one-man torpedo at Anzio and on the Normandy invasion coast. He is seen here in the uniform of Bootsmannsmaat wearing the Iron Cross First and Second Class and on the right pocket the German Cross in Gold, the highest decoration for bravery in the Third Reich.

The wreckage of a *Marder* destroyed by explosives.

Linse-pilot Oberbootsmann Herbert Berrer (left) with *Neger*-pilot Walter Gerhold (right) on the occasion of their award of the Knight's Cross. Between them is ObltzS Leopold Koch, chief of K-Flotilla 361.

Grossadmiral Dönitz awards decorations to members of K-Flotilla 361. Far left is Korvettenkapitän Frauenheim.

More than 50 years later: former Kriegsmarine one-man torpedo pilots before a *Marder* in the Bundesmarine Weapons School at Eckernförde. Amongst them are Horst Berger (4th from left), Helmut Bierbrauer (5th from left) and Walter Gerhold (6th from left).

Korvettenkapitän
Hans Bartels.

Midget German submarine Type XXVIIA *Hecht*.

The *Molch* cabin. Above it projects the steel cylinder in which were located the periscope and magnetic compass. The rectangular glass panel below the tower is a modern addition to afford museum visitors a view into the cabin interior.

A finished *Seehund* on trestles either at the shipyard or in the Konrad bunker, Kiel, May 1945.

Seehund on sea trials.

Kptlt Hermann Rasch.

Fregattenkapitän
Albrecht Brandi.

Midget submarine *Delphin* in
towing trials or seawater tests,
1944/1945.

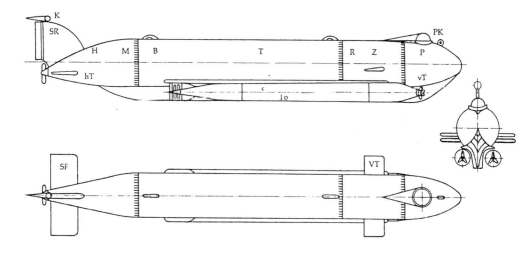

Profiles of *Schwertwal* I.

Key

P   = pilot room
Pk = plexiglass cupola
Z   = engineer's control room
R   = regulating tank
T   = Ingolin tanks
B   = Fuel tanks

M = Walter machinery room
H = stern section
K = master compass
vT = forward trim tank
hT = aft trim tank
SR = rudder

SF = stabilizers
VT = forward hydroplanes
To = Walter torpedoes
      (K-Butt)

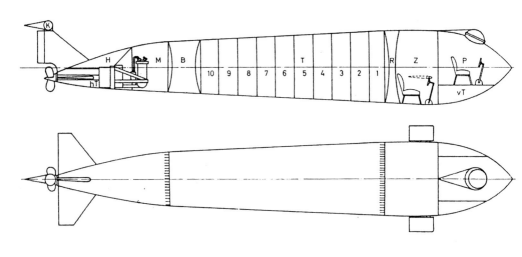

Schwertwal II with improved streamlining.

Key

P = pilot's cabin
Z = engineer's control room
R = regulating tank
T = 1 to 10 Ingolin fuel
     tanks (10 tonnes)

B = fuel tanks, 1 tonne
     Deakalin
M = engine room (Walter
     turbine drive)
H = stern section

K = master compass
vT = forward trim tank
hT = stern trim tank

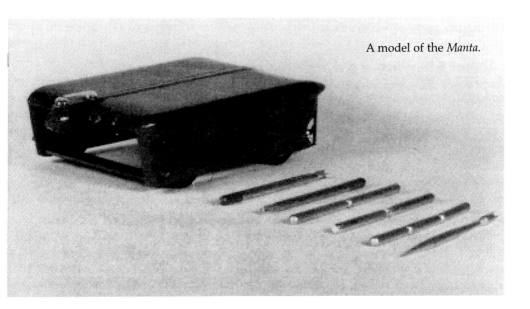

A model of the *Manta*.

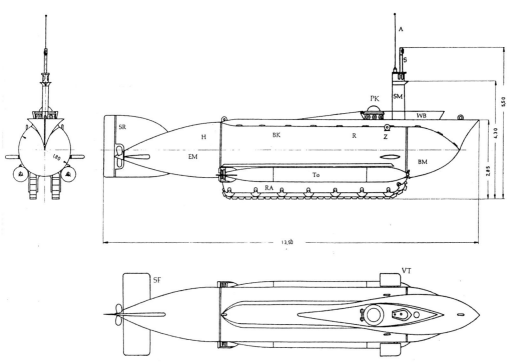

The amphibious craft *Seeteufel* with caterpillar track/propeller drive.

Key

BM	= gasoline motor	RA	= caterpillar tracks	SR	= rudder		
Z	= control room (2 men)	WB	= breakwater	SF	= stabilizers		
R	= regulating tank	Pk	= plexiglass cupola	VT	= forward hydroplanes		
Bk	= battery room	SM	= snorkel mast	To	= 2 torpedoes		
H	= stern section	S	= periscope				
EM	= electric motor	A	= Ultra short wave antenna				

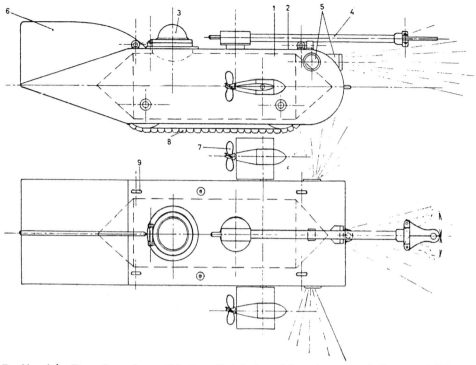

Profile of the Deep-Sea submersible *Grundhai* designed for salvage work down to 1,000 metres.

Key

1 = pressure hull for divers
2 = casing and dive tanks
3 = access hatch with cupola
    for all-round vision

4 = electro-magnetic grab
5 = three searchlights
6 = stabilizers
7 = active hydroplanes

8 = caterpillar tracks
9 = lifting hooks

Rittmeister Konrad von Leipzig, chief of the Brandenburg *Küstenjäger*.

Kptlt Helmut Bastian, awarded the Knight's Cross on 3 November 1944 as head of a *Linse*-flotilla.

LtzS Alfred Vetter, Group Leader, K-Flotilla 211, was decorated with the Knight's Cross on 12 August 1944 for his *Linse* attack of 8 August. He was also mentioned in the Wehrmacht report of 15 September 1944.

A *Linse* unit before an operation.

Kapitän zur See Werner Hartmann (photo dates from when Korvettenkapitän).

An Italian MTSMA explosive boat being lowered into the water.

Proven K-Verband *Linsen* operators with Grossadmiral Dönitz, here seen greeting LtzS Alfred Vetter.

MTSM boats on exercise.

A heavy assault boat of the Brandenburg *Küstenjäger* unit in the harbour at Santa Lucia.

Frogmen at a display for Grossadmiral Dönitz (second right) showing an interested admiral – possibly Heye – his watertight Junghans diver's watch/compass.

This photograph of German frogmen was taken on 16 November 1944, probably during training at List on Sylt. Notice the Junghans watches.

A frogman demonstrating
the swimming position.
Notice the veil
camouflaging the face.

German frogmen wearing
full-face mask.

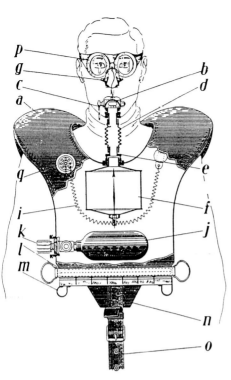

The Dräger compact oxygen rebreathing apparatus.

Key:
A = airbag
B = mouthpiece
C = tap
D = flexible hose
E = demand valve
F = potash cartridge
G = nose clip
I = spiral wire
J = oxygen bottle
K = hand-wheel
L = opening
M = spring clip
N, O = belt
P = protective goggles
Q = excess pressure release valve

German frogmen in captivity at Remagen respond to questions. Other sources state that these are *Linse* pilots.

The weather was too stormy: in a fresh breeze vision through the periscope was negligible. K-Verband Command remarked additionally that the use of *Molch* in winter in the Scheldt was barely feasible because the cold reduced the efficiency of the accumulators by 30%, and this meant that even with a long tow the operations zone was out of reach.

Finally, on the night of 22 February 1945, fourteen boats sailed, four under their own power from Hellevoetsluis, ten from Scheveningen to Schouwen Island under tow. All were headed for the inner Scheldt. Six *Molch* failed to return. Two were sunk by British armed motor launches ML 588 and ML 901 four sea miles north-west of West Kapelle, and the third was destroyed by shore batteries at Flushing. The other three disappeared without trace. Two *Molch* which ran aground were blown up by their pilots. No successes were claimed. Oblt Pechel was returning with the tide when he ran aground on a sandbank and could not work his *Molch* free. He reached the safety of the channels between Goerre and Walcheren paddling the rubber dinghy.

The second operation was sailed in company with S-boats on the night of 12 March 1945. Sixteen *Molch* from Rotterdam departed Hellevoetsluis. Fourteen were lost, nine pilots failed to return. The causes of loss were enemy aircraft, British MTBs and the coastal batteries at Breskens and Flushing. No successes were reported. Nothing further is known regarding the activities of K-Flotilla 2/412.

Equally little is known of *Molch*-Flotilla 413. After basic training at *Lehrkommando 400* it was taken by Oblt Vieth to Assen in northern Holland, arriving on 22 December 1944, and held in readiness for operations against the Scheldt convoys. By virtue of the adverse weather no sorties were sailed until mid-March when it is presumed that some of the boats took part in the K-Flotilla 2/412 operation against Thames-Antwerp traffic, but this cannot be confirmed. It is also not known if the boats of K-Flotilla 413 were in the *Molch* reserve depot at Amersfoort which was bombed and seriously damaged on 3 February by Spitfire fighter-bombers of 2nd Tactical Air Command.

On Maunday Thursday 1945 what remained of K-Flotilla 413 was loaded along with some *Linse* explosive boats on transport for Germany: between Utrecht and Groningen the convoy squeezed through the advancing Allied forces and reached Oldenburg. Here a number of *Molch* and damaged torpedoes were left behind in a railway shed, and K-Flotilla 413 was then disbanded at Surendorf.

K-Flotilla 414 was operational at Wilhelmshaven in January 1945 and was probably transferred to Sæby in Denmark.

No documentation can be found for K-Flotilla 415, and only scanty information exists as to its fate. It is certain that during the training period at Surendorf between July and September 1944 the flotilla was commanded by Kptlt Graf Reventlow-Cri(e)minie. On completion of training, mainly in the theory and practice of midget submarine operations, navigation (including celestial), torpedo instruction and ship recognition, K-Flotilla 415 was taken over by Oblt Pülchen in September. Fleet engineer was Lt (Ing) Kroll, torpedo officer Lt Kernchen, head of shore personnel Oblt (Ing) Kaub, head of mechanics Stabsobermaschinist Frank. Nothing is known about where the flotilla was stationed or its operations.

Molch-flotilla 416 was formed at Surendorf on 12 December 1944 under the command of naval veteran ObltzS (Reserve) Friedrich Brechwoldt. Before the war he had served as mate aboard merchant ships and whale-catchers and held a ship's master's certificate. Prior to joining K-Verband he had served in the U-boat Arm. His deputy and half-flotilla chief was Oblt Dähne, the other half-flotilla was led by Lt Peschke. Group leaders were Lt Volland, Dehm, Jühlke, Hiob, Kessler, Maschke and Schweden, midshipmen Schenck and von Linde-Sudau. The midshipmen had served previously with K-Flotilla 415. At sea and in the workshops they had amassed extensive knowledge of the boats and their capabilities, problem areas and deficiencies, and those of their torpedoes. Medical care was in the hands of NCO Sanitätsfeldwebel Rauh. In mid-March 1945 standard training ended and the flotilla loaded its 30 boats and equipment on special loaders for Gettdorf near Kiel. On 25 March K-Flotilla 416 arrived at Arhus in Denmark. The unit was divided into three and prepared for trans-shipment to Norway.

The first group left aboard the ferry *Preussen* at 0030 on 31 March arriving after a stormy crossing in Oslo on 2 April. The second group followed on the steamer *Friedericia*, which sank after being mined, all equipment including 15 *Marder* one-man torpedoes being lost, but no lives. The third voyage, aboard the *Preussen,* passed off uneventfully. From the diminishing stocks of K-Flotilla 414, *Preussen* then brought replacement *Molch* to Norway from Sæby. The boats were loaded on two goods trains at Oslo, which left for Stavanger on 3 April. The senior officer of the shore personnel was killed in an attack by low-flying aircraft, his successor, Oblt (Ing) Otto Kansog, arrived later. On 20 April 1945 the last boats and men under Fähnrich von Linde-Sudau arrived with a fast convoy from Friedrichshaven to Larvik.

The flotilla was stationed at Sola where the *Molch* were kept in an aircraft hangar. Immediately the flotilla was at its authorized strength it was operational. The boats went down the launching apron of the seaplane base and were trimmed to the specific gravity of the water. On 17 April 1945, KptzS Beck, Chief of K-Staff Norway, who had served aboard the heavy cruiser *Prinz Eugen* before his detachment to K-Verband 10, raised the red alert 'Alarm on the Coast', but the flotilla's *Molch* saw no action. On 25 April 1945 certain Wehrmacht units in Norway capitulated to the western Allies who then took over the seaplane base. The men of K-Flotilla 416 were made PoWs without ever having sailed a mission.

In April 1945 K-Flotilla 417 was formed under Oblt ter Glane, but would not have completed its basic training course before the capitulation.

The midget submersible *Molch* was far from ready for service at the front when it was tossed into the fray. The seaborne trials and the few operations it sailed exposed the defects of its design. First and foremost, the trimming system which made submerged passage possible had not been properly thought through and displayed lethal deficiencies. Diving manoeuvres went awry, the boats could not be held at the desired depth, and either the *Molch* broke back through the surface or headed for the deep where the hull could not withstand the water pressure and was crushed. Fatal accidents were the consequence of these design failures. The *Molch* was too slow to escape the enemy if discovered. To manoeuvre more smartly, the boats needed more powerful motors. The fixed periscope had too restricted a field of view and in the mildest chop (sea state 3 to 4) the pilot could see nothing through it. The navigation was too primitive. Before every operation the navigation officers worked out the compass courses to be steered and wrote them on a wooden tablet. At least in the beginning *Molch* pilots were not sufficiently qualified and trained to handle an 8-tonne submersible.

As a result of these technical shortcomings and the lack of practice, relatively few missions were sailed and, so far as is known, no enemy ship was damaged or sunk by a *Molch*. Its effect on maritime warfare in the Second World War was nil.

Chapter Seven

The Pocket U-boat
Seehund

Development, Construction, Technology

U-boat Type XXVII B/5 or *Seehund* (seal) was the most successful small-scale submarine designed and operated by the Kriegsmarine. In contrast to all its forerunners which, with the exception of *Hecht*, were mere submersibles, *Seehund* was a straightforward U-boat. Made operational in numbers earlier in the war it would have represented a dangerous threat to Allied shipping.

It was the design of naval architiects Fischer and Grim. The latter was a young engineer who had been actively employed for several years at the Kriegsmarine naval shipyard at Wilhelmshaven, and had taken the post of consultant for small-scale submarines with K-Amt Berlin (located in Schell Haus on the Tirpitzufer). This office, headed by Otto Grim and designated 'k1Ue' had been created in 1942 shortly after a proposal was put forward to build a 100-tonne 'pocket U-boat'. It would be 25.33 metres long, 2.7 metres in the beam, have a draught of 2.34 metres and a surface speed of 9 knots. An armament of three torpedoes was envisaged. This project was not pursued but in 1943, after the attacks on *Tirpitz* by British midget submarines, consultancy office k1Ue was reactivated. Under great pressure the design for the two-man submarine *Hecht* was turned out while in parallel K-Amt worked on a series of ideas designated Type XXVIIB. These would have a long range, carry several torpedoes and have diesel-electric

87

drive. The first blueprints, completed in June 1944, bore a strong resemblance to *Hecht*.

The torpedo-like hull had a bow section for better sea-keeping when surfaced, and saddle tanks. Enlarging the keel to accommodate the batteries made more space available in the boat's interior. The two torpedoes were suspended from two grabs alongside the hull. A 22 hp diesel engine provided surface drive. Speed was designed to be 5.5 knots surfaced and 6.9 knots submerged.

The building contract for the three *Seehund* experimental boats U5001–U5003 was awarded to Howaldtswerke Kiel on 30 June 1944. Enthusiasm for the pocket U-boat was so great that orders and boat numbers for series production (U5001 to U6531) were allotted even before the designs had been submitted. The ministerial programme of June 1944 wanted a thousand. Schichau Werft at Elbing in East Prussia and Germania Werft Kiel would produce 45 and 25 boats respectively each month. Other centres for mass production were Simmering (Graz), Panker (Vienna), W. Schenk (Hall, Austria), CRDA Monfalcone (Trieste) and Klöckner-Humboldt-Deutz (Ulm).

The reality was different. Dönitz was not prepared to give *Seehund* priority over the large Type XXIII *Elektro-Uboote*. There were shortages of raw materials, skilled yard workers and transport bottlenecks. In the end, series production was concentrated mainly at Germania Werft and the Konrad bunker at Kiel no longer required for Type XXI and XXIII assembly. The three experimental boats were completed in September 1944 by Howaldt Werke. In the series production, Germania delivered 152 and Schichau 130 boats, the monthly basis being:

October 1944	35 boats
November	61
December	70
January 1945	35
February	27
March	46

A total of 285 *Seehund* were supplied to the K-Verband.

The *Seehund* displaced 14.9 tonnes. It was 11.9 metres in length and 1.7 metres in the beam. Fitted amidships was a small raised platform with ventilation mast, light-image reflective magnetic compass, peri-scope, hatch for crew access and side viewing ports. Later boats had a plexiglass cupola for navigation purposes pressure-resistant to 45 metres. Propulsion came from a Büssing 60 hp 6-cylinder heavy lorry diesel motor for surface drive and an AEG 25 hp electric motor for submerged travel. The diesel continued running submerged following a full speed alarm dive to 10 metres, in emergencies to 15 or 17 metres. This was possible because the diesel exhaust gases were expelled out-board through a vent at up to 2 atmospheres pressure. The critical depth was 20 metres, before which the engineer had to close the vent as rapidly as possible to prevent the external water pressure over-coming the exhaust pressure, entering the diesel and flooding it. The diesel fed on air in the boat. The crew would be deprived of breathable air if the diesel was kept running too long at depth. They could survive in air pressure of 550 millibars.

The *Seehund* had a range of 270 sea miles at 7 knots, if fitted with additional fuel tanks outside the hull up to 500 sea miles. Submerged, 63 sea miles was possible at 3 knots. Surfaced maximum speed was 7.7 knots, submerged 6 knots.

Seehund was the absolute zenith of contemporary pocket-submarine design worldwide. It could dive rapidly and be fully surfaced within four seconds. By six or seven seconds it could reach five metres. Great things were anticipated of it. The small hull would generally escape detection by radar, and not return an Asdic echo. When submerged at slow revolutions the electric motor would be barely audible to hydro-phone gear. Even depth charges with the most violent shock waves would probably pass it by. At least, that was what the designers hoped for, but in practice the assumption varied from the reality.

The free-flooding forward compartment of *Seehund* contained the dive tanks. A tunnel below the pressure hull between the stern-most dive tank and forward of the diesel bunker held two 8 MAL 210 battery sets. Within the pressure hull the arrangement was very similar to *Hecht*. Forward of the control room bulkhead was the battery room with six racks (six 8 MAL 210 batteries each of 32 cells). The control room contained the driving position and two seats, one behind the other, for commander and engineer. The latter had the control panel in front of him and on the order of the commander fired the torpedo. When attacking the boat ran at periscope depth. The two (later three) metre long revolvable periscope of first class construction was inbuilt. Its optical spectrum allowed the commander to search the skies before surfacing.

Armament consisted of two standard G 7e torpedoes hung from a retaining rail secured by two protective arms either side of the keel. This arrangement required the boat to be lifted from the water and landed for reloads. Before the war's end a *Seehund*-flotilla reportedly received the *Walter*-torpedo or *K-Butt*. On 28 November 1944 SKL reported that a *Seehund* travelled more than 300 sea miles during a four and a half day endurance voyage.

A further Type XXVIIB variant was the 'small U-boat K' designed for closed circuit circulating propulsion by naval architect Kurzak who had been appointed by OKM to investigate the possibilities at Germania Werft Kiel. A 15 hp diesel motor available in large numbers was adjudged suitable. A large 1,250-litre pressure flask in the keel supplied oxygen for the system. Seventy sea miles at 11–12 knots submerged was possible, 150 sea miles at an underwater cruising speed of 7.5 knots. After a discussion at OKM on 25 May 1944, Kurzak received a contract to develop the idea for a pocket U-boat. He chose the Daimler-Benz OM 67/4 100 hp motor. The engine (with an electric motor for slow running) would be ready-mounted on a common frame and slid into a stern box, secured with a few relatively accessible screws. Kurzak paid special attention to suppressing the resonance but found that four rubber shock absorbers in the corners of the frame sufficed. The designers hoped that this measure would be enough to eliminate the need for the slow-speed electric drive unit. The final result was a very light, simple engine.

Work on the *Seehund* closed circuit system was continued by naval architect Dr Fischer, head of the engineering bureau 'Glückauf' set up in the buildings of a girls' school at Blankenburg in the Harz. An important colleague in this Type 127 design was engineer Kurt Arendt.

Contracts for the prototype Type 127 were awarded to Germania Werft Kiel and Schichau Elbing. By the war's end Germania had three boats under contruction. These were to have received the *Seehund* conversion Büssing NAG-L06 diesel because so few Daimler-Benz motors were available. Bench tests confirmed that the Büssing diesel could be successfully substituted for circulatory drive purposes, but the war ended before the first prototype was ready.

90

Training of *Seehund* Crews

The *Seehund* crews trained at *Lehrkommando 300*, Neustadt/Holstein (*Neukoppel*) in a camp on the edge of the Wiksberg barracks, the home of 3 *U-boat Lehrdivision*. The exact date when this Lehrkommando was established is not certain but was probably at the end of June 1944. Presumably there was a forerunner, a small unit known as *Versuchskommando 306* which had the job of preparing the training of *Lehrkommando 300*.

First chief of *Lehrkommando 300* was LtzS Kiep, who had just completed training as a U-boat watchkeeping officer. His successor was Knight's Cross holder Kptlt Hermann Rasch (13 ships of 81,679 tons sunk as commander of U-106). His last boat had been the trainer U-393. Rasch was temporary operations leader of the *Seehund* base at Ijmuiden until relieved by FKpt Brandi.

The technical shore staff head, *Hecht* and later *Seehund* instructor was initially a midshipman, Oberfähnrich (Ing) Hinrichsen. Once the *Seehund* boats arrived he yielded the post to Flotilla Engineer KKpt Ehrhardt. On 4 October 1944 Oblt (Ing) Palaschewski took over from Ehrhardt.

From July 1944 the volunteers, and a sprinkling of pressed men, arrived at Neustadt. As was usual with K-Verband Command all wore field-grey for camouflage purposes. Tactical training began with the delivery of the first *Hecht* on 26 July. It was evident almost from the outset that trained U-boat men were needed to handle the boats. It was through human error and inadequate mastery of the techniques that the fatal accidents referred to in Chapter Four occurred. Therefore only U-boat watchkeeping and engineer officers, midshipmen, coxswains and senior engine room ratings who had undergone U-boat training qualified for *Seehund* training.

In September or October 1944 the first *Seehund* was brought to Neustadt. The training was typically hard and lasted eight weeks. It concluded with a Baltic navigation voyage over three days and torpedo-firing practice. For training purposes *Lehrkommando 300* had available the survey ship *Meteor*, used as a target, and the torpedo preparation ship *Frida Horn*, a former Horn-Line steamer. The leader of torpedo practice was Kptlt Hagemann assisted by Oblt Stepputat shipped aboard *Frida Horn*. Probably the air-sea rescue ship *Greif* was attached temporarily as an escort to this command before being used to evacuate refugees from the East in the last month of hostilities. Six other air-sea rescue boats from Köslin, KFKs and communications vessels worked the torpedo retrieval routine and as escorts on training and practice sessions. The exercises took place in Neustadt Bay and between Pelzerhaken and Timmendorferstrand. Later, in April 1945, training was transferred to Wilhelmshaven (*Graukoppel*) and directed there by KKpt Ehrhardt. A *Seehund* flotilla was transported by train to Aalborg in Denmark on 23 September 1944 and at the end of the year moved from Neustadt to Holland.

The *Seehund* Flotilla and Its Men
Lehrkommando 300 at Neustadt had the following officer corps:

Chief: Kptlt Hermann Rasch

Adjutant: Oblt Gerhard Hermeking

Camp Commandant: Oblt Willi Demmler

Training Officers: Kptlt Klaus Ohling, Oblt Helmut Wieduwilt

Navigation Officer: Oblt Ernst-Ulrich Lorey

Torpedo Practice Leaders: Kptlt Karl-Heinz Hagenau, Oblt Manfred Stepputat, Oblt Reinhard Pfeifer

Torpedo Officers: Oblt Willi Sebald, Lt Friedrich Weinbrecht

Acceptance Officer: Oberfähnrich Werner Hertlein

Medical Officer: Lt Dr Adolf Hollunder

The officers of *Übungsflotille 311* were listed in Chapter Four, *Hecht*.

The officers of K-Flotilla 312 included:

Flotilla Chief: Oblt Jürgen Kiep

Torpedo Officer: Lt Paul Reinhold

Pilots/Engineers: **Oblts** Rudolf Drescher, Klaus-Gert Krüger, Karl Wagener, Hans-Hellmuth Seiffert, Wolfgang Bischoff; **Lts** Dietrich Meyer, Benedict von Pander, Winfried Scharge, Paul Reinhold, Harro Buttmann, Alwin Hullmann, Günther Markworth, **Oberfähnrich** Korbinian Penzhofer

Which pilots and engineers were attached to K-Flotillas 313 and 314 can no longer be ascertained. From about February 1945 the *Seehund* crews were led as *5 K-Division*. The following men were known to have been involved in sea-going missions:

Officers
Oblts: Alfred Dierks (Flotilla Engineer), Horst Kuppler, Palaschewski, Heinz Paulsen, Wolfgang Ross, Karl-Heinz Vennemann, Wolfgang Wurster.

Lts: Hans Werner Andersen, Wolfgang Bischoff, Wolfgang Böhme, Harro Buttmann, Wolfgang Demme, Karl von Dettmer, Rudolf Drescher, Claus-Dieter Drexel, Siegfried Eckloff, Horst Gaffron, Gernot Göhler, Walter Habel, Martin Hauschel, Klaus-Joachim Hellwig, Helmut Herrmann, Willi Hesel, Hinrichsen, Horstmann, Max Huber, Alwin Hullmann, Wolfgang Jäger, Ludwig Jahn, Friedrich-Wilhelm John, Wolfgang Kähler, Kallmorgen, Herbert Kempf, Jürgen Kiep, Harald Knobloch, Konrad, Henry Kretschmer, Alfred Küllmeyer, Karlheinz Kunau, Giselher Lanz, Rolf Löbbermann, Günther Markworth, Dietrich Meyer, Friedrich Minetzke, Gerhard Müller, Ulrich Müller, Johann von Nefe und Obischau, Otmar Neubauer, Jürgen Niemann, Benedict von Pander, Werner Plappert, Heini Plottnick, Reinhold Polakowski, Werner Preusker, Winfried Ragnow, Gotthard Rosenlöcher, Felix Schäfer, Gerhard Schöne, Karl-Heinz Siegert, Wolfgang Spallek, Klaus Sparbrodt, Otto Stürzenberger, Hans Wachsmuth, Wagner, Hans Weber, Hans-Günther Wegner, Reimer Wilken, Willi Wolter, Götz-Godwin Ziepult.

Oberfähnriche: Friedrich Livonius, Korbinian Penzhofer, Streck.

Warrant Officers and Senior Ratings
Obersteuermann: Böcher, Fröhnert, Warnest.

Obermaschinist: Bauditz, Feine, Fröbel, Harte, Herde, Herold, Holst, Kässler, Nöbeling, Arno Schmidt, Stiller.

Maschinenobermaat: Langer, Sass.

Maschinenmaat: Baumgärtel, Hardacher, Heilhus, Heinicke, Heun, Jahnke, Köster, Leidige, Mitsche, Musch, Niehaus, Pawelcik, Pollmann, Radel, Reck, Rettinghausen, Rösch, Schauerte, Teichmüller, Vog(e)l.

Bootmaat: Köster.

Ranks unknown
Beltrami, Haldenberg, Huth, Knupe, Macy, Mayer, Schiffer, Schulz.

The Operations of the *Seehund* Crews

(Where known, the boat number and crew names are supplied, commander first, engineer second. The appropriate rank of each where known will be found in the preceding alphabetical listings.)

The *Seehund* base in Holland was at Ijmuiden, a district located at the entrance to the Noord Zee Kanal near the town of Velsen in the province of Noord-Holland. Velsen (population then 30,000) was an outlying suburb of Amsterdam. Besides being a large fishing port, it had jam factories, furnaces, steel and iron works, also cement, paper and chemical industries.

From 1940 Ijmuiden had been an S-boat base. The area seemed very promising for *Seehund* operations with its numerous tributaries and islands where the boats could be hidden from enemy air reconnaissance. The steadily growing importance of the port of Antwerp for the Allies meant that a huge number of shipping targets was available. The Noord Zee Kanal connected Amsterdam to the sea. It was constructed with a lock system designed to keep Amsterdam independent of the tides. Ijmuiden was at the seaward end of the system and had three locks of different sizes to accommodate all sizes of shipping traffic.

The HQ of K-Flotilla 312, the first *Seehund* flotilla, was located in an unheated two-storey building in the Rijkswaterstraat industrial area. An old mission house and the Velsen cemetery chapel served as the Operational Staff (later 5 K-Division) facility. The shore staff workshop was set up on the Hoogoven Pier, the crematorium and chapel made for a suitable food warehouse.

Aboard the boats neither roll-neck sweaters nor fur and leather jackets were effective against the Dutch winter. Since thick clothing hindered movement, the cold damp which filtered through the hatch and diesel air shaft made life miserable for the crews. Crew shipboard rations was concentrated fare poor in roughage and based on egg-white: pea-, lentil- and millet-soup cubes, rice with meat, dried vegetables, potato puree, dried egg powder, for sweet buns baked with cocoa, chocolate and almond nougat. Beverages were made from compressed bean coffee, Nescafé, compressed tea, some alcohol, also vitamin-C products, and naturally caffeine and cola nut extracts to aid alertness. Routine patrols could last up to four days and so a hotplate was installed for heating up rations as required.

Ashore the officers shared a house on the Kerkenweg in Driehus, the crews were later given a villa on the eatern side of the railway line to The Hague. The shore staff, about 100 men, were lodged in terraced housing near the small lock and in an hotel in the Velsenbeck Park. The *Seehund* were moored in the central lock alongside low-floating jetties.

A few days before Christmas 1944 some of the training staff were transferred to Wilhelmshaven (*Graukoppel*) and paired off to take over new boats. Operational leader of K-Flotilla 312 was Kptlt Hermann Rasch. The first six *Seehund* left Germany for Ijmuiden on Christmas Eve. Each day another group of six followed so that by the end of the year 24 *Seehund* had arrived at the Dutch base. On 29 December 1944 the flotilla was at readiness.

By order of Admiral Heye the first *Seehund* operation was scheduled for 1 January 1945 against Allied shipping in convoy lanes of the outer Scheldt between Ostend and the Kwinte Bank to position 3°10′E, and from the south coast of England against the Antwerp-bound traffic west of 10°50′E and south of 52°N. The boats would run parallel to the Dutch coast to the Hook of Holland, then pass through the eastern Hinder Kanal to reach their operational area off Ostend. From 1700 the *Seehund* fleet – 18 boats – transited the small lock at Ijmuiden to embark on an operation expected to last three to five days. It was heavily overcast and rainy, the wind light, sea state Beaufort 2–3, but then the weather deteriorated rapidly, the wind increasing to storm force. Icy rain rattled down on the submarines, pitching and tossing in the rising seas. Vision became worse as the first combers swept the boats' hulls. The catastrophe was about to begin.

Shortly after sailing, when still in sight of land the first casualty occurred when a *Seehund* hit a mine and blew up. U-5035 was forced to return with a leaky propellor shaft. Contrary to assurances that they would be invisible to radar, from intercepted enemy wireless traffic transmitted at Ostend and in the Scheldt it was soon evident that that was not the case.

The majority of the boats reached the operational area where they achieved a single success, Paulsen + Huth sinking the British trawler

95

Hayburn Wyke, 324 tons, at 2225 on 2 January. On their return the boat struck a mine off Ijmuiden and both lost their lives. Also that day Andersen + Hardacher in U-5327 ran aground a mile west of Domburg on the enemy-occupied island of Walcheren. A farmer hid them but later they were captured by Dutch Resistance fighters after a brief firefight. The British seized the boat.

Hertlein + Haun had rudder damage. The destroyer HMS *Cowdray* discovered the submarine and fired on it from a quadruple-barrelled gun on the bow. The crew abandoned and were picked up by the British. Another *Seehund*, number unknown, was sunk on 2 January at 2002 by the frigate HMS *Ekins* north-east of Ostend.

On 4 January at about 1230 Kallmorgen + Vogel ran aground south of Katwijk while returning to base. The crew survived.

Scharge + Rösch had no luck. After a bomb exploding near the boat had caused little damage, they were forced to dive and depth-charged by two corvettes. Scharge ordered a torpedo fired at one of the pursuers. The torpedo stuck in the grabs. Later the diesel began to splutter, and the boat stranded off Scheveningen. After Scharge fired distress flares the crew was rescued by a naval flak battery on the evening of the seventh operational day.

U-5305 Penzhofer + Heinicke found no targets. On the return voyage the diesel broke down and the boat was run aground on the island of Voorne. Both swam to the mainland.

On 2 January U-5309 von Pander + Baumgärtel spent twelve hours in the vicinity of buoy NF8 being hunted by MGBs. The magnetic compass and diesels had failed after a depth charge attack. Sailing for home on battery drive only they eventually ran the boat aground off the Hook of Holland. A KFK brought them home.

A difficult time was experienced in U-5024 by Markworth + Spallek. After receiving serious damage from depth charging and bombing they were forced to run the boat aground on a sandbank off Goerre island. The two crew, who had spent a long time in the icy water, were found unconscious by a Wehrmacht patrol in a rubber dinghy.

Löbbermann + Plappert were surprised four miles north-east of Zeebrugge at 1655 on 5 January by a patrol boat, probably HMS *Samarina*. The crew was forced to abandon, were picked up by the British and brought to Ostend.

A terrible drama must have unfolded in one of the boats of the first wave. On 3 January the two crew were finished physically and mentally, their nerve gone. According to the commander's account, at the request of the engineer the commander shot him dead and then fired a bullet into his own head. This wound was not fatal. The commander was later found adrift on the wreck of an MTB (how this came about, and whether the boat was British or German, is not explained) and he was taken to a military hospital. The outcome of the court-martial (the survivor of a suicide pact is guilty of murder) is unknown.

On 5 January while in the Noord Zee Kanal a *Seehund* torpedo discharged itself, hitting a lighter and damaging a harbour defence boat.

Hullmann + Hinrichsen in U-5013 had failed to find any ships on their first voyage. Their rations were ruined, compressed air and oxygen used up. The hatch was open, following seas washed over the boat partially flooding it, and it had sunk in 18 metres. After a superhuman effort the crew managed to raise her an hour or so later and ran into Ijmuiden on 5 January totally exhausted. After that Hinrichsen was given a shore appointment.

In this first operation, K-Flotilla 312 lost sixteen *Seehund* and eighteen men, an appalling statistic. K-Verband Command and OKM were horrified. Kptlt Rasch was ordered before Grossadmiral Dönitz to deliver a personal report. Despite these heavy losses, a new operation was planned for 9 January 1945.

Between 1830 and 1930 on 10 January, four *Seehund* sailed for Margate on the Kent coast. A fifth boat dropped out with trim problems. Two of the four boats returned prematurely. Wegner + Wagner had compass failure in U-5311, Stürzenberger + Herold were tracked by radar, damaged by aircraft and pursued by two MLs. Both these boats put back into Ijmuiden on 11 January.

South of the Kentish Shoals (naval grid square AN 7935), Kiep + Palaschewski sank a collier of about 3,000 gross tons at 1500 on 12 January in heavy seas, wind force 5–6 with persistent snow showers. This was at the entrance to the Thames estuary. The name of the ship could not be established as Kiep turned away at once in compliance with his orders. The sinking was confirmed by the *B-Dienst* which had been monitoring British radio traffic. The boat returned safely to Ijmuiden on 13 January.

Krüger + Bahlmann stranded at 1330 on 14 January off Zandvoort and had to destroy the boat with explosives.

In better weather on 17 January ten *Seehund* set out. Nothing was achieved and all boats returned safely. By 20 January the number of operational boats at Ijmuiden had risen to 26, these reinforcements arriving despite the closure of Schichau Werft at Elbing in the face of the Russian advance in Prussia.

Between 1400 and 1600 on 21 January ten *Seehund* left Ijmuiden in three groups for the Dumpton and Elbow Buoys, South Falls, Lowestoft and Great Yarmouth. This operation reported no successes, nearly all boats had technical problems. U-5033 Bischoff + Hellwig had a defective diesel vent, U-5339 Kempf + unknown had both compasses fail. U-5368 Drescher + Bauditz had a faulty diesel, another boat was losing lubricant, another collided with a buoy. Von Dettmer's boat had to break off the mission when the engineer said he could not go on because of seasickness. This boat then stranded about 7 sea miles south of Ijmuiden and had to be blown up. Aboard U-5334 Ulrich Müller + Niemann the bilge-pump, light-image compass and trimming switches all failed. The boat was pursued by an aircraft working with British search groups and had to be run aground in a sinking condition on 23 January off the Hook of Holland after the torpedoes had been discharged to aid buoyancy. The boat was destroyed by explosives.

Another *Seehund* crew had tragic bad luck. The boat reached the operational area but entered the Thames estuary as the result of a defective compass. A torpedo was fired at a ship and missed. On 22 January the boat regained the North Sea. After two days voyaging blind the *Seehund* arrived south of Lowestoft where the launch ML 153 tracked her and attacked with depth charges. The boat waited on the bottom and eventually escaped. When night fell the commander decided to surface. He was not aware that the current had drifted the boat northwards to Great Yarmouth, and on 25 January, heading in the wrong direction, he ran the boat aground on Soroby Sands. After nearly three days attempting to refloat her and living in the stinking interior the crew gave up and fired their distress flares. The Trinity House lighthouse tender *Beacon* came out to assist.

On 19 January SKL reported on the current state of preparations for further *Seehund* operations which were presently being made extremely difficult by north-westerly storms preventing sailings. A deluge at Petten in Noord Holland breached dykes and displaced sand dunes.

The last *Seehund* operation of January 1945 began on the 19th at 1500 when ten of the dwarf fleet left the small lock at Ijmuiden in two groups. Operational zones were the crossing points for Allied convoys near the Dumpton Buoy and the sea area of the South Falls sandbanks. The orders were to return to base if the weather worsened, especially if the wind backed to the south-west. The wind soon strengthened to gale force with a sea state varying from 5 to 10. It was overcast with very poor visibility – not good weather for a *Seehund*.

The area of operations was naval grid square AN 8744. Only two boats got there. On 30 January U-5335 Stürzenberger + Herold discovered a convoy of three steamers and escorts. Before they could fire the escorts forced the boat to dive. Later heavy seas caused the boat's return. The other *Seehund*, Ross + Vennemann, put back on 30 January and reported having torpedoed a collier between the Dumpton Buoy and the Margate roadstead. There was no official confirmation for the claim.

None of the other eight boats found the enemy. U-5342 Böcher + Fröbel abandoned the voyage after only three hours with damage to couplings. Schulze + Macy put back on 30 January with a leak astern. Weber + Knupe were losing lubricating oil and feared that the diesel would seize up. U-5338 Wachsmuth + Feine were unable to find the operational area through navigational difficulties. Seiffert + Stiller searched the Goodwin Sands without reward, U-5332 Wolter + Minetzke broke off because of the rough seas in the Margate road-stead: Krüger + Bahlmann returned for the same reason, in U-5041, Kretschmer + unknown found his engineer so totally incapacitated by seasickness in the sea conditions that he could no longer assist in running the boat.

In January 1945, 44 *Seehund* voyages were sailed and ten boats were lost. At the beginning of February three boats operated off Ramsgate. On 3 February Wolter + Minetzke in U-5332 claimed sinking a ship of 3,000 gross tons off Great Yarmouth, but *B-Dienst* was unable to confirm.

On 3 February 1945 Kptlt Rasch was relieved of command as Flotilla Chief and appointed head of *Lehrkommando 300* at Neustadt.

99

Presumably his wolf-pack tactics had let him down and led to unacceptably high losses. The new chief of K-Flotilla 312, and later 5 K-Division, was FKpt Albrecht Brandi, an experienced U-boat officer who, on 23 November 1944 as the second Kreigsmarine recipient (Wolfgang Lüth was the first, 9 August 1943) received the Diamonds to his Knight's Cross with Oak-leaves and Swords. At the outbreak of war Brandi had been 1WO aboard the minesweeper M1 (commander, KKpt Bartels). Subsequently he went to the U-boat Arm and as commander of U-617, U-380 and U-967 had sunk 25,879 gross tons of merchant shipping, two destroyers, the fast minelayer HMS *Welshman*, a Fleet tug and a naval trawler. After leaving the U-boat Arm, Brandi was appointed Admiralty Staff Officer to Commanding Admiral Eastern Baltic, and had been a Staff Officer with K-Verband Command since 1944. His assistants were KKpt Heinrich Stiege and Kptlt Karl Born.

On that same 3 February 1945 an operation previously prepared by Kptlt Rasch was due to begin. As if to usher in the change in command, Ijmuiden was bombed. No *Seehund* was damaged. The Allies did not target the locks to avoid flooding Velsen. This resulted from a secret agreement between the Allies and Dutch to prevent unforseeable consequences for the city of Amsterdam.

At 2330 eight *Seehund* left for the Thames estuary, the crossing and assembly point for Allied convoys. This operation had no success.

U-5368 Wilken + Bauditz had navigation problems after being tracked by radar and attacked by aircraft.

U-5033 Bischoff + Hellwig and U-5326 Knobloch + Leidige were forced to return with technical problems.

U-5339 Kempf + unknown stranded north of the Hook of Holland on 7 February. The boat had to be destroyed, the crew was rescued. The same day U-5329 Ulrich Müller + Niemann returned to Ijmuiden having failed to reach the operational zone.

U-5311 Wagner + Wegner ran aground about 10 sea miles north of Ijmuiden.

U-5348 Dietrich Meyer + Schauerte reached the operational area despite the weather and scouted the Thames-Scheldt route for ships in vain. This shipping lane was well lit by night by a string of light-buoys every two miles. On the way home Meyer surfaced alongside the hull of a patrol boat. The commanders of both vessels were so taken aback that neither reacted in time. No action ensued. U-5348 escaped and reached Scheveningen on 8 February.

U-5344 Livonius + Pawelcik also returned to base on 8 February after having been depth-charged in the operational zone by MGBs.

A new operation against the Thames-Scheldt route began on 10 February when eight *Seehund* sailed: by nightfall U-5363 (Buttmann + Arno Schmidt), U-5337 (Horstmann + Nitschke) and Lt Polakowski's boat were all back at Ijmuiden with technical problems. They were joined on the morning of 12 February by U-5335 (Kunau + Jäger), and 13 February by U-5347 (Sparbrodt + Jahnke) because of thick fog.

Schöne + Sass in U-5347 were attacked by aircraft at 2330 on 10 February off the Hook of Holland. Six bombs exploded close to the boat putting out both compasses. Nevertheless they reached the operational area but were foiled by thick fog. The boat was losing fuel and trailing lubricant. Early on 13 February the bunkers and batteries were drained. Schöne put his command aground on the island of Texel, about 30 sea miles north of Ijmuiden, and destroyed it with explosives.

U-5349 (Kähler + Harte) was discovered beached at Castricum north of Ijmuiden by Wehrmacht forces at 1500 on 16 February. There was no sign of the crew.

U-5345 failed to return, nothing further is known.

These failures must have prompted a rethink at K-Verband Command. The so-called wolf-pack tactics practised by the large U-boats in their heyday and to a limited extent by the *Seehund* were no longer viable, not least because the boats had no radio. This ruled out centralized direction or even agreement between the respective captains. Moreover the problem of radar had been grossly under-estimated, and the plethora of technical defects which was causing many boats to put back prematurely pointed to the need for a better standard of maintenance and preparation for operations.

FKpt Albrecht, a willing listener, sent his boats out only in small groups. What he could not influence however were the strong defences protecting even the smallest convoys, and the enemy's immense aerial presence day and night.

On 12 February five *Seehund* sailed to attack the convoy traffic heading for Antwerp. U-5332 (Wolter + Minetzke) and U-5342 (Börchert + Fröbel) put back with technical problems the same day.

U-5354 (Streck + Niehaus) was depth-charged in the operational area, counting 259 explosions. The boat was badly damaged but got back to Ijmuiden on 16 February, finally running aground inside the harbour mole.

U-5361 (Ziepult + Reck) attacked convoy TAM 80 off North Foreland on 15 February, torpedoing and seriously damaging the Dutch tanker *Liseta*, 2,628 gross tons. Reck was found unconscious on the beach at Voorne island on 23 February, eight days later. There was no sign of the boat, the remains of Lt Ziepult washed up at Ijmuiden in April 1945.

U-5356 (Preusker + unknown) failed to return from this mission.

At 0830 on 16 February four *Seehund* left Ijmuiden to attack shipping in the western Scheldt, supported at night by 15 *Linse* explosive boats.

U-5363 (Buttmann + Arno Schmidt) and U-5332 (Wolter Minetzke) returned on 18 February: Wolter had attacked a convoy of landing ships but the escorts had driven him off.

U-5041 (Kretschmer + Radel) was sunk. The circumstances are not recorded. Kretschmer was captured, Radel did not survive.

U-5337 (Horstmann + Nitschke) disappeared without trace. The crew was declared dead on 23 February.

Since the *Seehund* was no more successful than the *Biber* in the Scheldt, K-Verband returned to the concept of operations on more open waters. On the afternoon of 19 February 1945 three *Seehund* set off for the Dumpton Buoy.

Wachsmuth + Feine in U-5097 lost their bearings in adverse weather. The boat was so severely damaged by a bomb near-miss that it could not longer submerge, and eventually drifted ashore at Egmond aan Zee, ten sea miles north of Ijmuiden. The crew was rescued by a flak detachment, the boat destroyed.

U-5342 (Böchert + Fröbel) failed to return. The crew was declared dead on 1 March 1945.

The last operations of February remain confused but there were successes. The crews had become hardened by their earlier experiences and now they had some luck. The various accounts as to the number of *Seehund* at sea between 21 and 26 February differ, but was probably eight.

102

Gaffron + Köster fired both torpedoes at a destroyer at 2300 on 22 February. A hit was observed, *B-Dienst* reporting a probable sinking which the British side disputes.

U-5367 (Ragnow + Vogel) fought their way through heavy seas in the Channel, breakers restricting visibility. At about 0600 on 23 February they heard Asdic. East of the Goodwin Sands visibility deteriorated. Towards evening a flashing buoy appeared on the starboard hand. Then a Hunt-Class destroyer was seen approaching bow-on. Dive, torpedo ready! The destroyer pounded overhead and kept going. Lucky! The sea state was now 6 to 7. The bunkers had emptied, the batteries were drained. U-5367 drifted towards the enemy coast. The crew abandoned the boat and swam through thin ice to shore where gunners took them prisoner.

Habel + Rettinghausen were lurking near the Dumpton Buoy. Their compasses were malfunctioning, Habel was navigating by the occasional V-1 which passed over and the stars. Suddenly the destroyer *Mecki* appeared. Both torpedoes were fired – missed. MGBs dropped patterns of depth charges near them for twelve hours. Having escaped, off the Hook of Holland they hit a mine. Though waterlogged the boat stayed afloat. On 24 February they made Ijmuiden.

Sparbrodt + Jahnke in U-5330 had returned because of a blocked fuel line. They sailed again next day and on 23 February, five sea miles north-east of South Falls near the East Dungeon Buoy, found the French destroyer, *La Combattante*. At 1028 a single torpedo was fired at 600 metres range. Eighty seconds wait with bated breath then – a hit between bridge and funnel! The destroyer went down swiftly. MGBs rescued 118 members of the 184-man crew.

U-5365 (Hermann + Holst) returning from the operational area ran aground near the German artillery battery at Katwijk. Holst remained with the *Seehund* while Hermann paddled ashore in the inflatable dinghy. A Dutch lifeboat came out with a salvage crew and the *Seehund* was towed into Scheveningen.

The numbers of the other boats cannot be determined. The following enemy ships were sunk:

22 February, 17 sea miles east of North Foreland, a *Seehund* attacked convoy TAM 87 and sank the armed landing ship LST 364, 2,750 gross tons.

24 February, 0930, 3 sea miles off North Foreland, the British cablelayer *Alert*, 941 tons, was torpedoed by a *Seehund* and sank immediately with all hands.

26 February 0530. The steamer *Rampant* from convoy TAC sank following an explosion near buoy NF8. Ships of the convoy saved 46 crew.

26 February 0955. The steamer *Nashaba* was sunk near buoy NF7. 24 survivors were picked up.

In February, there were 33 *Seehund* voyages sailed and only four boats were lost. For the first time, midget submarines had inflicted important losses. At Ijmuiden it rained decorations. On 27 February in a reshuffle at Staff Operations, Lt Hullmann relinquished the chart room to Oblt Seiffert who held the post until 20 April, when Lt Sparbrodt took over.

In March K-Verband Command began to feel the pinch. Fuel was becoming scarce. The number of *Seehund* operations declined and were only sailed in small groups or singly as rolling operations. SKL could not, or would not, recognize the disastrous war situation. On 27 February the Chief of Torpedo Production addressed Dönitz on the subject of equipping the *Seehund* with the so-called *Spinne* torpedoes. Tactical trials had been carried out with this weapon at Neustadt and had been assessed as promising. The main difficulty was the inadequacy of torpedo production.

SKL demonstrated the extent to which it had become a stranger to reality by proposing *Seehund* operations in the Mediterranean. Following a request by C-in-C South West on 1 March 1945, OKM thought it should set up a base on the coast of the Ligurian Sea by the beginning of April from which 80 *Seehund* would operate. Immediate steps would have to be taken to install heavy duty bilge pumps because of the different specific gravity of seawater in the Mediterranean. Nothing came of this idea.

The successes at the end of February must have encouraged FKpt Brandi to continue the struggle with much greater numbers. In favourable weather on 6 March a number of *Seehund* sailed in a joint operation with seven *Biber* to attack shipping in or bound for the Scheldt. The *Seehund* were to find their targets off Great Yarmouth near the Elbow Buoy and off Margate where the Thames-Scheldt traffic assembled into convoys.

The boats of Ross, Gaffron, Göhler, Drexel and Markworth returned shortly after sailing with the usual variety of technical problems.

A *Seehund* was sunk on 7 March 26 sea miles east of Ramsgate by MTB 675, another fell victim on 10 March to a Beaufighter off Goerre. The same day the frigate HMS *Torrington* and MTB 621 sank two *Seehund* off the South Goodwin lightship, one of these being U-5374, Siegert + Keilhues being taken prisoner.

At 0951 on 11 March a British escort vessel sank Lt Neubauer's boat half a mile off the Kellet Buoy, the crew being rescued. The same day two other *Seehund* were lost, one off Ramsgate, the other 17 sea miles north of Dunkirk.

On their first voyage, on 11 March Huber + Eckloff damaged or sank the freighter *Taber Park*, 2,878 tons, during an attack on convoy FS 1753 off Southwold (naval grid square AN 7668).

At 1125 on 12 March John + Teichmüller were surprised in fog by the coastal patrol vessel HMML 466. John was captured, Teichmüller gunned to death.

U-5336 (Hauschel + Hesel) was surfaced in a strong gale, the hatch continually swept by high seas. The *Seehund* crashed from wave to wave and icy cold reigned in the boat. They dived. Suddenly Asdic and screw noises were heard. Down came the depth-charges. Hauschel came to periscope depth, sighted a warship and fired a torpedo. It stuck fast in the retaining grabs, its propellor speeding the *Seehund* towards the enemy ship. Sweating with the effort and panic, they finally managed to steer the boat away and ran for it to the north-east. After being at sea seven days their oxygen was very low. Land came into sight. Soldiers with foreign steel helmets were seen. Artillery rounds greeted their arrival – the boat was off the Canadian-held island of Walcheren. With their last reserves of strength Hauschel and Hesel steered away from the hostile coast and made Ijmuiden on 12 March. The engineer had to be lifted out and stretchered ashore.

On 12 March off West Schouwen a fighter-bomber gunned Lt Böhme's boat. It burned and both crew perished.

On their return to base in U-5064, Kugler + Alois Schmidt reported having sunk a steamer of 3,000 to 4,000 tons.

On 10 March SKL had decided to use *Seehund* submarines to supply the starving German garrison at Dunkirk. K-Verband Command received orders to fit out three boats to carry transport cylinders of provisions, batteries, limpet mines and mail. The boats were to be ready at Ijmuiden on 15 March.

On their return to base on 13 March, Fröhnert + Beltrami reported having sunk a steamer in the Thames estuary. They had also survived a depth-charging.

The same day U-5377 was lost, von Neefe und Obischau + Pollmann were saved: U-5339 (Kempf + unknown) was depth-charged and sunk off Buoy NF5: off Harwich on the same day a *Seehund* ran into five boats of 165th Minesweeping Flotilla and after being forced to dive in a hail of 2-cm and 7.5-cm followed by depth-charges, the boat was lost at position 52°01′24″N and 01°53′24″E.

None of the three *Seehund* known to have been off Margate on 16 March returned. On 18 March *B-Dienst* reported a British signal describing large quantities of oil and wreckage found near the Margate coast, and four empty lifeboats. What ship this was and its cause of loss remains a mystery.

On 21 March in light fog, U-5366 (Hauschel + Hesel) discovered a convoy assembling in grid square AN 7663 between Lowestoft and Great Yarmouth. At 0330 Hauschel torpedoed a Liberty freighter which exploded three minutes later. The whole sea was lit bright as day, the victim must have been carrying munitions. U-5366 touched bottom at Egmond aan Zee during the night of 24 March but reached Ijmuiden undamaged.

Gaffron + Köster got caught up in a battle between German S-boats and British MTBs and MGBs on 22 March. The *Seehund* was fired on and the tower was damaged, making the boat undiveable. The crew abandoned and were picked up by the British. The same day Göhler + Kässler were attacked and sunk by a fighter-bomber shortly after leaving Ijmuiden.

At 0452 on 22 March, MTB 394, while lying stopped on listening watch about 23 sea miles south-east of Great Yarmouth, was rammed by a *Seehund*. The British opened fire into the mist, heard cries for help and picked up two German submariners.

At 1920 on 24 March U-5264 fired two torpedoes at a destroyer near the South Falls sandbanks and missed.

On 25 March the British motor launch ML 466 was torpedoed by a *Seehund* and exploded. There were no survivors. The attacker may have been the boat of Meyer + Schauerte which had left Ijmuiden two days previously and failed to return, although Wagner + Wegner or Plottnik + Mayer who were in the area on 24 March are also possibles.

At 1200 the same day Warnest + Nöbeling came under attack from motor launch ML 1471 near Tamarisk Buoy. Warnest decided that attack was the best form of defence and responded with two torpedoes which missed. He escaped, however, and returned to base.

On 26 March in grid square AN 7956, Küllmeyer + Raschke torpedoed the steamer *Newlands*, 1,556 tons, which sank at once. The boat returned to Ijmuiden on 27 March.

On 25 March at 1440 Beaufighter Q of RAF 254 Squadron sank a *Seehund* about 17 sea miles north-west of the Elbow Buoy.

At 0231 on 26 March the escort destroyer HMS *Puffin* pinpointed a *Seehund* by Asdic about seven sea miles off Buoy 4. The submarine surfaced, rammed the stern of the destroyer, slid along the hull and exploded, tearing a great hole in the destroyer's forecastle, damaging the keel. *Puffin* remained afloat and picked up the two Germans from the water. After an inspection ashore, the destroyer was declared a constructive total loss.

On 27 March ML 586 sank a *Seehund* west of Walcheren.

On 30 March a *Seehund* sank the coaster *Jim*, 833 gross tons south-east of Orfordness. Twelve of her crew of twenty survived. Another *Seehund* was sunk by the harbour defence vessel HDML 1471.

On 27 March three *Seehund* left Ijmuiden to supply the German garrison at Dunkirk. The boat of Fröhnert + Beltrami began to flood and being undiveable returned to base. They sailed again the following midday. Weather was extremely bad with enormous seas. The storm lasted seven days: Fröhnert's boat reached Dunkirk on the last day of the tempest and was guided through the coastal minefield by the stern light of a naval trawler. Both crewmen were admitted to the military hospital with exhaustion. After their recovery they were received by Admiral Frisius. On 9 April they sailed, and reached Ijmuiden despite air attacks and a flooded diesel.

In summary it may be said that the fighting between hunters and hunted became particularly bitter and resolute in March 1945.

Seehund boats sank or damaged five steamers of about 15,000 tons. A patrol boat was torpedoed and a destroyer written off as a total loss after being rammed. On the debit side, 5 K-Division lost at least 15 *Seehund* and 30 men dead or prisoner.

Before the beginning of April 1945, Anglo-American forces reached north-west Germany and were virtually surrounding *Festung Holland*. Additional *Seehund* at readiness in Wilhelmshaven naval base and U-boat bunkers on Heligoland island prepared to sail for Holland, transport by road or rail being no longer possible. Heavy air attacks on K-Verband bases caused damage to buildings but the midget submarine force escaped unscathed. After the weather improved sorties were sailed from 4 April with great determination. By the end of the month 36 individual missions had been been sailed to the English east coast, the Scheldt Esturary and to Dungeness near Dover.

On 8 April, 5 K-Division had 29 boats at Ijmuiden, only half of them operational. Four others arrived on 20 April, 14 on 1 May from Wilhelmshaven, and another two from Heligoland.

Two boats sailed, one each on 5 and 6 April respectively, for the Thames-Scheldt route. U-5366 (Hauschel + Hesel) returned on 8 April with no successes to report, the other boat was sunk, probably on the 6th. Nine *Seehund* sailed at 2130 on 7 April to attack convoys between Dungeness and Boulogne. Bischoff + Hellwig failed to return and were presumed killed in action on 19 April. U-5332 (Wolter + Minetzke) ran aground at Calais. After destroying the boat, they surrendered. Rosenlöcher + Musch remain missing. The boats of von Pander + Vogel, Ross + Vennemann and U-5074 Schöne + Sass returned to base, the latter boat being undivable after a Martin Marauder bombed it at 0630 on 8 April.

The operations of these and a number of other boats can only be assembled in fragmentary form:

9 April, 0531. A *Seehund* torpedoed the tanker *Y17* from convoy TAC 90 eight cables off North Foreland Buoy NF5. The tanker burst into flames after an explosion and sank. There were no survivors.

9 April: Near Dungeness, Buttmann + Arno Schmidt attacked convoy TBC 123. Buttmann sank the freighter *Samida*, 7,219 gross tons with one torpedo, and seriously damaged the US freighter

Solomon Juneau, 7,116 gross tons, with the other. The *Seehund* was subsequently sunk by ML 102 east of Dover. The body of Schmidt drifted across the North Sea and washed up on the island of Föhr, to be interred at Wyk cemetery.

Another *Seehund* was sunk this day by Beaufighter W of 252 Squadron RAF.

Off Orfordness, a *Seehund* sank the British cable-layer *Monarch*, 1,150 gross tons.

10 April: Pander + Vogel reported having sunk a tanker of about 1,000 tons. Penzhofer + Schulz attacked a destroyer in the South Falls area. The torpedo failed to release and dragged the submarine to the target, where a collision ensued. The destroyer stood off and machine-gunned the *Seehund*. The submarine escaped and made Ijmuiden on 12 April.

11 April: East of Dungeness a *Seehund* attacked convoy UC63B, damaging the freighter *Pat Wyndham*, 8,580 gross tons. The same day the attacker was sunk by ML 632.

U-5071 (Hullmann + Schiffer) was heading for home when attacked from the air. Splinters damaged the torpedo warhead, which did not explode, and the boat made Ijmuiden on 12 April.

U-5070 (Markworth + Spalleck) discovered a destroyer escorting a refrigerator ship of about 3,000–4,000 gross tons off Dungeness near buoy C6. Markworth fired both torpedoes and dived immediately to 15 metres. After 50 seconds there was a deafening explosion. The *Seehund* settled on the bottom at 26 metres, screw noises overhead. A four-hour long depth-charge inferno began. U-5070 survived.

At 0828 a *Seehund* was seen by escort vessel HMS *Guillemot* three miles off North Foreland Buoy 1. ML 586 gave chase and sank the submarine at 1330 hrs. Later, at 1945, ML 585 sank another *Seehund* near the South Falls.

12 April: Two *Seehund* including U-5366 (Hauschel + Hesel) headed for the Thames-Northbound and Thames-Scheldt crossing point. In U-5366 the bilge pump failed, but Hesel carried out repairs under difficult circumstances. On 13 April Hauschel sighted a convoy. Both torpedoes were fired and missed. The boat put into Ijmuiden at 1700 on 18 April.

Between 0758 and 1020, aircraft attacked several *Seehund* at position 52°N 02°E and claimed one sunk.

109

At 1630 Mosquito H of 254 Squadron RAF, Wellington V of 524 Squadron and Beaufighters M and U of 236 Squadron attacked and sank a *Seehund* 25 sea miles west of the Hook of Holland.

13 April: Barracuda L of 810 French Squadron sank a *Seehund*.

U-5090 (Kunau + Jäger) arrived at Ijmuiden after finding no targets around Dungeness and surviving a day-long depth-charge attack. During the delivery voyages from Wilhelmshaven to Ijmuiden, the boat of Schäfer + Wurster was sunk. The boats had sailed after being informed that 500 RAF bombers had attacked Heligoland in waves.

14 April: Four *Seehund* including U-5074 (Schöne + Sass) and U-5364 returned to Ijmuiden from unsuccessful sorties.

The losses continued. The destroyer HMS *Garth* sank a *Seehund* off Orfordness: on 18 April a land battery at Blankenberghe sank another. A third boat was found beached and abandoned on the 19th. The Konrad + Kaldenberg *Seehund* which had sailed on 10 April began to founder after being attacked by a fighter-bomber. Konrad was killed. Kaldenberg threw the body of his commander into the sea intending to use it as a float in an attempt to swim for shore. On the way he was found by a British patrol boat and rescued.

At midday on 16 April the tanker *Goldshell*, part of convoy TAM 40, sank north of Ostend after a violent explosion: it could not be attributed definitely to a *Seehund*.

While running for Ijmuiden a *Seehund* ran out of fuel and battery power. After drifting for days the rations came to an end. The current took the boat towards the minefields off Katwijk. On 24 April the crew, having written their farewell messages and put the bottle into the sea, abandoned the submarine. Wehrmacht shore personnel spotted them. Their voyage lasted ten days and is the longest *Seehund* patrol on record.

On 29 April off Walcheren the steamer *Benjamin H Bristow* was sunk either by a mine or *Seehund* torpedo. The last definite torpedoing of a ship by a *Seehund* occurred on 23 April 1945 near the South Falls. This was the *Svere Helmersen*. The last *Seehund* to be lost to enemy action was sunk in a depth-charge attack south-east of Lowestoft on 29 April by the corvette HMS *Sheldrake*.

Because of the war situation, K-Verband Command cancelled the *Seehund* training programme on 27 April. Under the protection of the two auxiliaries *Frida Horn* (Kptlt Hugo Holm), and *Meteor*, the VP boat VS 517 (Kptlt Paul Masch), the naval trawlers KFK 203 (Lt Otto

Klähn) and KFK 204 (Lt Alfred Laon) and a few air-sea rescue boats, the training *Seehund* were escorted from Neustadt to Eckernförde and then to Grafensteen in Denmark. The Danes refused to admit them and referred the German convoy back to Neustadt. The training division eventually surrendered at Surendorf.

On 28 April 1945 the Dutch operations terminated, although several *Seehund* continued to act as blockade breakers into Dunkirk. On 2 May 1945 four boats undertook the dangerous journey and reached the port before the capitulation. On 6 May 1945 the German units in Holland struck their flag. The Royal Canadian Hastings and Prince Edward Regiment of 1st Canadian Division took over Ijmuiden. About 5,000 Wehrmacht personnel went into captivity.

The Balance

The *Seehund* pocket U-boats sailed 142 missions from Holland and accounted for about 93,000 gross tons of shipping (British sources estimate 120,000 tons). They were therefore the most successful German midget submarines. These results could not affect the outcome of the war, but if the *Seehund* had been developed and operational as little as six months earlier, it could have caused Allied shipping grave problems, particularly at the time of the invasion of Normandy. In any case they forced the continuing use of hundreds of escort vessels to protect convoys. The operations led to high losses in personnel and materials. The greatest respect is due to the brave men who accepted the challenge to fight an overwhelmingly superior enemy dominating the sea and air.

Note

In early 2001 the research ship *Deneb* of the Federal German Hydrographic Office (BSH) discovered a sunken *Seehund* off Fehmarn in the Bay of Lübeck. It was raised on 11 May 2001 and taken to the naval arsenal at Kiel for examination. The two crew, who could not be identified, were interred in the Lübeck military cemetery. The *Hamburger Abendblatt* reported on 14 April 2003 that the restoration of the boat by Herr Peter Tamm was expected to be complete by the summer of 2003, just as the original German edition was going to print.

Chapter Eight

Unfinished Developments

Between the end of 1943 and the first months of 1944 naval architects began to design new midget surface craft and submarines. Most of the forerunners which had seen frontline service had been too primitive to achieve important successes: in particular speed and range had been poor and the torpedoes carried too slow. The latter carried only half the normal complement of batteries to save weight.

The Central Naval Construction Office (*Hauptamt Kriegsschiffbau*), the torpedo research institute (TVA) at Eckernförde, the Walter Werke at Kiel and other centres were all largely independent of each other and worked without much consultation with K-Verband. For this reason in July 1944 Admiral Heye set up *Versuchskommando 456*, the purpose of which was to harmonize the development and construction of new vessels, and to monitor and approve practices used.

V-456 was stationed at Kiel-Tannenberg, close to Walter Werke. Its personnel consisted of naval architects, engineers, machine builders, technical designers and qualified tradesmen in particular welders, coppersmiths and electricians. They worked with civil engineers, especially Professor Hellmuth Walter[1] and his colleague Dr (Ing) Harald Schade, and selected TVA torpedo mechanics. Under the supervision and control of V-456, the following projects were developed, built and tested.

The One-Man Torpedo *Hai*
While *Neger* and *Marder* were under development, TVA personnel worked on an improved one-man torpedo. Initial considerations

113

focussed on a manned torpedo of the Type T IIId. This *Dackel* (pointer dog) was to have been towed by a U-boat. Next came *Hai* (shark) which displaced 3.5 tonnes, was 11 metres long and 0.53 metres in the beam. At 4 knots the speed was too poor to have promise. An *Ingolin*-motor was thought possible but nothing came of it. One experimental boat was built.

The vessel consisted of a torpedo head and tail with two torpedo central sections. The *Hai* was thus simply an elongated *Marder*. The length would have allowed more batteries to be carried to improve speed and radius of action. A standard G7e attack torpedo would have been slung below the carrier. The length/diameter ratio of the *Hai* was so unfavourable however that the boat was almost unmanoeuvrable. The *Hai* was a poor sea boat and the project was accordingly abandoned. The TVA experimental boat (actually a manned weapon) was destroyed by explosives at *Blaukoppel* (Lübeck) at the war's end.

The Midget Submarines *Delphin* I and II
In May 1944 Admiral Heye held talks with the head of the machinery test institute at Berlin Technical University (*Versuchsanstalt für Maschinengestaltung*), Professor (Ing) Cornelius, on the building of a new midget submarine. They came up with a fast one-man boat with a favourable shape for submerged travel, displacement 2.5 tonnes, length 5 metres and 1 metre in the beam. Propulsion would be supplied by a closed-circuit circulation motor.

Within a few days Dr (Ing) Haug produced the sketch of a droplet-shaped hull with plexiglass cupola. The hull-form would provide very fast submerged speed for low output. Dive and trim tanks were unnecessary because the boat could submerge by virtue of its dynamic shape. The project received the name *Delphin*. In July 1944 a model based on the blueprints was tested in the wind-channel of the towing-tanks at the Hamburg Ship Testing Institute HSVA (*Hamburger Schiff-bauversuchsanstalt*). The results were considered very promising.

Despite the sceptics who doubted the viability of the project, Karosseriefabrik Ambi-Budd at Berlin Johannishal received the order for three experimental boats. The firm had great experience in light construction work and had made fuselages for the V-1 and V-2. Ambi-Budd now proceeded using the principles of modern automobile bodyworking. The nose, motor room and stern sections of the *Delphin* were produced on special presses contrary to normal shipbuilding practice.

The cylindrical central section and the frames were made by rolling 2.5–4 mm thick steel sheets. The bow was welded to the central section but the central section and motor room were screwed together, a departure in midget submarine construction. It was found necessary to elongate the hull somewhat to accommodate the motor which still languished in the design stage.

In order to gain practical experience in the first instance, the experimental boats were propelled by standard G7e torpedo motors. In the autumn of 1944 Flender Werke at Lübeck tested the water-tightness and HSVA the towing qualities of the new boat before sea-water trials began. The first submerged runs were made in the Trave estuary. It was found that when running on the surface the plexiglass cupola caused a degree of instability which was rectified by the installation of a dive tank. In trials the boat achieved an underwater speed of 17 knots. On 18 January the first experimental boat was destroyed in collision with an escort vessel.

The armament was to have been a 500-kg explosive in the bow, later changed to a towed mine of the same weight. Contrary to a torpedo, this towed mine did not prejudice the streamlined advantages of the hull form. The *Delphin* had a 1.32 metre tall, fixed snorkel through which fresh air was admitted into the cockpit and then sucked into the motor room during surface travel. The maximum speed possible with the snorkel was 14 knots. The snorkel vent was worked by an electromagnet or mechanically by a foot pedal.

In autumn 1944 Dr (Ing) Urbach of the Berlin Technical University began testing an Otto closed-circuit motor. Initially he used the Junkers KM8 torpedo motor, but when this proved too demanding of current he switched to the 2.5 four-stroke 80-hp Opel Kapitän. In a second trial period between mid-October and mid-December 1944, the rheostat was redesigned in a simpler and more suitable form for series production. This cut the high consumption of fuel and oxygen and made the whole installation more efficient. A sucker pump ensured that the closed circuit system was largely independent of the atmosphere. The motor gave no trouble and could be switched as required between fresh air and closed-circuit irrespective of the engine revolutions. Endurance testing was not possible then (1945)

115

because of fuel shortages. The motor was never fitted into a *Delphin* experimental boat.

Meanwhile experiments had been undertaken to determine the submerged characteristics of the *Seehund* or 'Closed-circuit circulation engine-*Seehund*' if given the *Delphin* hull shape. New designs, *Delphin W* and *Grosser Delphin*, retaining most of the new methods of building and the mechanical fittings, were in preparation. One- and two-man versions were planned, but no further progress was made.

Technical details

	Delphin I	*Delphin* II
Experimental boats	3	None
Displacement	2.8 t	7.5 t
Length	5.5 m	8.7 m
Beam	1.0 m	1.3 m
Drive	32 hp closed circ.	100 hp diesel (80 hp closed circ.)
Speed (surfaced)	17 knots	18 knots
Range (submerged)	300 sea miles	400 sea miles
Torpedoes	One	Four to five
Crew	One	One or two

The *Delphin* was a pure submarine, i.e. it could submerge without flooding tanks. To dive the pilot turned two stumps projecting laterally along the hull. The crew of *Delphin* II would have been up to five men. The boat could carry five torpedoes. Rockets were another possibility. The *Delphin* was not completed by the war's end. The two surviving Ambi-Budd experimental boats were taken by road transport to Pötenitz in the Trave estuary where they were destroyed by British troops on their arrival on 1 May 1945.

The Midget U-boat *Schwertwal* and the K-*Butt* Torpedo
On 1 July 1944 designers at Walter Werke, Kiel began work on a project for a new and extremely fast midget submarine. In *Schwertwal* (Orca) they were planning an underwater hunter for submerged enemy submarines. The first prototype would serve in the main to evaluate how the boat handled at fast underwater speeds and to try out the 800 hp engine unit specially developed for seawater injection by the torpedo-

engine manufacturer Wal-Torpedotriebwerk. The *Schwertwal* propulsion unit, a BO V-1 turbine of the standard 55 hp Walter torpedo fitted with improved bearings, central oil lubrication and an additional jet ring provided a top speed of 30 knots and a range of 500 sea miles at 10 knots cruising speed.

The hull, based extensively on aviation streamlining experience, was tested in the wind tunnel of the aviation research institute (*Luftforschungsanstalt*) at Braunschweig and in the towing channels at HSVA. The control position and control room were located in the bow section. Between the forward and stern bulkheads was the engineer's compartment with regulating tank, the *Ingolin* fuel bunkers were abaft the rear bulkhead. *Ingolin*, so-called for Professor Walter's son Ingo, contained hydrogen peroxide (H_2O_2), when unthinned an extremely explosive, colourless, oily liquid able to be mixed with water. The central section with the fuel tanks was free-flooding so that the pressure at depth was equalized as fuel was consumed. This ensured that the engine worked at the same efficiency at all depths.

The compartmentalization was a safety feature which allowed the crew to be located well forward of the machinery plant. Had an explosion occurred in the combustion chamber aft, the crew would have been relatively well protected and, after jettisoning a major part of the ballast (the forward part of the outer keel), the foreship would have risen to the surface. The pressure-resistant bulkheads of the regulating tank provided a double bulkhead astern for safety. In the event of leaks from the fuel tanks, the escaping fuel would have been so thinned by mixing with the water of the free-flooding central section as to be practically harmless.

The machinery plant was located abaft the fuel bunker bulkhead. At the stern was the tail unit with rudder and fixed stabilizers. The hydroplanes were either side of the control room forward. The torpedoes fitted sheer below the hull to avoid compromising the streamlining and so cut speed. The 350-shp double propellor proved inadequate and gave only 25.6 knots at best. A 500-shp single screw with a maximum turning moment of 215 mkp was in preparation. In common with ordinary submarines, *Schwertwal* had a regulating tank to compensate for changes in weight, and fore and aft trim tanks for diving and surfacing dynamically, thus dispensing with the need for dive tanks.

117

Since the high speeds did not permit the use of a periscope, a forward-searching Asdic was in development. An aircraft gyro compass installation manufactured by Patin of Berlin adjusted automatically in the various axes and worked without problems on trials. The master compass was located in a streamlined mounting on the rudder head.

By the end of April 1945, the *Schwertwal* I prototype was ready for practical trials. The testing of all systems on land and the engine test stand were completed, the latter having achieved the required endurance output of 800 hp. In order to prevent the boat falling into the hands of the enemy it was brought to Bosau near Plön and scuttled. Two months later the British raised it and condemned it for scrap after a brief examination.

The project for *Schwertwal* II with more pronounced streamlining had commenced at the beginning of 1945. The 18-tonne boat was to have been 13.5 metres in length with a cross-section of 2 metres, maximum underwater speed 32 knots. The enlarged hull form allowed a more roomy accommodation and the installation of a small 25 hp electro-drive motor for slow manoeuvring and cruising at 8 knots. *Schwertwal* II remained on the drawing board.

The armament was to have been two fast K-*Butt* torpedoes (Butt = turbot) but other underwater weapons were also planned: a torpedo with reverse thrust which worked on the rocket principle and was for use against submerged submarines. ELAC of Kiel was developing a kind of Asdic sound location device. Propelled mines for use against submarine-chasers had entered the testing stage, planes were on hand to try out rocket batteries and flame-throwers for use on minor surface vessels. Various ground-, anchored- or towed mines were also planned. TVA Eckernförde had obtained good results in trials of a provisional towed mine consisting of a torpedo head and tail which when under tow descended to a pre-set depth by use of a torpedo depth-setting apparatus. At Surendorf standard artillery rockets were test-fired from submerged over a 500-metre range.

The K-*Butt* torpedo was designated Type T XIII G7ut. It was weight-equalized, i.e. when ready to fire displaced the same weight as the surrounding water. This was a very important advance for midget submarine use, particularly on *Schwertwal*. At the end of its run it would float once the propellant was used up. As a practice torpedo

118

Technical Details of *Schwertwal*

	Type I	Type II
Displacement	17 t	18 t
Length	12.0 m	13.5 m
Beam	2.2 m	2.8 m
Pressure hull	1.3 m	
Drive	Walter turbine	
Machinery output	800 hp	T. 800 hp
Top speed	30 knots	32 knots
Range	500 s/m	500 s/m
Maximum depth	100 m	100 m

Equipment: Gyro-stabilized compass automatically adjusted for depth and yaw, depth-sounder with forward search facility UT and hydrophone installation, electric motor for slow speeds. Course and speed printer. Dräger air purification equipment.

Armament: Two 53.3-cm torpedoes as *Schwertwal* I, K-*Butt* torpedo 50 knots/3,000 metres, or four mines, or underwater rocket battery.

Crew: Pilot and engineer as *Schwertwal* I.

---

it was thus easy to retrieve. This modern weapon with high speed and accuracy was to have become the standard torpedo for German midget submarines. A normal attack torpedo weighed 300 kgs. Once fired from a midget submarine, the sudden enormous weight loss caused the submarine to rise to the surface and thereby reveal itself. Large U-boats compensated for the weight change by flooding the torpedo tubes, but a midget submarine was too small to compensate the difference. What had been needed therefore was a weightless torpedo with great promise. The K-*Butt* fulfilled the hope.

The normal attack torpedo was unsuitable for *Schwertwal* because the boat was faster. The torpedo had to have a speed advantage over the submarine which fired it, or the submarine had to reduce speed to launch the torpedo. This involved some risk because the speed of the *Schwertwal* was its greatest asset. There was therefore no alternative to arming the *Schwertwal* with the Walter *Golden Turbot* torpedo, which with its small propellant tanks fitted neatly against the long

119

hull of the *Wal*. The 500 hp turbine gave the K-*Butt* 50 to 60 knots if the depth regulator was fitted. Its extraordinary range was three kilometres. After successful testing of three prototypes it was declared 'ready for the front' and given the go-ahead for series production at Walter Werke Kiel and Ahrensburg. About 100 were completed in April 1945 but none were used operationally.

Midget U-boat Type XXVIIF/F2

Following favourable results in the development of the Walter turbine with seawater injection it was obvious that in the forseeable future a similar unit would be available for long-range torpedoes, and the torpedo-turbine assumed greater significance as the drive for a fast midget U-boat. Therefore in the summer of 1944, K-Amt ordered the construction of a torpedo-shaped midget submarine designated Type XXVIIF. Its torpedo would be located sheer in a cavity below the hull. The pilot sat in the bow section at a control panel with periscope.

During travel, the boat became lighter as the *Ingolin* was used up, but no regulating tank was fitted since at its relatively high speed the weight loss would be compensated for dynamically. No dive tanks were installed. At the outset of a voyage the boat's operational displacement would be compensated for by disposable buoyancy tanks. Once the design stage was completed, the projected Walter turbine with seawater injection was far from series production, and the project was suspended. Instead, a previous idea to design a midget submarine for the proven Walter-torpedo-turbine with freshwater injection was taken up as project XXVIIF2. The boat had to be larger if freshwater injection was used and since weight could no longer be compensated for dynamically, a regulating tank had to be added. This increased the submerged displacement to 7.9 tonnes for a design 11.28 metres long and 1.05 metres in cross-section.

The new design resembled XXVIIF. The Hamburg testing unit carried out towed trials of the larger version in August 1944. Despite having the torpedo fit a moulded cavity on the underside of the boat, the increase in resistance caused by the torpedo was considerable. At 20 knots it was around 50 hp, a third of the total resistance of the boat without torpedo, while the torpedo's own resistance was only 16 to 17 hp. The other 34 hp was lost to the unfavourable contrary

120

arrangement of boat and torpedo. A total of 300 hp output provided a submerged speed of 22.6 knots without the torpedo and 20.4 knots with it. All developments in the autumn of 1944 not having priority were to be restricted. The boat's poor range, the grim war situation and the disastrous situation in industry in the autumn of 1944 all led to the decision of K-Amt not to pursue the project.

The One-Man Submarine *Tarpon*

This project was for a small, very agile boat with two torpedoes lodged forward one above the other. The boat's length would reduce to four metres once the torpedoes had been discharged. A purely electric drive was envisaged giving a range of 100 to 150 sea miles. It was thought that a depot ship or possibly land vehicles would present the best solution for maintenance and transport to the launching point. The boat was also considered a possible for commando operations, entering weakly defended harbours and so forth. Only a sketch was prepared, even a model was now beyond the limited capacity of industry.

The Submarine-Catamaran-MTB *Manta*

The *Manta* project resulted from a collaboration between Hellmuth Walter GmbH and *Versuchskommando 456*. The intention was to combine various progressive ideas found in earlier midget U-boat designs. The principal objective was to avoid water resistance caused by having torpedoes slung alongside the hull, and overcome the difficulties of lowering the craft into the water.

The *Manta* was a catamaran formed from three torpedo-shaped cylinders joined by a horizontal deck. The central cylinder had a cabin in the nose for two crew and a diesel generator. The remainder of the central cylinder, and the two external cylinders, were principally tanks for the fuel and *Ingolin*. Trim and regulating tanks were also fitted. The propulsion system was a *Schwertwal* II plant located in each of the side keels below the outer cylinders. Besides diesel-electric for cruising a diesel-hydraulic version was also discussed. The side keels were to take two large aircraft wheels each. On these the 50-tonne catamaran would enter the water independently. Adjustable surfaces were fitted between the side keels for planing on the surface.

121

The designers envisaged:

1. surface planing (max. 50 knots with Walter drive)
2. snorkel travel (10 knots, diesel-electric)
3. underwater maximum speed (30 knots, Walter drive)
4. underwater slow speed (8 knots max. with electric motor and four torpedo battery racks.

The specialist estimated range at about 1,180 sea miles, at top speed around 320 sea miles. The wing surfaces between the outer cylinders had four tubes for torpedoes or mines, so that the *Manta* was well armed. Equipment included automatic compass adjustment, sounding equipment and hydrophones similar to the *Schwertwal*. The model was not tested.

Although the *Manta* embodied many interesting ideas, the project showed just how far the military collapse had induced some designers, knowingly or not, to flee the Third Reich and enter the realms of fantasy. After the military decision-takers had for years continued to misunderstand or dismiss perfectly viable projects with scepticism, they now went ahead with any crazy idea which happened to catch their fancy.

Midget MTBs – The Midget E-boat *Wal*

While work proceeded full out on new midget submarines, there were various parallel schemes for coastal surface craft. These included the *Wal*. The 9-metre long planing hull had a 750 hp aircraft engine for a speed of up to 40 knots. Range was 250 sea miles. The two crew would have two torpedoes and two rocket launchers at their disposal. The boat completed its trials but was overtaken by *Wal* II and III. The latter were 10 metres long and could be built in wood or steel. Crew, armament and performance were all similar to *Wal* I, but the range was greater at 350 sea miles. Forward-looking plans had a four-man crew and an MG as an additional weapon. After good test reports and the completion of one wooden and one steel boat, the Boizenburg Werft began series production, but the *Wal* never saw action.

Float-boat *Torpedoschlitten*

With a 600 hp aircraft engine the 'torpedo-toboggan' would have had a top speed of 40 knots and a range of 300 sea miles. Series production would have presented no problem for the boat was little more than a

122

simple welded construction of floats. The two-man crew would fire two torpedoes and retire. A simple principle but a very dangerous weapon. First trials were reported as 'very promising' but too late.

The Midget MTB hydrofoils *Sachsenberg*, *Tietgen* and *Zisch*

Sachsenberg was a two-man torpedo-carrier. The design had originally been rejected by the Kriegsmarine but found favour as industrial capacity sagged. Some improvisation appears to have been introduced. The boat was driven by a 750 hp aircraft engine providing 50 knots and a range of 250 sea miles, but could not sail in anything stronger than a fresh breeze. The spray it threw up was visible far and wide, although this would not have been a significant handicap in night attacks. Various experimental boats were built, even one of 80 tonnes. The K-Verband tried out a small version but it came too late for series production.

Tietgen was a small unmanned explosive boat with outriggers similar to the *Torpedoschlitten*. The warhead would have been 500 kg explosive delivered by collision at 50 knots. An experimental boat was completed before the capitulation but had no motor or remote control fitted.

Zisch was a planing hull with four collapsible hydrofoils. It was not a naval development, but a project of the Wankel firm at Lindau on Lake Constance, where a small experimental version impressed on its trials on the lake.

Float-borne Torpedo Substitute

The increasing shortage of torpedoes led to the development of a substitute for use by S-boats and destroyers. This was a remote- or wire-controlled single seaplane float or pair propelled by a V-1 Argus engine. The craft would have carried 600 kg explosive to the target at 60 knots.

The *Seeteufel* Amphibian

The Eckernförde Nord TVA experts had soon realized that for attacks on shipping manned torpedoes were an interim solution lacking much promise. In the spring of 1944 engineer Alois Lödige, having evaluated the experience gained to date, set out to design a special midget submarine which embraced the tactics and operational requirements of the time. His boat was fitted with caterpillar tracks and so could overcome the difficulties inherent in getting down to the water and of land transportation, especially in difficult sectors near the front.

With few assistants Lödige built an experimental boat ready for trials by July 1944, only four months after the concept emerged. Flotillas of these *Seeteufel* (sea-devils), also called *Elefant* for their plump outline, were to be stationed in protected sheds at readiness. Here they could also be maintained technically and prepared for operations. From the sheds they would trundle down to the shore under their own power. The boats were as mobile as panzers, could traverse heavy terrain, and flatten a path to the beach, thus dispensing with the need for harbours or cranes. Once in the water propeller drive would be engaged to make the vehicle into a midget submarine. The bottom keel of the double keel opened to stow the caterpillar tracks, thus ensuring that the boat had a fine streamlined form. In this way the boat was very stable, and on land or the seabed had a firm base.

Technical Details

Overall length:	13.5 metres
Overall beam:	3 metres
Total weight:	20 tonnes
Machinery:	Gasoline and diesel motors
Output:	Gasoline 80 hp, diesel 250 hp, electric motor 30 hp
Maximum speed:	10 knots
Cruising speed:	6 knots
Range:	about 500 sea miles, with diesel 1,000 sea miles
Depth:	50 metres
Armament:	2 torpedoes or 2 mines
Other:	on land with caterpillar tracks, about 20 kms/hr
Crew:	Two

Snorkel mast with ventilation mast and mirror-compass. Periscope with target optic and magnification glass for torpedo aiming. Dräger air purification system.

Versuchskommando 456, which monitored all maritime ultra-light developments, carried out extensive trials, diving tests, torpedo firing exercises and speed tests over the measured mile in Eckernförde Bay with the experimental boat. The *Seeteufel* excelled. In the water it proved very agile and easily manoeuvrable. The location of the hydro-planes forward was found very good during submerged passage. The various axes were arranged similar to aeronautical practice and the control surfaces worked by a manual stick. In the cockpit the controls were sited prominently, the faces of indicators and dials given luminous paint. The pilot, who sat below the main hatch, had all-round vision. Voyaging at periscope depth while using the snorkel the pilot could see the mast easily and by lining up a red mark could hold the desired snorkel depth. At greater depths recourse was had to an easily visible depth gauge.

The boat trimmed for diving could dive and surface dynamically. It responded immediately to every touch on the hydroplanes. During surface travel the hatch could be opened. For better vision, especially at night, the commander could make the necessary calculations for a torpedo shot using binoculars. Data such as enemy course and speed would be shouted down to the engineer in the control room or passed by internal telephone. The second man then worked out the firing angle on the attack calculator and adjusted the periscope so that when the commander saw the target 'enter' the crosswires he could order the torpedo fired at exactly the right moment. Light through the periscope was dim and left something to be desired.

The surfaced and snorkel speed of the *Seeteufel* was 10 knots, submerged with electric drive 8 knots. On land with the tracks 10 or more kms/hr. For submerged passage *Seeteufel* was equipped with dive-, trim- and regulating tanks. To assist trimming, the boat had a spindle system with an adjustable battery rack amidships. All tanks could be monitored and operated from the control room. In trials the boat reached a depth of 21 metres.

A fixed compass installation and the periscope were housed in a non-magnetic casing, the snorkel was made of non-magnetic material so as not to interfere with the compass. The compass indication was reflected by mirror into the control room, the compass rose was illuminated – during passage the control room would be in darkness so as to enable vision through the tower ports. The figurework on all armatures, indicators and depth gauges was luminous.

The *Seeteufel* could fire standard G7a or G7e torpedoes without the danger of being forced to the surface by the weight loss when a torpedo was discharged. The designers had provided for a quick-flooding tank amidships to equalize the loss of 300 kgs torpedo weight and so remain at the required depth.

The snorkel sucked fresh air through the mast into the control room and from there into the motor room. This provided the crew with fresh air while also removing poisonous gases.

These outstanding results were the subject of a conference in August 1944 between Admiral Heye, the head of the Carl Borgward automobile manufacturer and its Bremen director, Kynast. This firm, which had been active for years in the field of torpedo manufacture, received the contract for the series production of *Seeteufel*, beginning with three prototypes. Twenty diesel-electric boats would follow. How far this work progressed is not recorded; by the end of the war no second *Seeteufel* had made its debut.

The Deep-Sea Salvage Vessel *Grundhai*

During the hasty training of U-boat crews, especially in the training flotillas, there were occasionally diving accidents and other break-downs which resulted in U-boats sinking to great depths from which the crews could no longer be saved.

The Kriegsmarine had at its disposal the armoured salvage vessels of the Kiel firm Hagenuk. These were considered very modern, but their limit was 150 metres, for at greater depths the moving joints became immobile because of the water pressure. Accordingly a new salvage vessel, the midget submarine *Grundhai* (bottom shark) able to work down to 1,000 metres, found its way to the drawing board.

Technical Details:

Length:	3.6 metres
Beam:	2 metres
Weight:	1.5 tonnes
Drive:	Two electric motors, output 3 hp each
Endurance:	With cable connection to the surface, battery life about 20 hours
Operational depth:	1,000 metres
Other equipment:	Four-wheeled caterpillar track for carriage on land or on deck, magnetic grab arms, 3 search-lights

126

Grundhai had all the usual fixtures found on a U-boat such as regulating and trim tanks. The boat was not streamlined: from above it looked rectangular, from the side aspect it tapered aft to a point, while the bow was rounded. Flat aluminium plating was used for the outer casing. The two electrically operated hydroplanes could be operated independently of each other. This made possible unlimited movement underwater and laterally by working the port and starboard screws and manoeuvring the hydroplanes. This was important for operating the electro-magnetic grab-arm at the sea bed.

Floats or inflatable bags could be hooked on for lift. To raise the casualty three different sizes of lifting bag were planned for weights of 250, 500 and 1,000 tonnes. Thus to raise a 500-tonne U-boat two inflatable bags with a lifting capacity of 250 tonnes each would suffice. The bags were 14 metres tall and 8 metres in diameter, cone-shaped and tapered towards the bottom end. Air was pumped in under pressure through a hose from the mother-ship at the surface. The bottom-most part of the air bag was equipped with a release valve to spill excess air and so avoid the balloon bursting through overload.

Communication between the mother-ship and *Grundhai* was by telephone cable and UT equipment for morse and short signals. The boat had an air purification system supplying atmospheric air allowing the crew to breathe freely without the need for *Jägermasken* and potash cartridges.

By the war's end *Grundhai* had not left the planning stage. As with so many other Kriegsmarine projects, it came too late. K-Verband Command occupied itself with a large number of ideas and projects. In the complicated conditions of the war economy of the latter war years it would have been a better policy to have concentrated on a few very promising ideas realizable in the short term.

Note
1 For this scientist's extraordinary career see Möller, Dr (Ing) Eberhard: *Marine-Geheimprojekte*, Motorbuch, Stuttgart, 2000.

Chapter Nine

The Explosive Boats of the Kriegsmarine

History, Technology and Tactics

Besides one-man torpedoes and midget submersibles, K-Verband Command also operated *Sprengboote*, or explosive boats. The historical predecessors of these so-named *Linsen* (the word in German means 'lens' or 'lentil') were the fireships, small sailing vessels loaded with easily ignited substances (tar, pitch, cotton waste, oakum or oil) which were sailed or rowed towards the target vessel. In proximity to the latter the cargo was set ablaze and the fireship made fast to the victim by hooks or chains. Fireships were used at the siege of Syracuse in 413 BC and even in the early 19th century formed part of the regular inventory of the various battle fleets.

In 1909 the German Imperial Navy awarded the Lürssen Werft a contract to build a 9-metre long experimental explosive boat *Racker* (villain) with a top speed of 27 knots which would be controlled using two 50-metre long wires run from a spool.

The second experimental boat, the 11-metre long *Havel*, also developed by Lürssen for remote control and equipped with 100 hp engines, achieved a speed of 33 knots at Schwerin in 1911. The trials headed by Kptlt Ehrhardt were not considered satisfactory.

After the outbreak of World War I the German Navy revived the programme and in 1915/1916 seventeen remote-controlled boats (FL1 to FL17) were constructed. Most of them saw action on the Flanders coast. They carried a 700 kg charge and were operated by means of a 16-mile long (later 27-mile long) cable from a land station. Even after the introduction of radio, however, remote control proved unreliable and was not a suitable alternative to having personnel available to make decisions on the spot.

In the Second World War it was not the Kriegsmarine but experts of Brandenburg Regiment zbV 800, a special unit of the German Abwehr, which took up the concept. On 27 September 1939 Dr Theodor von Hippel, then Hauptmann on the Staff of Abwehr/Ausland II, obtained approval to form a company of experienced men for the impending campaign in the West, and on 15 October Admiral Canaris, Abwehr head, told him to proceed. The task of this special unit was to be commando operations behind enemy lines often wearing enemy uniform. Operations involved blowing up bridges, railway tracks and ammunition depots, kidnapping persons of prominence, taking prisoners for interrogation purposes and later anti-partisan work.

The recruitment centre was the QM-General Barracks of the former Brandenburg Feld-artillerie Regt at Brandenburg, from which the unit derived its name and which grew to division size during the course of the war. Volunteers, many of them from the Abwehr, were trained at Gut Quenzsee.[1]

In 1941 the Army Weapons Office (*Heereswaffenamt*) ordered the production of explosive boats similar to the Light Assault Boat 39 built of light spruce. These were the forerunners for the later *Linsen* of the Kriegsmarine.

In February 1942, Regt Brandenburg zbV 800 set up a maritime unit with the cover name 'light engineer company' (*Leichte Pionier-kompanie*) aboard the sail training brigantine *Gorch Fock* moored in the Osternot harbour at Swinemünde. Amongst those reporting to the unit were Kriegsmarine small-boat pilots who had carried out landing exercises in the Bansin-Heringdorf area. After successful completion of induction training the company – or individual squads – were deployed in various theatres of war. At the end of 1942 at Langenargen on Lake Constance the Brandenburg coastal infantry unit (*Küstenjäger*) was formed from the 'light engineer company' and other elements from the regiment. The *Küstenjäger* was composed of four companies, and included the explosive-boat pilots. The Brandenburgers called these 'explosive speedboats' (*Ladungsschnellboote*).

130

The unit fought under its commander Rittmeister Konrad von Leipzig (a native of German South West Africa, now Namibia) in various theatres of war. The home garrison was Langenargen, the HQ at Schloss Montfort and the boats were kept at nearby Baggersee. In the spring of 1944 the *Küstenjäger* transferred to the Italian naval base at La Spezia on the Ligurian coast, and in April 1944 were used alongside *Neger* one-man torpedoes against the Allied bridgehead at Anzio, but achieved no successes. The spruce-built craft found the rough seas very heavy going.

After the K-Verband came into existence, Admiral Heye applied for the boats to come under K-Verband jurisdiction. On 15 April 1944 OKW/Wehrmacht Command Staff ruled in a very wordy piece of prose:

... The operational and tactical conditions of the naval war require uniform operational control of all naval units by the Kriegsmarine. Accordingly, all development work, completion, trials and operations of all special fighting machines (naval) for coastal deployment and at sea are the responsibility of the Kriegsmarine. These machines include in particular special fighting machines (naval) and small fighting machines (naval) as for example one-man boats, remote and wire-controlled explosive-carrying speedboats.

The operational groups for special fighting machines of the OKW/Amt Abwehr or Brandenburg Division which were previously responsible for preparations and operation of special fighting machines (naval) are to be transferred gradually into the Kriegsmarine (Naval Operations Section).

This order does not apply to operations of special fighting machines (naval) on rivers and lakes. Deployment and testing of these boats – insofar as they resemble or are assimilated to boats passing to the Kriegsmarine – is however the responsibility of the Kriegsmarine or is to be carried out jointly with the Kriegsmarine.

As the initial measure, the development and deployment of large explosives-carrying speedboats is to be transferred to the Oberkommando der Marine ... and the above mentioned term 'explosive-carrying speedboat' is to be understood to mean the *Linsen* explosive boats.

K-Verband Command took charge of the thirty existing *Linsen*. Brandenburger Major Goldbach, the inventor and leader of the *Linsen* units, was transferred into the Kriegsmarine and given the equivalent rank of Korvettenkapitän. All other *Küstenjäger* were allowed to choose freely between remaining with their unit or transferring into the Kriegsmarine,

The K-Verband soon discovered that the Brandenburger explosive boats were too light for sea service, and an improved *Linse* was developed by naval designer ObltzS F.H. Wendel, head of the K-Verband Design and Testing Bureau.[2] In 1941 Wendel had designed for the Luftwaffe parachute arm a 10-metre long motor boat capable of being dropped into the sea from a Go 242 heavy glider.

The new *Linse*, more powerful and stable, displaced 1.2 tonnes. It was 5.75 metres in length and was powered by a 3.6-litre Ford 95 hp Otto motor V-8 giving 3,300 revolutions driving two Voith-Schneider propellers. The boat could turn on the spot. Range was 80 sea miles at 15 knots cruising speed. Maximum speed was 31 knots.

The 300 kg (later 480 kg) charge was stowed in four metal containers in the stern of the boat. A metal frame ran around the boat holding a spring 15-cms from the gunwhale. At 80 kgs pressure, the spring activated a timer to detonate the explosive. When a collision occurred with the target ship – the pilot would have jumped off previously – the bow portion was destroyed while the heavy stern section sank with the explosive and motor. By means of a pre-set delay timer the explosive would be detonated after 2.5 or 7 seconds by when the explosives would have reached a depth close to or below the ship's bottom.

The three-man command boat was equipped with an ultra short-wave transmitter (7-metre band, manufacturer Blaupunkt). The radio beam of the high frequency transmitter was modulated with various low frequency tones. Each tone was an order. The *Linse* receiver filtered out the tones into relays which translated them into steering orders. An attack *Rotte* consisted of a command boat and two *Linsen*. The two command boat crewmen looked after the radio direction equipment while the *Rotte*-commander picked up the pilots from the water.

The new *Linsen* were built as from the end of May 1944. By October that year 385 boats had been completed, a total of 1,201 were built altogether. Six to ten yards were involved ranging from Flensburg to East Prussia, for example the Engelbrecht Werft at Berlin Grünau, Elbing and Rostock, also the Kröger Werft at Stralsund, Elbe and Weser. Trials were run mainly on Lake Constance.

On 26 March Kptlt Ulrich Kolbe was transferred from 5 S-boat Flotilla to the K-Verband, and in April 1944 at Lübeck's Dassower Wik formed K-Flotilla 211 with about ten *Linsen*. His orders were to work out the tactics and train the personnel. Improvisation was the order of the day, for example there were no trailers to get the *Linsen* to the beach and into the water. And the radius of action of the boats was only eight sea miles at full speed. This led to the transfer of the flotilla to the barracks of the seaplane base at List on Sylt. Here the weather and sea conditions proved unsuitable for training and another move ensued to the new *Lehrkommando 200* at Priesterbeck in Mecklenburg, cover-name *Grünkoppel*.

The base was the former barracks of a former RAD (*Reichsarbeitsdienst*) camp in the hamlet of Speck am Specker See whose ten farms were about ten kilometres east of Lake Müritz. The base was hidden away in the Langenhorst Forest, a large nature reserve. In May 1944 the flotilla had a permanent staff and sixty boats were on hand for training after fifty reinforcements arrived by train from Berlin Grünau and from Königsberg in East Prussia.

From July 1944 the head of *Lehrkommando 200* was Kptlt Helmut Bastian who had been deprived of his latest command when the torpedo boat *Möwe* was sunk in the big air raid on Le Havre. Later *Lehrkommando 200* was transferred to Plön in Holstein, cover-name *Netzkoppel*. Bastian had a double function as head of the *Lehrkommando* and operational leader of the *Linse* K-Flotillas. In March 1945, after all *Linse* flotillas had been formed, he took over 4 K-Division, vacant after partisans at Rotterdam assassinated the former encumbent FKpt Josephi.

A *Linse* flotilla consisted of four groups. Each group had four command boats and eight *Linsen*. Thus the strength of a *Linse* flotilla was 16 command boats and 32 *Linsen*. The attack formation was the pair, or *Rotte*. On the run towards the enemy, the command boat held the centre position, the two *Linsen* close in either side so that target and attack details could be shouted across. The pilots were issued lifejackets and later foam-rubber suits for protection against the effects of lengthy immersion in cold waters. A paratrooper helmet was worn. The *Linsen* were equipped with one-man inflatable dinghies and night rescue lamps. A wrist compass and illuminated chart helped navigation in the event of a return to base.

The *Rotte*-leader was helmsman of the command boat. His two crew were responsible for controlling the two *Linsen* after the pilots had jumped out. During the attack each used an ultra short-wave transmitter in a black box balanced on the knees. The remote control operated on different frequencies. By working a lever the *Linse* would receive the following instructions:

1. starboard rudder
2. port rudder
3. stop engine
4. start engine
5. slow ahead
6. go faster
7. blow up the boat, if the attack was a failure.

The ultra short-wave device was the steering gear fitted to the German Army's *Goliath*, a remote-controlled explosives carrier on tracks used against enemy armoured vehicles, bunkers and other targets.

To outwit enemy defences the *Linse* had two trumps: speed and manoeuvrability. At night, at the beginning of the attack phase when the pilots could only make out a target as a shadow, their boats would creep up on the enemy ship throttled back to 12 knots so as to avoid premature detection. When the target was confirmed, the *Rotte* headed full out at 30 knots for the enemy. The pilots checked the course, primed the detonator and switched on the remote control unit. A few hundred metres short of the target they jumped upwards and outwards away from their *Linsen*. Control of the two boats now passed to the command boat crewmen. At the stern of the pilotless *Linse* was a green lamp, and a red lamp stood further forward. Both lamps could only be seen from astern. The two lights and the target had to be aligned for a hit.

Once the attack terminated a search would be made for the *Linse* pilots in the water. Their lifejackets would have a small lamp to aid this endeavour. As soon as the pilots were aboard the command boat it would turn away at full speed and within seconds lay a 30-metre broad smoke screen from a stern installation. That was the theory, the practice would often turn out to be more complicated.

The *Linsen* Flotillas

Lehrkommando 200 was composed of the following personnel:

Chief: Kptlt Ulrich Kolbe, later Kptlt Helmut Bastian

Adjutant: Lt Fritz Engelhardt

Instructors: Kptlt Johann Rheinfeld, Lt Max Becker, Lt Günter Brunsch, Lt Rainer Jäckle

The training flotilla *Grünkoppel* was led by Oblt Herbert Seipold and Oblt Emil Taddey.

The Readiness Unit Waren/Müritz was responsible for supply and formed part of the *Linse*-Command. The officers were:

Commander: Kptlt Heinrich Schlüter

Adjutant: Oblt Günther Runge

Camp Chief: Kptlt Eduard Lunte

Company Chief: Kptlt Hermann Rademacher

Medical Officers: Kptlt Dr Gerhard Maschewski and Oblt Gerhard Lück

The following operational flotillas were formed during 1944 and 1945 (listing incomplete):

K-Flotilla 211 (formed April 1944)

Flotilla Chief: Oblt Helmut Plikat

Group leaders: Oblt Karl-Heinrich Schrader, Lt Alfred Vetter

Leader of the *Rotten*: Officer-applicant (R) Fritz Schöpfleuthner

Flotilla Engineer: Lt Max Becker

K-Flotilla 212 (formed July 1944)

Flotilla Chief: Kptlt Helmut Hinte

Group leaders: Oblt Heinz Günzerndt, Oblt Karl Feigl, Oblt Winfried Hempel, Lt Norbert Bunge

Leader of the *Rotten*: Oberfähnrich Hans-Georg Willenbrock

K-Flotilla 213 (formed July 1944)

Flotilla Chief: Kptlt Dr Ernst Rosefeldt

Leader, remote-control platoon: Oblt Otto Schmidt

Group leaders: Oblt Werner Johst, Oblt Hans Krämer, Lt Hans Philipp, Lt Gert-Karl Mehlhorn

Leader of the *Rotten*: Officer-applicant (R) Erich Mach

K-Flotilla 214 (formed November 1944)

Flotilla Chief: Kptlt Ludwig Vellguth

Group leader: Lt Karl-Friedrich Mand

K-Flotilla 215 (formed November 1944)

Flotilla Chief: not known

Leader remote-control platoon: Oblt Schädlich

Group leaders: Lt Hans-Joachim Heim, Lt Walter Kirchner, Lt Wolfgang Reussner, Officer-applicant (R) Hans-Kraft Uhlendorf

K-Flotilla 216 (formed August 1944)

Flotilla Chief: Oblt Erich Doerpinghaus

Leader remote-control platoon: Lt Peter Schlumberger

Group leaders: Lt Wolfgang Thum, Oblt Hans Krause, Oblt Arnim Theopold, Lt Wolfgang Ehrensberger

K-Flotilla 217 (probably formed October 1944)

Flotilla Chief: Oblt Dr Ulrich Müller-Voss

Leader remote-control platoon: Lt Alfred Mohr

Group leader: Oblt Gerhard Gress

K-Flotilla 218 (formed November 1944)

Flotilla Chief: Kptlt Christoph Schiekel

Group leaders: Lt Heinrich Brauer, Lt Hans Dieckmann

K-Flotilla 219 (formed January 1945)

Flotilla Chief: Kptlt Kiehn

Group leaders: Lt Erich Kudielka, Lt Friedrich Glahr

K-Flotilla 220 (date of formation not known)

Flotilla Chief: not known

Group leader: Lt Maximilian Arbasser von Rastburg

K-Flotilla 221 (formed March 1945)

Flotilla Chief: Oblt Ekkehard Martinssen

It was not possible to provide the officer corps in all cases. The flotillas to which the following officers were attached cannot be ascertained: Flotilla engineers Oblts Bernard Uphues, Oblt Richard Grossjohann, Oblt Hans Duckstein; Remote-control platoon leader Lt Diether Wolf; Consultant Oblt Fritz Eccard.

Sonderkommando *Hydra*

In addition to the *Linse*, K-Verband Command was working all out on an improved version of a midget motor torpedo boat, *Hydra*. This craft was 12.5 metres in length, 3 metres in the beam, weighed 8.5 tonnes and drew 60 centimetres. It was of an elegant whale-shape with low silhouette and closed-over upper deck for good seakeeping. The drive was a 750 hp aircraft motor providing the boat with 36.5 knots in sea conditions up to Force 4. Range was 400 sea miles. Two stern torpedoes and an MG or rocket launcher made up the armament.

The following officers were some of those involved in the training programme: Oblts Rudolf Bock, Friedrich Klein and Günter Nuyken; Lts Kurt Berg, Wilhelm Festing, Walter Gatermann, Hans-Rudolf Marchand, Hans Pecht, Bernd Schirrmacher, Fritz Heinrich Schulz, Werner Sudermann and Bernhard Zeidelhack.

1 *Hydra*-flotilla under Oblt von Eicken was ready for the front in the spring of 1945 but never saw action. It lay in wait at Kolding, Denmark and later Langballigau. The flotilla surrendered to the British at Glücksburg.

Linse Operations on the Normandy Coast

On 6 June 1944, K-Flotilla 211 under Kptlt Ulrich Kolbe headed for Le Havre. Its personnel numbered 250. The shore staff under Flotilla Engineer Max Becker included engineers for motors and equipment, radio and remote control, an explosives detachment, a radio crew to maintain radio liaison with Staff, a medical team, cooks, carpenters, flak, motor-cycle despatch riders and lorry drivers.

On 19 June the flotilla's ten command boats and 24 old *Linsen* arrived at Bolbec, a village east of Le Havre and set up camp in the grounds of an old shipyard on an inlet of the Seine. On the night of 20 June they moved to their intended launching point at Honfleur. The new *Linsen* with good seakeeping qualities and greater fuel capacity were not yet available, and so the *Brandenburg* boats, poorly suited for sea work and having a range of only 20 sea miles, were pressed into service with supplementary fuel tanks.

The first attack was planned for the night of 25 June. That evening at Le Havre R-boats took in tow eight command boats and nine old *Linsen*, one *Rotte* to each R-boat. One of the *Linse* collided with R-46 and exploded, sinking the R-boat and two command boats. The probable cause was failure to disconnect detonator leads after the electrical checks.

Despite the mishap the operation went ahead, and at first all went well. The boats had cast off and the individual towing parties (one R-boat and three to five *Linsen*) headed for the release point off the Orne estuary. Most failed to make it here because as soon as they cleared the harbour and the R-boats picked up speed the small *Linsen* found themselves struggling in fairly rough seas. Towing warps parted, some boats had electrical equipment short-circuit through swamping, others capsized. One crew after another headed back to the coast. Of the eight *Rotten* which started, only two remained viable. They set off in search of enemy shipping but returned next morning with no successes to report. The next attempt in July was equally unrewarding.

By the beginning of August 1944, K-Flotilla 211, now commanded by Kptlt Helmut Bastian, had 16 command boats and 32 new-type *Linsen*. On the night of 2 August as previously described in the section on one-man torpedoes, they took part in a combined operation with S-boats and *Marder*. This attack on congregated Allied shipping off Courselles sur Mer, the British and Canadian landing beaches *Juno* and *Sword*, caused chaos amongst the Allies. To sow more confusion the *Linsen* set adrift plexiglass cupolas with artistic heads painted on the insides. Bobbing up and down on the waves, they imitated perfectly the visible part of one-man torpedoes.

Two *Linsen* rammed and sank the landing ship LCG 764. At 0115 hrs a *Rotte* of two boats crewed by Funkmeister (Radio Warrant

Officer) Lindner, Funkmaat Preuss, Hauptgefreiter Arbinger and Ober-gefreiter Gorzawski attacked two ships. After an explosion a tanker sank. Other vessels sunk on this night remain the subject of debate as to which German boats were responsible. The operation claimed two command boats, 16 *Linsen* and the lives of one officer and seven men. The last *Linse* attack in Normandy followed on 8 August in favourable weather conditions. Towards midnight 12 command boats and 16 *Linsen* started out from the Dives estuary where they had hidden out in a small wood near Novelles, a village between Lizieux and Pont l'Eveque 4 kilometres from the front.

The battle reports claim three ships sunk: the freighter *Iddesleigh* near anchorage H-20,[3] the workshop ship *Albatross* and a mine-sweeper. Because three boats of 2 S-boat Flotilla fired long-range *Dackel* torpedoes towards Allied shipping in this area, and boats of 6 S-boat Flotilla were also active in the vicinity, the successes cannot be attributed for certain. Four *Linsen* crews failed to return.

While Kptlt Bastian was in Berlin making his report, group leader LtzS Alfred Vetter, the flotilla medical and transport officers took half of 3 Group and some stragglers (therefore almost two Groups) to Germany via Nancy and Strasbourg. On 23 August the remainder of K-Flotilla 211 arrived at Plön where, at Fedderwardsiel, the flotilla rested and re-formed.

Operations in the Mediterranean and Adriatic
Linse units fought in the Mediterranean and Adriatic, initially with the Italian X-MAS Flotilla under Prince Julio Borghese, who remained loyal to the Germans after Badoglio's Italy went over to the Allies in 1943.

Operations opened in August 1944 with attacks on the Allied landings fleet in southern France. The German groups were equipped partly with captured or newly-built Italian MTM (*Motoscafo Turismo Modificato*) explosive boats and MTSMA (*Motoscafo Turismo Silurante Modificato Allargato*) small MTBs, and partly with German *Linsen*. Depots and assembly centres were set up at Verona and Padua for boats arriving from Germany at the end of September 1944. The history of *Linse* operations in the region remains fragmentary. As the result of the confused military situation in Italy, the Italian Army had capitulated. Elements continued to fight with the Germans, but details

139

of boats, launching points and crews are absent. Often the boats were lent out for commando operations. A large number of explosive boat crews died in action or failed to survive so-called Yugoslav 'prisoner-of-war' camps. So far as is known no War Diaries have survived.

K-Flotilla 213 was the first *Linse* unit to head for Genova. On 18 October 1944 lorries carrying 48 *Linsen* arrived at San Remo and were parked in the roomy flower market near the harbour. The flotilla was directed by Operational Staff South under KptzS Werner Hartmann, whose HQ was located in an hotel at Levicio near Trieste.

Between 24 August and 10 September operations were sailed in the Bay of St Tropez. No successes were claimed and thirteen boats were lost. In an operation on 30 September from Corsini the boats were towed out by naval lighters. Nothing was achieved and only two command boats returned, the others having fallen foul of the weather at sea. The remaining boats removed to San Remo, arriving on 18 October. On 20 October a British destroyer bombarded the flower market, destroying all the *Linsen*, four MTM boats and 20 lorries. The boat-less flotilla now moved to Verona to join the flotilla Staff and await new boats. Not until 22 November was it declared operational again.

On 23 November the 60 boats at Verona were attacked by seven fighter-bombers. The raid was a failure, no *Linsen* were damaged and one aircraft was shot down by flotilla flak. Whether any missions ensued in November 1944 is unknown.

According to French reports, on 11 December 1944 south of Cap d'Antibes nine French minesweepers were engaged by two German 'assault boats' – possibly explosive boats – of which one came alongside to surrender in damaged condition, and was sunk after the crew was taken off.

On the night of 3 December 1944 in a fiasco in the Adriatic off the Albanian coast, S-boats of 1 and 2 Groups/3 S-boat Flotilla (1 Group ObltzS Backhaus with S30, S36, S58, S60 and S61: 2 Group ObltzS Buschmann with S151, S152, S154, S156 and S157) intending to attack Allied naval units landing on the island of Lussin were unaware, due to the collapse of the telephone network, that K-Verband units were active in the same location. K-Verband boats attacked the S-boats, forcing them to turn away sharply. Very few combined operations were sailed subsequently.

On 10 January 1945 at 2309 a warship, probably the French destroyer *La Fortune*, reported having been attacked by a German explosive boat 15 miles south of San Remo. On the night of 16 January, 33 *Linsen* sailed from La Spezia. Ten were lost. Before the end of the month the survivors were withdrawn to Verona and sent to Plattensee (Balaton) in Hungary for operations on the Danube. For this theatre of operations, *Missions on European Rivers*, the K-Staff for Special Operations under KptzS Düwel with HQ at Kammer am Attersee had jurisdiction. On 8 March 1945 K-Staff South was transferred to KptzS Böhme, command office at Levicio. 6 K-Division was stationed at Pola in the Adriatic.

At the end of 1944, virtually the entire Albanian and Yugoslav coast as far as the entrance to the Gulf of Fiume was held either by the Allies or Tito's partisans. The only part of the Mediterranean over which the Kriegsmarine exercised some control was the Ligurian Sea between La Spezia and the Italian border with France, and the northern Adriatic. During the last six months of the war in this region, offensive operations were carried out mainly by K-Verband. On 24 April 1945 San Remo was evacuated. The only success in the period was damage inflicted on the French destroyer *Trombe* on 17 April.

Linse Operations in the Low Countries

After the K-Flotilla operations in Normandy and the loss of the French Channel coast, K-Verband Command concentrated its efforts against the French-Belgian coast. Nearly all *Linse*-Flotillas now reported there for operations: at the beginning of October 1944 the first 62 *Linsen* arrived at the Dutch port of Flushing.

On the night of 5 October a group from K-Flotilla 214 is reported to have sailed from Flushing with MEK 60 as convoy protection for KFKs (naval trawlers) running supplies into the beleaguered enclave at Dunkirk. This was Operation *Kamaraden*. The other four groups of K-Flotilla 214 were ordered to attack British minesweepers off the Scheldt estuary. All missions terminated in failure. Soon after the KFK escorts sailed two of its boats were sunk in error by harbour patrol vessels. As the KFKs considered the *Linsen* to be a liability, the operation was called off.

Because of deteriorating weather, heavy seas and wind strength 5 the other groups were unable to fulfil their mission. 26 boats were

141

forced to return, 14 ran ashore on German-held territory and were destroyed by their crews. The remainder were recalled to Rotterdam, two boats being sunk on the way by fighter-bombers. On 12 October K-Flotilla 215 arrived at Groningen with 60 boats, and transferred two days later to Rotterdam. Ten days later 28 *Linsen* of this flotilla were transported by lighters to Flushing and ordered to sea the same night to attack shipping on the Flanders coast. After sailing they drew fire from a British coastal battery at West Kapelle and the little armada broke up in confusion. Fourteen *Linsen* which had become separated from their command boats returned to base, but the fate of all the rest is unknown. On 24 October two groups from K-Flotilla 215 were sent with supplies for Dunkirk, another four boats with gun parts for Kadzand. These groups were also dispersed by artillery fire from the land.

After another operation against the Allied landing area at Zuid Beverland failed on 26 October when all boats ran aground off Terneuzen, towards 2000 hrs next evening K-Flotilla 215 set out for a fresh assault on the traffic unloading from the Scheldt into the bridge-head at Zuid Beverland. *Linsen* rammed an unloading quay and sank two lighters: the outer mole was also rammed and a 600-ton lighter under tow destroyed. Three *Linsen* were destroyed by the enemy in these attacks and one *Rotte* ran aground near Zuid Beverland. The Germans suffered no losses in personnel. On 31 October two *Rotten* from K-Flotilla 215 sailed for the last operation of the month in the western Scheldt. Off Terneuzen they sank a troopship, an ammunition ship, an AA lighter and a searchlight barge.

On 1 November 152 Brigade of 52nd British Infantry Division and 4 Special Service Brigade landed on the island of Walcheren. General-leutnant Daser's 70 Infantry Division was defending the approaches to Antwerp and their coastal batteries held off the British until being finally overwhelmed on 8 November. Flushing was occupied by a Polish division.

On the night of 3 November two groups of K-Flotilla 212 moved from Dordrecht to Zierikzee. Nine of these boats were forced to return to Dordrecht, five stranded and six reached Zeipe. The difficult situation caused another move, from Zeipe to Hellevoetsluis, which now became the only outlet for *Linsen* operations. The boats, equipment and remaining personnel of K-Flotilla 215 were evacuated from Flushing in barges. K-Flotilla 214 was at Groningen.

On 20 December, K-Flotilla 215 transferred with 60 *Linsen* to Oslo to operate against British MTBs from Levanger in Trondheim Fjord. To compensate for its absence, 96 *Linsen* were brought to Holland from other flotillas and distributed amongst the bases at Den Helder, Scheveningen and Hellevoetsluis.

Because of a shortage of Ford motors, in November 1944 only 222 *Linsen* were completed instead of the planned 350. Another 80 followed in December. These were the last to be built for a grand total of 1,130. Despite the shortfall Dönitz decided to transfer 24 *Linsen* to the Plattensee in Hungary in support of the Army. Meanwhile on 5 December K-Flotilla 215 arrived at Arhus in Denmark and was ready to embark for Oslo on 20 December, on 5 December also 12 *Linsen* left Hellevoetsluis for a raid but were wiped out in the Meuse estuary by fighter-bombers.

A sortie on the evening of 17 December with a force of 27 *Linsen* went awry when four boats flooded and sank in heavy seas. The others returned to base. Once the weather improved these same 23 boats made for the Scheldt the same night. Three ran aground off Goerre. Only three reached the area of operations where they attacked a destroyer but missed.

21 *Linsen* sailed on 19 December but were soon fogbound: seven *Rotten* had motor problems or ran aground on sandbanks without reaching the attack zone. One boat was sunk by a destroyer near Walcheren, a *Linse* claimed sinking a ship with two funnels.

On 21 December 1944 Kptlt Bastian reported that the boats could no longer be considered operational without a full overhaul, but nevertheless at 2300 on Christmas Eve nine *Linsen* set out for the western Scheldt in extremely cold weather with drifting ice. Next day the three command boats returned, the six explosive boats having been destroyed by their crews. On 28 December the *Linsen* units at Hellevoetsluis were ordered to transfer to Scheveningen because of the growing danger of air attack and the icy conditions.

The operation by 12 *Linsen* on 9 January 1945 was abandoned at sea due to poor visibility and high swell: one boat remained unaccounted for. The subsequent attack by K-Flotilla 212 which began at 1540 on 13 January from Hellevoetsluis was abandoned after a number of boats were machine-gunned and damaged by fighter-bombers. Nothing else is known of the January 1945 operations. In February only two sorties were attempted because of adverse weather. On 19 February 15 *Linsen* took part in a combined night operation with *Seehund* submarines from Hellevoetsluis. Nine boats returned because of fog, the other six had no success to report, two of the boats were written off. Two days later, on 21 February, nine *Linsen* took part in a combined operation in the western Scheldt with *Molch* submarines: six boats put back with engine damage, the other three returned after finding no targets.

After a slight improvement in the weather, five missions were sailed in March.

On the night of 10 March, six *Linsen* set out to attack the Allied anchorage off Veere on the north coast of Walcheren, but were driven off by coastal batteries. Two boats stuck on a sandbank.

On 6 March it was reported that a transport of *Marder* lures destined for Italy had been destroyed by fighter-bombers at Rosenheim in Bavaria. These were actually mines made from a *Marder* glass cupola and containing an explosive charge. They would explode if rammed after being mistaken for a *Marder*.

On 12 March five of seven *Rotten* reached the operational zone in the Scheldt estuary. The only contact with the enemy was a failed attack on a patrol boat. Three command boats and seven *Linsen* were destroyed by fighter-bombers while returning. The same night S-boats transported three *Linsen* to attack a convoy 18 sea miles off the Thames estuary, but no details of the operations have survived. The command boats with the crews were stranded near the Goerre lighthouse on their return and were machine-gunned by fighter-bombers. There were no survivors, eleven bodies were recovered.

On 23 March four *Rotten* set out for North Foreland buoy NF8 on the Thames-Scheldt convoy route. This was a long voyage resulting in three *Rotten* failing to arrive and a fourth grounding on Schouwen island.

In March 1945, 66 *Linse* individual missions were sailed.

In April 1945 Holland was encircled by the Allies. Reinforcements could no longer be brought up by road or rail. Fifty-one *Linsen* remained at Hellevoetsluis and Scheveningen. In this last full month of the war they sailed four operations.

On the evening of 11 April five *Rotten*, fifteen boats in all, left Hellevoetsluis to attack ships anchored at Ostend. Four *Rotten* reached

144

the operational zone but one returned with engine damage. Two of the surviving three *Rotten* made contact with the enemy. After missing a patrol boat the two returned, the third was not heard from again. According to other reports the frigate HMS *Ekins* sank two boats.

On the following night seven *Rotten* left to repeat the operation against ships found sailing independently or anchored at Ostend. The boats turned back for bad weather. Two boats with a special mission to land German agents ashore were foiled by the high swell.

On 17 April four *Rotten* searched for enemy shipping in the Scheldt estuary. Two turned back with technical problems. No successes were claimed. Two other *Rotten* entered Dunkirk harbour despite the moleheads being in enemy hands. The boats manoeuvred unscathed through the great cemetery of ships to reach the besieged German garrison after negotiating a wire entanglement laid by the British. The *Linsen* brought butter and *Panzerfäuste*. On 18 April they returned to base safely. The famine in the enclave had grown so serious that the fortress commandant had asked Naval Command West if flour used for bread-making could be supplemented with tree-bark or sawdust. He was told to use finely chopped straw.

On the night of 20 April 1945 the last *Linse* operation was sailed when 12 boats set out for Dunkirk. 25 sea miles north of Ostend they were intercepted by British patrols. The frigate HMS *Ekins* sank six boats, the others put back to Hellevoetsluis.

In April 1945 in the North Sea-English Channel theatre 171 *Linsen* voyages were sailed. The *Linse* explosive boats achieved few successes, but their crews proved their bravery and great devotion to duty in operations carried out in the dead of night, in cold and ice, and against an overwhelmingly powerful enemy.[4]

Notes

1 For a comprehensive history of the Brandenburgers and their coastal infantry unit see Kurowski, Franz: *Deutsche Kommandotrupps 1939–1945, Brandenburger und Abwehr im weltweiten Einsatz*, Vols 1 and 2, Motorbuch Verlag, Stuttgart, 2001–2003.

2 For the technology and history of explosive boats and other midget units, with many sketches and illustrations see Harald Fock: *Marine Kleinkampfmittel*, Koehlers Verlag, Hamburg, 1982.

3 This ship was run ashore to prevent her sinking, and was torpedoed on the beach by a *Seehund* later that month.

4 After 1945 various navies studied German and Italian explosive boat operations and developed their techniques and tactics. The Israeli Navy in particular admired German-Italian K-force ideas and introduced them locally with noteworthy success. See Mike Eldar: *Israels geheime Marine-kommandos,* Motorbuch Verlag, Stuttgart, 2000.

Chapter Ten

K-Verband Assault Boats

Formation and Training

The daring activities of the assault boats and their crews remain obscure. Few details and facts have emerged from that period. Most men of these units fell in action, were murdered by partisans or failed to survive captivity in Eastern Europe. The War Diaries were destroyed or have been lost. Therefore very little knowledge of their operations has been preserved. Additionally the history of the assault boats is allied closely to that of the frogman and naval sabotage units (MEKs) and cannot always be separated out.

The K-Verband assault boat flotilla was formed and trained at three locations: *Lehrkommando 600* (List/Sylt, *Weisskoppel*), *Lehrkommando 601* (Sesto Calende, Laggio Maggiore, Italy) and *Lehrkommando 602* (Sta. Anna, Stresa Aerodrome, west bank of Tessin estuary).

Head of *Lehrkommando 600* was Kptlt Heinz Schomburg, the unit being known occasionally as *Sonderkommando Schomburg*. He had been head of K-Verband Command Naval Appointments Division at Lübeck and before taking charge of the *Lehrkommando* was liaison officer for German Naval Command Italy to X-MAS Flotilla.

Amongst others the following instructors served at *Lehrkommando 600*:

Kptlt Richard Rett; Oblts Gerd Prensemeyer, Walter Hesse; Lts Erhard Beyer, Ernst Haeusler, Walter Ertel.

The following assault boat flotillas were formed:

147

K-Sturmboot Flotilla 611
Flotilla Chief: Kptlt Wilhelm Ulrich

Pilots: Lt Hans Gercke, Georg Kulow, Walter Schiedl, Ulrich Pagel; Officer-applicant (R) Bernhard Meier

K-Sturmboot Flotilla 612
Flotilla Chief: Kptlt Ernst Wilhelm Witt

Pilots: Oblt Wolfgang Dallwig, Lts Hans-Hermann Priesemann, Horst Eichhorn; Officer-applicants (R) Karl Geschwandtner, Max Hofer

K-Sturmboot Flotilla 613
Flotilla Chief: Oblt Wilhelm Gerhardt

Pilots: Oblt Johann Kruse, Lt Christian Hansen, Oberfähnriche Gerhard Jänicke, Hans-Peter Johannsen, Fritz Kraus, Heinz Krieg, Manfred Kurek, Officer-applicant (R) Karl-Gustav Hoff; Rank unknown, Heinz Kroohs.

Of K-Sturmboot Flotillas 614 and 615 nothing is known except that the latter came into existence in March 1945 under Oblt Friedrich Böttcher. It is somewhat confusing that until August 1944, Flotillas 611 to 613 had generally been known as *Sturmbootflotillen* 1, 2 and 3.

The training of assault boat pilots was as uncompromising and comprehensive as that of the German naval sabotage units (MEKs).[1] Boxing, wrestling, judo, long distance swimming, fast marching, shooting and hand-grenade throwing were to the forefront in the sporting curriculum. Pilot training began on Italian MAS boats. Continuation training followed at Stresa on the SMA boat, a development of the MTSM. Knowledge of the so-called SA-boat groups is scanty:

Group 1: Oblt Freiherr Leopold von Troschke

Group 2: Oblt Karl-Heinz Ritschke

Group 4: Oblt Karl Beier, Lt Arnim Bayer, Lts (S) Helmuth Möhring, Rudolf Veurel, Walter Wangerin, Alfred Ziegler

Group 12: Oblt Hans Gimbel

It is not impossible that these were all Abwehr men.

148

Light and heavy assault boats were used by Wehrmacht assault pioneers for river crossings. A powerful outboard with hand tiller was used. These boats were also used by the Brandenburg *Küstenjäger* for coastal work. In Italy the K-Verband used mainly Italian, or copies of Italian, midget MTBs, e.g. one or two-man SMA-type boats. The armament of the two-man assault boat was two small-calibre stern torpedo tubes, but for close-in fighting hand-grenades and *Panzer-fäuste* were also used.

Operations on the Ligurian Coast

The assault-boat flotillas were controlled by K-Staff South at Levicio. The first to arrive on the Italian Riviera was 1 Sturmboot Flotilla on 15 August 1944, commanded by Kptz Werner Hartmann. Those serving at Staff included Kptlt Thiersch, No. 1 General Staff Officer (1a), Oblt Haertling (adjutant), Marineoberstabsarzt Dr Heinz Neumann (flotilla surgeon) and Kptlt Heinz Schomburg, head of the *Sonderkommando*. MEK 80 Supply headed by Kptlt Krumhaar and KFZ Süd (Vehicles South) also came under this umbrella. MEK 80 had a complement of about 350 men and fought for a long period as infantry in the anti-partisan role on the coastal slopes of the Appenines. X-MAS Flotilla was attached to MEK 80.

Chief of K-Staff South West, at Ville Franche near Nice in August 1944 and later at Opicina on the Adriatic, was KKpt Haun, whose task at the time was the formation and operational planning for the German-Italian flotillas. Operations of 1 Sturmboot Flotilla com-menced on 16 and 17 August 1944 from San Remo against the Allied invasion fleet but claimed no successes. After six one-man and fourteen two-man additional assault boats arrived on 20 August, a fresh attack was made off the bridgehead on the night of 25 August. A large ship five miles south of Cannes, a destroyer and a patrol boat three sea miles east-south-east of Cap d'Antibes were claimed hit. Sinkings could not be confirmed because of the strong defences are doubtful. All assault-boats returned safely. Italian boats reported having hit a cruiser, after which they were driven off.

In a sortie on the night of 27 August a hit was claimed on a British MTB or patrol boat: a small ship, presumably an escort, was claimed sunk. The following night eight 2-man boats operated without success against the bridgehead. On the return leg the Italian boats were fired on by destroyer Bofors but not hit. In the night operation a German assault boat attacked a gunboat at 12 metres range. The *Panzerfaust*[2] failed. After numerous hits the German boat caught fire but the flames were soon extinguished. Whilst hurling a hand-grenade the second pilot then fell overboard but reached his base after a three-hour swim.

On 28 August 1944 German Naval Command Italy announced with regard to the operational opportunities for small units that the principal landing places of the Allied invader lay between St Tropez and Marseilles and were out of range. The convoy traffic between Corsica and that stretch of coast was strongly escorted east of the line Cannes-Calvi, however, and the assault boat operations there on moonlit nights seemed very promising. Despite this evaluation, on the night of 30 August a single one-man and eleven two-man assault boats left Monaco to attack the bridgehead. The German boats slipped through the British defence line of five gunboats off Ville Franche but found no worthwhile targets. Nine boats returned to Mentone, one to San Remo after surviving an air attack and another reached Monaco. One boat was abandoned off Cap Martin, salvage was attempted.

On 10 September a mixed force of six German and Italian assault boats launched a fresh attack supported by 14 *Marder* manned torpedoes but this failed because of the strong air and sea defences. Four days later, on 14 September, boats of 1 Sturmboot Flotilla hunted from San Remo but found no targets. The flotilla was 18 boats strong at that time.

After a long inactive pause, on 11 December five two-man, 16 one-man and three Italian MAS boats sailed for the Bay of Ville Franche, but bad weather forced an early return. An MAS boat was disabled and boarded by the enemy. A German assault boat was scuttled by its pilot after receiving damage, the pilot was then captured.

After an unsuccessful sortie along the Ligurian coast on the night of 20 December, K-Verband Command reported to SKL:

Further preparations for *Sonderkommando Schomburg* in the framework of the Western Offensive has run into difficulties because the relevant Army offices have apparently not been notified of its mission and to some extent consider its operations inopportune. The Admiral K-Verband has therefore ordered the *Sonderkommando* disbanded and released for other pressing duties.

150

On the night of 10 January 1945, two of five two-man assault boats fought enemy destroyers off San Remo. Neither scored a hit. All German boats returned to base undamaged. A week later on 17 January two assault boats got close inshore south-east of Nice and encountered a string of eight patrol boats. The lay of the harbour could not be determined. At the same time other assault boats attacked Livorno, Viareggio and Piscina di Pisa. Loud explosions were heard but whether ships were sunk or damaged is not known.

The last attack on the Ligurian coast occurred on the night of 22 April 1945 when Sturmboot Flotilla 611 *Hitler Jugend* attacked Allied shipping off Livorno in company with *Linse* explosive boats. The German vessels were probably tracked by radar, fired on and either sunk or forced to withdraw. Some crews were picked up by Allied warships but the other survivors, unarmed, who swam ashore were murdered there by partisans.

Operations in the Adriatic
In autumn 1944 the Sturmboot flotillas received new, improved stepped-planing boats. The first trials of these were run at Fiume on 6 October. Crews were drawn from *Lehrkommando 600*. The new craft were simple but robust and very manoeuvrable. They weighed in at 600 kgs, were 6.3 metres long and could manage 30 knots, gasoline consumption being 15 to 20 litres. The turning circle was a favourable 60 to 75 metres diameter. 3 Sturmboot Flotilla under Oblt Gerhardt took over the first boats.

2 Sturmboot Flotilla under Kptlt Witt was to operate from Pola. On 26 October the naval transport chief agreed to supply a transport vessel to the forward base at Lussin. On 2 November the flotilla transferred from Sesto Calende to Opicina and arrived at Pola on the evening of 3 November with 23 MTM and 3 SMA boats. An MTM pilot was killed in an accident on the way. After six assault boats had reached Lussin-Piccolo, all survived a machine-gun and rocket attack by Mosquito fighter-bombers. That same day, 20 November, 2 Sturmboot Flotilla was sent out to search for survivors from the German hospital ship *Tübingen*, which had been attacked and sunk. One boat was lost to bad weather.

On 24 November, sixteen assault boats and nine boats of 3 S-boat Flotilla arrived at Pola to attack shipping anchored off the Dalmatian

151

islands of Dugi and Otok, but the operation was called off for bad weather.

On the night of 3 December assault boats of 2 Flotilla set out for Pola to engage enemy naval units reported in the Cigale area near Lussin, but nothing was achieved. Two days later in a fresh sortie the Punta Nera lighthouse was destroyed. The Allies had converted it into a military radio station. The crew escaped.

On the night of 16 December, MEK men were landed from assault boats on the islands of Isto and Meiada: on the following night other assault boats, protected by two S-boat groups, attacked Meiada. While the S-boats were forced to withdraw by heavy fire at 0045, Sturmboot crews blew up the quay and storage sheds at Zapuntelo.

In the last known operation in the Adriatic on 18 and 19 January 1945, involving an attack on Zara by nine S-boats and assault boats of K-Flotilla 612, the assault boats were forced to abandon the attack with engine breakdowns. Even the SMA boats, copies of Italian midget MTBs with 52-cm torpedo tubes built in Germany, could not cope with the heavy seas. Off Zara, S-boats duelled with a large ML escort and received several hits.

Notes

1 For comprehensive coverage of assault and explosive boats, MEKs and frogmen in the Italian theatre see Lau, Manfred: *Schiffssterben vor Algier, Kampfschwimmer, Torpedoreiter und MEK im Mittelmeer 1942–1945*, Motorbuch, 2001. Manfred Lau was himself a K-Verband frogman.
2 A powerful German infantry anti-tank weapon fired from the shoulder. The armour-piercing *Panzerfaust 100* weapon available at the time had a range of 100 metres.

Chapter Eleven

The German Frogmen

Frogmen and divers were an important component of the K-Verband. The men were given the most intensive training, particularly in underwater demolition with emphasis on shipping, bridges, buildings and so forth. The Italians were the most experienced in the field, and the Kriegsmarine profited from their knowledge. The Abwehr and the SS-RSHA (Reich Security HQ) were first in the field to train frogmen, however. From 1942, SS-RSHA Abt.VIa-c maintained close links with Italian counter-intelligence and the X-MAS Flotilla. This special unit of the Italian Navy had begun training German frogmen, mainly from the Brandenburg Division. In the spring of 1943 a demonstration of underwater diving activities was held for the Abwehr at the Berlin Olympic Pool. A Lt-Cdr Wolk took part. This man was a representative of the Italian Navy, a Volksdeutscher of Russian origin – although others describe him as a White Russian emigré – domiciled in Italy.

The exhibition was the idea of an NCO, Alfred von Wurzian, an experienced diver who had taken part in the 1939 underwater expedition to Curaçao in the Caribbean arranged by the renowned researcher Hans Hass. The war disrupted the expedition and its participants had many adventures on their return to Germany. In 1942 the underwater research was continued in the Aegean and von Wurzian – meanwhile conscripted into the German Army – was given leave to participate. At his instigation a new underwater breathing gear manufactured by the Dräger firm of Lübeck was tried out for military use and found satisfactory. It was von Wurzian's ambition to set up an elite unit of swimmers and divers. In contrast to its predecessors, the Dräger set

153

weighed only 4 kgs and allowed a diver to remain underwater for about an hour at depths down to 25 metres.

Unteroffizier von Wurzian obtained the agreement of his superiors to present his idea to the Kriegsmarine in 1942, but SKL turned it down since they could see no present use for such a unit. The Army (OKH) visited next by von Wurzian was of the same opinion but suggested he approach the Abwehr. Here he encountered interest and was ordered to arrange the exhibition in the Olympic Pool. It is said that in conversation with Lt-Cdr Wolk he learned for the first time of the existence and operations of the Italian 'Gamma' frogmen.

Wolk offered to have the Italians train German volunteers, resulting in the despatch by the Abwehr of the first German swimmers to X-MAS Flotilla at La Spezia. Von Wurzian had been transferred meanwhile to *Abwehrtruppe 204* under Rittmeister Erwin Graf Thun and was seconded together with well-known sports swimmers such as Richard Reimann, Erwin Sietas, Herbert Klein, Kurt Kayser, Gerd Schmidt, Manfred Laskowsky, Heinz Lehmann and Walter Ernst, some of whom had swum at the 1936 Olympics. Lt-Cdr Wolk was in charge of training.

In December 1943, an SKL commission attended a frogmen demonstration at La Spezia naval base in order to assess the standard achieved. It proved highly successful. Four Italians and three Germans, amongst them von Wurzian, attached mock limpet-mines to the keel of a destroyer unnoticed. The commission was enthusiastic. From 2 January 1944, thirty members of the Brandenburg *Küstenjäger* in Greece, together with Abwehr and SD men, were order to Termoli for a 10-week training course.

Training began with acclimatization exercises in the main pool followed by hours of swimming in the Venice lagoon. Besides the energy sapping currents, the muddy seabed was useful for walking exercise wearing lead boots. Finally there were plenty of shipwrecks around for practice attacks.

As members of the K-Verband, frogmen fell within Kriegsmarine jurisdiction. On 21 June 1944 the former K-Verband medical officer, Marinestabsarzt Dr Wandel, was appointed chief of *Lehrkommando 700* at Venice, and he remained in this post until January 1945 when he was replaced by KKpt (V) Hermann Lüdtke. Besides this sea-training camp there were other diving schools at *Lehrkommando 704*

154

Valdagno, north of Verona, and *Lehrkommando 702* Tölz an der Isar, where there was a Waffen-SS training academy. Amongst those attached to *Lehrkommando 700* were training leader Oblt Karl-Josef Küsgen, training officer Alfred von Wurzian, now in the rank of Leutnant zur See, and group leaders LtzS Albert Lindner, Günter Heyden,[1] Rolf Frohus, Rolf Drechsling and Walter Christ.

From November 1944 frogmen were trained at List on Sylt island (*Weisskoppel*). The first training site in Venice was the abandoned monastery of San Giorgio on the small island of Alga. The cloisters were converted to resemble a wounded soldiers' convalescence home. Oberfähnrich Fritz Kind and five men made the place habitable for its true occupants. In February 1945 the unit removed to the lagoon island San Andrea at the entrance to Canal Grande near the church of Santa Maria Salute. From here practice charges were used on the sunken wrecks of the freighter *Tarnpico*, the tanker *Ilivia* and on a steel net.

The *LK 704* Valdagno school in northern Italy was located in a complex of the Manzotti textile factory. It consisted of a sports stadium and swimming hall. The German *Pig Group* led by Otto Lehmann using the improved *Maiale* Type SSB human torpedo was stationed here. The group, which had come from Kappeln, one of the naval sabotage training schools, consisted of five midshipmen, senior NCOs and nine ratings. Lehmann's representative was Oberfähnrich (later LtzS) Wirth.

The *LK 702* diving school at Tölz was founded in the *SS-Junkerschule*, the officer training academy (the later Flint Barracks of US Special Forces) on Sachsenhauserstrasse in the Lettenholz neighbourhood. The barracks had been erected in 1936 and conformed to the most modern technological ideas of the time. It was equipped with a light athletics stadium, football pitch, tennis court, sports and equestrian halls and a 25-metre pool for swimming and highboard diving.[2] Schulze-Kossens, the last German commander of the school, stated that frogman training took place between 2200 and 0600 for security reasons. In his book he spoke expressly of Kriegsmarine men in groups of up to twenty. No instructor of the *Junkerschule* training staff was allowed access to the nightly training sessions.[3]

Volunteers accepted provisionally for frogman training were subjected to physical and intensive psychological suitability tests. Mental

155

fitness, a good voluntary attitude, confidence, firmness of purpose, perseverance and the will to succeed were demanded in order to meet the levels required for acceptance.

The frogman's wardrobe consisted of woollen underwear and a two-part rubber swimsuit with shoes and gloves attached. The overlap of the two parts was covered by a nine-inch wide stomach band. Over the rubber suit the diver wore a canvas protective suit, and the rebreathing apparatus was buckled on over this. The oxygen was good for a four-hour stay submerged using potash cartridges to purge the exhalations of poisonous content.[4] Swim fins, a compass, the water-resistant Junghans watch/compass and a diver's knife completed his equipment. After smearing the face with a black fatty cream and pulling the dark-green camouflage veil over the head he was ready for work.

To maintain body warmth during a long period of cold water immersion, if needed a fur jacket and cotton thermals could be worn over the under-suit. The problems of hypothermia were under urgent consideration in the autumn of 1944. The crews of all descriptions of naval vessels were particularly exposed to cold and very low temperatures, and in September 1944 the Kriegsmarine had begun testing clothing for protection against cold. These were initially trials with Luftwaffe foam suits in which K-Verband volunteers reported good buoyancy in the floating position and a distinctly improved feeling of warmth. A short while later there was a further improvement with the introduction of woollen plush underwear for frogmen.

The history of military diving began in the first half of the 19th century after August Siebe, a German who had emigrated to England in 1837, invented the first closed diving suit. In the Second World War the firms of Siebe Gorman & Co and Dunlop developed new equipment in the form of thin, pliable suits and an underwater oxygen set which released no bubbles.

The frogman's diving technique involved releasing at least a part of the air trapped in his thick underclothing to allow him to sink. For this purpose he would lower himself to the neck in the water and open the neckband of the diving suit a little. The water pressure working against the body forced the air upwards and out of the suit. Enough air would be expelled until only enough buoyancy remained to keep the face above water in the horizontal position. The swimming style

156

involved lying on the back but slightly inclined to one side, keeping the arms inactive and allowing the swim fins to do the work. Once within the enemy's range of vision, the frogman ceased all activity and drifted with the current towards the target, thus moving no faster than debris in the water, so deceiving even an alert sentry. Once the frogman arrived at his objective he placed the mouthpiece of his breathing set in his mouth and operated the small handwheel to open his oxygen bottle before submerging.

Frogman training was generally free of problems and was exercised with the greatest self-discipline. The only major trouble encountered by Dr Wandel was with SS men of Otto Skorzeny's *Jagdstaffel Oranienburg*. Admiral Heye explained later:

> ... The primary cause of this problem was that the SS sent so-called 'probationers' for frogman training. Most of them had been convicted and demoted for various offences committed at the front but could regain their honour by a 'proving act', i.e. by means of an especially dangerous mission. This was kept secret from the Navy and we only found out later after some unsavoury incidents had occurred involving these 'probationers' ...

In the spring of 1944 Sturmbannführer (R) Otto Skorzeny was commander of the newly-formed *Jägerbataillon 502* from which the *Jäger* groups were drawn. His contact with Heye is described in his book[5] thus:

> One day I received the order to pay a call on Vizeadmiral Heye ... I was told that a number of suitable men from my *Jägerbataillon* should take part in his training groups. I soon had a good working relationship and trust in the man. The basic ideas which the Admiral explained to me were convincing and thrilling.

The talk was about various vessels and K-Verband methods. Some of Skorzeny's men were at Anzio as *Neger* pilots. The following extract from his book shows his relationship to the Kriegsmarine:

> The survivors of the Anzio mission were ordered to report to Grossadmiral Dönitz' HQ to receive their deserved decorations.

157

It was a noble gesture by the Admiral that he should invite me to attend this small celebration in person so as to honour the members of my battalion. All Kriegsmarine men involved were then my guests at Friedenthal. It was a happy, drunken gathering of brothers such as only occurs between real old sea-dogs ...

Skorzeny went on thus:

... in Valdagno I took part in the training of the Italian frogmen ... with great merriment these men watched my first attempts with the breathing gear. As I had long been a water rat, I was able to acquit myself decently ...

Whether there were SS frogmen is doubtful. Probably there were men who had joined Skorzeny's units from the Abwehr or the Brandenburgers, or were subordinated to them. Skorzeny wrote:

All the work of *Abwehr Abteilung II* on the fronts (in 1944) was now falling apart ... more important and interesting for me was the fact that men of the Brandenburg Division were volunteering in large numbers for my units. They were all the active type of soldier who no longer felt at home in the mundane frontline and now as before wanted to be at readiness for special missions.

Writing of the operations against the Waal bridges at Nijmegen in September 1944, Skorzeny said:[6]

A common operation by Kriegsmarine frogmen and men made available by ourselves caused a lot of excitement at the time. It was led by Hauptmann Hellmer, an *Abwehr II* officer, who was directly responsible to myself.

The internal power struggles between the Abwehr of Admiral Canaris, later executed for treason, and the SD, now striving for a leading role in the State intelligence apparatus, culminated eventually in a split developing between the Kriegsmarine and SS frogmen units, and in January 1945 Dr Wandel was relieved of command as chief of operations.

In mid-April 1944 the military situation had deteriorated to such an extent that the Venice training camp was placed under the jurisdiction of the local naval commander. On 25 April 1945 the *Lehrkommando 700* installations were destroyed by explosives: on 27 April the last five SSB and SLC manned torpedoes were sunk in the lagoon.

After failing to reach the mainland over the Mestre dam, and skirmishing with partisans, the men of *Pig-Group Lehmann* at Valdagno were brought out aboard lighters in the last German naval convoy. At Trieste they joined the one-man torpedo flotilla stationed at Sistiana 20 kilometres to the north-west and erected a defensive line along the Adriatic coast to resist the advancing New Zealanders. Eventually the Group fell back on Trieste and surrendered on the outskirts of Opicina.

In all, the Kriegsmarine trained about 450 frogmen. The following chapter considers their operations linked with the MEKs, the naval sabotage units.

Notes

1 Post-war Günter Heyden, born 1925, was first chief of the Bundeswehr Frogman Unit and retired in the rank of Fregattenkapitän. See Probst, Wilhelm: *Kampfschwimmer der Bundesmarine*, Motorbuch, 2003.

2 This was one of the most advanced pools in the world. The temperature was kept at 28°C because the SS wounded practised there. This is physiologically the ideal temperature for swimming training, as became generally known in the 1950s and 1960s, the recipe for success preached by US trainer Gambril therefore being nothing new. After the war 3 US Army under General George Patton set up its HQ in the *Junkerschule*. Patton described it as: '... an installation of unique conception, such as I have never seen before, and if I had to plan an HQ for an Army, I would copy this ...' See Schulze-Kossens, Richard: *Militärischer Führernachwuchs der Waffen-SS – Die Junkerschulen*, Nation Europa Verlag, Coburg, 1999.

3 Schulze-Kossens, *ibid.*, p. 156.

4 This was probably the Italian gear or the Dräger dry-suit with breathing mask introduced later. The 1943 Dräger equipment used by frogmen was a closed-circuit rebreathing system safe to 13 metres and good for forty minutes underwater. Military divers other than frogmen used different equipment. Lau, Manfred, *op cit*, and Welham, Michael: *Kampfschwimmer*, Motorbuch, 1996.

5 Skorzeny, Otto: *Wir Kämpften, wir verloren*, Helmut Cramer Verlag, Königswinter, 1973, pp. 10–15 and 34–35.

6 Skorzeny, *ibid.*, pp. 54–57.

Chapter Twelve

The MEKs – Naval Sabotage Units

Development, Training, Structure

As with other light naval units, the MEKs were formed late in the war. As commandos and naval sabotage troops they operated behind enemy lines close to the coast, attacking harbour installations, bridges, ships, supply depots, ammunition dumps and other worthwhile targets.

The idea was never discussed at OKM until 16 September 1943, the motive for the deliberations being the operations by their British counterparts. During the period from February to July 1942, British forces had launched three commando raids of this kind between Boulogne and Le Havre and collected important intelligence on German defences. In the course of these raids a number of enemy personnel had been captured and paperwork confiscated by the Wehrmacht. This led to certain conclusions being drawn regarding the development, structure of commando units and the tactics of their operations. The evaluation laid the foundations for the equivalent German squads (MEKs – Marineeinsatzkommandos).

The first MEK came into being at Heiligenhafen on the Baltic at the end of 1943. The training camp was barracks immediately behind the beach. Later, as the company grew in size, the artillery barracks was used as a training ground. Oblt (MA) Hans-Friedrich Prinzhorn was the first commando leader. In the summer of 1942 he had been a member of an assault squad which crossed the Strait of Kerch in the Crimea to attack Soviet positions on the Kuban Peninsula. Before his move to the K-Verband, Prinzhorn had been an instructor at the Kriegsmarine flak training school. By the end of 1943 the first thirty officers and men of all ranks were installed at Heiligenhafen, and the training lasted into the spring of 1944. It followed the British commando-training manual very closely, a fact to be kept strictly secret. Each man was required to sign a pledge to this effect. There was no leave and it was not permitted to leave the confines of the camp. All civilian contacts had to be broken off.

The instructors were infantrymen and engineers with frontline experience particularly against the Soviets. Training in sniping and explosives handling was made as realistic as possible. Sports, swimming and judo instructors taught methods of unarmed combat and how to overwhelm enemy sentries silently: experts gave instruction in motor vehicles and radio, specialists taught the use of life-saving devices and oxygen breathing gear, linguists passed on their knowledge of the vernacular used by enemy soldiers. Each man had to be an all-rounder. Candidates who flunked the course were returned to their unit without ever having really understood the purpose of what had been taught at Heiligenhafen. After completing training, the successful men were distributed between the various MEKs.

The authorized strength of an MEK was one officer, 22 men and 15 vehicles (3 radio cars, two amphibious and one catering vehicle, the other vehicles being for transport, equipment and ammunition). Rations and ammunition was to be sufficient for six weeks. In January 1944 Kptlt (S) Opladen's men were instructed in their missions and the first three units (MEK 60 – Oblt (MA) Prinzhorn, MEK 65 – Oblt Richard and MEK 71 – Oblt Wolters) transferred to waiting positions in Denmark and France. Subsequently each MEK, depending on its assignment, received an influx of personnel for special missions, e.g. one-man torpedoes, midget submarines, *Linsen* and assault boat pilots, canoeists and frogmen. An MEK might eventually be 150 strong.

MEKs existed before the K-Verband did. They had been set up by the Hamburg Abwehr office, to which they were accountable. These units were: MAREI (Kptlt (S) Opladen) and MARKO (Oblt Broecker). Both units were absorbed into the K-Verband as MEK 20.

As time went on other MEKs were formed. MEK 30 (Kptlt Gegner); MEK 35 (Kptlt Breusch, November 1944–March 1945, Kptlt Wolfgang Woerdemann, March 1945–End); and MEK 40 (Kptlt

Buschkämper, August 1944–March 1945, Oblt Schulz, March 1945–End). This unit was formed at Mommark in Denmark on the island of Alsen (*Gelbkoppel*) with 150 men for special assignments.

Others were:

MEK 70 – nothing known
MEK 75 – KptzS Böhme
MEK 80: Kptlt Dr Krumhaar (March 1944–End)
MEK 85: Oblt Wadenpfuhl (January 1945–End)
MEK 90: Oblt Heinz-Joachim Wilke

There are said to have been other MEKs, e.g. MEK Werschetz and MEK zbV. Leaders of these units may have been Oblt Rudolf Klein, Lts Alexander Spaniel and Wilhelm Pollex amongst others.

The training of MEK men was carried out at a training establishment at Kappeln and Heiligenhafen. Hand-to-hand infantry fighting training was held at Bad Sülze/Rostock, Stolp and Kolberg in Pomerania. Kappeln had the following officer corps:

Commander: KKpt Heinrich Hoffmann

Chief at Staff: Kptlt Erich Dietrich

Adjutant: Lt Günther Schmidt

National Socialist Leadership Officer (after 20.7.1944): Lt Gustav Weinberger

Medical Officer: Kptlt Dr Rudolf Neumann

Company chiefs: Kptlt Friedrich Adler; Oblts Werner Schulz, Hermann Ibach, Eckehard Martienssen, Hans-Günter Beutner; Lt Gerhard Zwinscher

Training Officer: Oblt Hans Diem

At Heiligenhafen the training staff was:

Commander: Kptlt Friedrich Jütz

Camp commandants: Kptlt Heinrich Schütz, Oblt Eberhardt Sauer

Instructors: Oblt Hans-Friedrich Prinzhorn; Lts Erich Kohlberg, Hainz Knaup, Herbert Vargel, Kurt Wagenschieffer, Hermann Baumeister; Oberfähnriche Georg Brink and Anton Ibach.

163

MEK Operations in the West

In June 1944 the Allies at Caen in Normandy succeeding in crossing the Orne and Orne-Sca Canal to the east, and built a bridgehead posing a severe threat to German units. The Allies 'pumped' 10,000 men into this bridgehead. Their supplies were brought up over two intact bridges. Their AA defences were so strong that no attack by the impoverished Luftwaffe stood any chance of success. German engineers were unable to reach the bridges cross-country.

On Thursday 22 June 1944 the Battle for Caen began. It was General Montgomery's intention to encircle Caen by crossing the high land with its dominant landmark Hill 112 south-west of the city and then the River Odon. This important sector was being stubornly defended by 12 SS-Panzer Division *Hitler Jugend* led by SS-Oberführer Kurt 'Panzermeyer' Meyer.[1] The demolition of the strategically important bridges was to be the proving test for MEK 60. Oblt (MA) Prinzhorn was given a platoon of frogmen from Venice. As the result of a road traffic accident, this platoon had been reduced in size from ten men to six. Its leader, LtzS Alfred von Wurzian, had been forbidden to take part in the operation because he was too valuable as an instructor.

The assignment was to destroy two bridges at Benouville which British airborne troops had captured in the early hours of the Invasion. The commandos consisted of two groups of three frogmen: *Group One* – Feldwebel Kurt Kayser, Funkmaat Heinz Brettschneider and Obergefreiter Richard Deimann; *Group Two* – Oberfähnrich Albert Lindner, Fähnrich Ulrich Schulz and a third man whose name has not been remembered.

The operation was scheduled to begin from Franceville at 2300 on the night of 14 August 1944. Each group was to take a torpedo – actually a time bomb package inside a torpedo-shaped container – to a specific bridge. Things started badly and got worse. When the 800 kg torpedoes were let down to the surface of the river on pulleys, they sank at once. No allowance had been made for the changed specific gravity in fresh water. Floats were improvised from empty fuel barrels to salve the torpedoes. The frogmen now entered the water, two to tow, one to steer, a torpedo.

Prinzhorn's group, which was to attack the further bridge over the Orne, passed carefully below the enemy-held first bridge. It was another 12 kilometres to the main bridge, which all believed to be the

164

crucial structure. Here they were to anchor their torpedo to the central pillar. After strenuous effort they attained their objective, moored the torpedo about a metre above the bottom on the central pillar and set the timer. Four hours later they were back at MEK. Too soon, as Prinzhorn was to discover. A revision of the map had brought to light the sorry fact that a third bridge, the real objective, had been omitted. The explosive had been set below the wrong bridge. It detonated punctually at 0530 hrs.

Events were equally dramatic for Lindner's group. Towing the torpedo was sheer torment. Suddenly the third man lost his nerve as they swam past the enemy on the bankside. He could not be convinced to go on and swam to shore. The two midshipmen proceeded with the operation alone. After passing a wooden hindrance designed to intercept drifting mines they reached the first bridge, anchored the torpedo and set off for MEK on foot. When this bridge also blew up at 0530, the British scoured the area for the saboteurs. Once Lindner and Schulz had to hide up in a latrine trench to avoid capture. It was the following evening before they reached the canal, where a weaker current allowed them to swim back. The third man had attempted to make his way back independently, had been shot by the British and died of his wound in captivity.

At the end of August 1944 the Allies had pushed onwards and eastwards. They took Honfleur near Le Havre with its formerly German coastal battery *Bac du Hode* sited on the south bank of the Seine between Honfleur and Trouville. This battery now menaced the German garrison in Le Havre. A Naval artillery assault squad had set out cross-country to retake the battery and had been wiped out in a firefight with the British. MEK 60 now received orders to destroy the battery. After Prinzhorn had been frustrated by engine breakdown in an attempt to cross the Seine aboard an infantry assault boat, he obtained two *Linsen* speedboats from K-Verband. These were fitted with double noise-suppressors and could make eight knots at slow ahead.

On the night of 26 August 1944 the operation began. Aboard the *Linsen* were Prinzhorn, seven MEK men and a naval artillerist who knew the locality well. At 0050 the agreed light signals flashed out from Le Havre, and they paddled their rubber dinghies through a mine-field to land. They came ashore too far west and had to negotiate the beach area on foot. By 0230 they were within 100 metres of the battery. The men slipped past the sentries and got into the bunkers. Hastily they set their explosives on the three heavy guns and in the magazine and fled. Four minutes later the charges exploded and the battery was destroyed.

At the end of August 1944 the German military resistance in France collapsed. Within a few days, fast Allied units had broken through northern France and into Belgium. Antwerp fell after a short battle and would not serve the British as a useful port for supplies. Although Antwerp lay well inland at the eastern end of the Scheldt, it was tidal and this influenced the port operations to a considerable extent. Besides an open harbour the city had a large network of docks. The Kruisschans Lock ensured that the water in the main harbour remained at a constant height. All ships arriving and departing had to pass through it.

MEK 60, now re-located in the Low Countries, was called upon again. Its task this time was to destroy the two principal locks – Kruisschans and Royers. Putting them out of commission would seriously disrupt Allied supply, reducing unloading capacity by five-sixths while it lasted.

After assessing the situation, it was clear that only an attack by frogmen held out any hope for success. The enemy had sealed off the last kilometre of the lock approaches with net barriers. The difficult currents in the Scheldt made it impossible for swimmers to do the whole journey there and back swimming. It was therefore decided to transport the frogmen to the lock entrance aboard *Linsen* boats. Both river banks were held by the enemy, but it was essential that the passage remained undetected. A dark, overcast night, or fog would be best. Moreover a floodtide was needed, the noise made by the engines pitted against the strong ebb would be too great. This would also ensure that the frogmen saboteurs would arrive at the lock gates at high water, enabling them to work below the walkway, beneath the feet of enemy sentries.

To blow up the 35-metre wide lock gate, K-Verband had developed a torpedo-mine. The necessary tonne of underwater explosive was to be carried in an elongated aluminium container the filling of which – mostly ammonia gas – was calculated to ensure that the torpedo mine would float with 30 to 40 grams negative buoyancy just below the surface, where it would be easily manoeuvrable in calm water. Two men would swim towing the torpedo while the third steered it from astern. At the appropriate time the mine would be flooded by opening a pressure valve, sinking to the river bed: a button would start the timer running for the detonator.

The operation began on the night of 15 September 1944. The pilots of the two *Linsen* were Prinzhorn and Oblt Erich Dörpinghaus of K-Flotilla 216. With motors suppressed for noise the boats set off towing the torpedo mines. Visibility was barely 30 metres and both *Linsen* were soon lost to sight in the murk. The boats motored slowly upstream and separated in search of their individual locks. At the ten kilometre mark Dörpinghaus' crew began peering through the gloom and thought they could make out the lock entrance.

While Dörpinghaus moored his *Linse* to a convenient post the three frogmen, Feldwebel Karl Schmidt, Mechanikermaat Hans Greten and Maschinenmaat Rudi Ohrdorf slipped into the water and prepared the torpedo mine. With great effort they swam the last kilometre under-water towing their elongated charge. Suddenly Schmidt's clothing snagged on a submerged object and tore. Now he had to wage a constant battle against buoyancy loss. The first major obstacles they overcame were a net barrier then a steel-mesh net: two more hind-rances and they were at the quay wall. They moved along it until striking their heads against the lock gate, their objective.

They flooded the torpedo mine and accompanied its descent to the bottom, about 18 metres below. After activating the detonator they surfaced and swam off. Returning to the *Linse* Schmidt became so exhausted that he had to be towed by boat hook. Some 75 minutes later they were back with Dörpinghaus. Once the *Linse* set off a motor boat approached them suddenly from the fog. Dörpinghaus put the *Linse* to full ahead and quickly lost sight of the stranger. It was in fact Prinzhorn's boat, his men not having succeeded in finding the Royers lock gate. At 0500 a tremendous explosion shook Antwerp harbour. The lock gate was wrecked and the passage of seagoing vessels had to be suspended for several weeks until the damage had been repaired.

In September 1944 the Allies concentrated on capturing the Dutch towns of Arnhem and Nijmegen by means of strong airborne operations.[2] This was to be the springboard for the Allied advance to the north and west into the heartland of Germany. Whereas at Nijmegen 82 US Airborne Division had taken intact the bridges over the Waal

167

(the main tributary of the Rhine delta), the British 504th Parachute Regiment had run into stiff opposition at Arnhem, and only on the north bank of the Waal had they been able to establish a bridgehead. On the road to Arnhem they were in possession of an area about three kilometres deep, but south of Elst their progress had been stopped by SS panzer units.

In order to destroy the important bridges, men from MEK 60 (Oblt Prinzhorn) and MEK 65 (Oblt Richard) were to form a special operational team to included *Linsen* and frogmen. After a thorough evaluation both officers concurred that 3 tonnes of explosives would be required for each of the mighty bridge pillars. This would need to be brought up in two 1.5-tonne torpedo-mines, each loaded with 600 kg of the special dynamite *Nebolith*. The pillars were over 11 metres tall and almost four metres in diameter. They would have to be forced upwards out of the jambs in which they were embedded, and only two simultaneous, violent explosions on opposite sides of the pillars could provide the necessary turning movement.

Two torpedo mines had to be joined for each tow: at the destination they would be separated and a packet of explosives placed either side of a pillar. Three bridges, one railway and two road bridges, were to be attacked. Two frogmen were sent to reconnoitre the length of the approach. They reported that the current was too strong for swimming in the return direction and they had had to walk back. An Abwehr liaison officer now arrived on the scene. Hauptmann Hummel was also known by the name Helmers and had been active as a commando leader at Valdagno and Venice. He mounted a major reconnaissance with two assault boats from *Jagdkommando Donau* crewed by Lt Schreiber, Bootsmaat Heuse and two junior NCOs, Krämer and Kammhuber. The loud engine noises betrayed them, and in an exchange of fire Heuse was killed. The British were now alerted and set up a floodlight barrier. The bridges were illuminated, the sentries reinforced and searchlight beams roved the region.

It seems probable that Hauptmann Hummel was the Hauptmann Hellmer mentioned in Skorzeny's memoirs who not only led the operations but swam a reconnaissance himself:

The bridgehead extended for about seven kilometres either side of the bridge. The left bank of the Waal was occupied completely

168

by the British. One night Hauptmann Hellmer swam the required reconnaissance alone . . . fortified by good luck, he swam between river banks occupied both sides by the enemy, and then returned to his own men.[3]

On the night of 29 September twelve frogmen entered the Waal about ten kilometres upstream from Nijmegen and began towing the torpedo mines towards the bridges. The first group consisted of the experienced Funkmaat Heinz Brettschneider (MEK 60, Orne bridges operation) and senior privates Olle, Jäger and Walschendorff. The team was almost at the railway bridge, their objective, when they discovered about 200 metres before it a pontoon bridge, complete but for the central section, which was in the process of erection across the breadth of the river. They passed by the sentries unnoticed, and between the pontoon bridge and the railway bridge Brettschneider gave the signal to separate the explosive packets. The lines fore and aft were cut, the only tie being the long line which had to go round the pillar. Once all was set the swimmers set out on the walk back to base. An hour later the mines exploded – but the bridge held.

The two other groups towing four mines towards the road bridges fared no better. These eight men were: Obermaat Orlowski, Boots-mann Ohrdorf, Bootsmann Weber, Feldwebel Schmidt, Steuer-mannsmaat Kolbruch, Obergefreiter Dyck and Gefreiten Gebel and Halwelka. One group drifted into a jetty, drawing the immediate fire of a British sentry. The attempt to link up the mines between the bridge columns failed because of the strong current. One of the men managed to open a valve and so sink the mine which exploded an hour later, blowing a hole of 25 metres diameter in the bridge. Of the twelve frogmen in the three groups only Brettschneider and Jäger reached the German lines at Ochten. The other ten were taken prisoner by the Dutch Resistance who were covering the south bank of the Waal.[4]

This action did not close the Nijmegen chapter. On 15 and 16 October 1944 two *Marder* one-man torpedoes and two *Linsen* set out with six torpedo-mines in tow. This force turned back nine kilometres short of the road bridge on account of technical problems. A second attempt with two operational and one reserve *Linse* on the night of 24 October was also called off after the mines sank one kilometre into the tow and exploded harmlessly five hours later. Subsequently paratroop-engineers made a bold attempt to destroy the road and pontoon bridges. The idea was to use mines to blow a channel through the Waal net barriers after which a float loaded with explosives would be moored to the bridge to blow a hole in the roadway overhead. The attack began on 20 November. Thirty-six mines were set adrift in the water between 1815 and 2000. Echo measuring devices would confirm the explosions in the net and the cable tension. The first operation failed because of a storm, and was repeated with eleven mines. At 0530 the float followed through and at 0657 an explosion occurred. Luftwaffe air reconnaissance photographs showed that a torpedo net had disappeared while large sections of the second and third barriers were no longer visible. The road bridge, though damaged, held however.

Earlier, on 15 November 1944, MEKs 60 and 65 had launched an attack on the Moerdijk Bridge between Dordrecht and Breda. Nothing is known regarding this operation or its outcome. Otto Skorzeny[5] described another frogman operation on the Rhine which did not proceed beyond the planning stage:

After the Invasion succeeded, the concern was expressed at the highest levels of Government that the Allies despised Switzerland's neutrality and might invade Germany from Swiss territory. This idea emerged when the German western front came to a standstill in September 1944. At that time the front ran more or less along the Reich border. On orders from Führer HQ I had to begin preparations for such a contingency within a few days. My frogmen were to be held at readiness on the Upper Rhine in order to destroy the Rhine bridges at Basle the moment Allied troops set foot in Switzerland. This purely defensive measure would help the German leadership gain time to erect a front line opposite Switzerland and parry a future attack from this neutral territory. It was a region which had never been occupied heavily by German troops. A few weeks later the whole scheme was cancelled and the men recalled when it became clear that under no circumstances would the Allies embark on the feared adventure through Switzerland.

On the night of 12 January 1945, MEK 60 put 240 mines into the water at Emmerich, it being hoped that these would do the trick and destroy the bridges at Nijmegen. The mines were to be towed by 17 *Biber* midget submarines, the periscopes of which would be camouflaged as drifting moorhen-nests. Each *Biber* had to tow 272 kgs of explosives which would be cast off below the bridges. The mines were fitted with light-sensitive cells and as soon as the charges were overshadowed by the bridge, the change of light intensity would set off the detonators. The operation was planned by KptzS Troschke. Herr Bartels, master of the ferry *Lena,* which shuttled between Emmerich and Warbeyer, towed the *Biber* out of the harbour every day for their practice runs.

Kptlt Noack, a senior midshipman, a leading seaman and Obergefreiter Josef van Heek sailed the first mission each submerged with eight mines in tow. They failed to reach the bridges. Next evening, Noack, again leading a team of four *Biber*, made a second unsuccessful attempt. On the third occasion eight *Biber* got to within a kilometre of the nearest Nijmegen bridge but tangled in the net barriers. Seven *Biber* stuck fast on the river bed, two of the boats had to be destroyed. Eight of the pilots in the operations froze to death in the ice-cold water. The road bridges at Nijmegen remained standing to the end.

In March 1945 the situation in the West was unpredictable because the front was so fluid. On 9 March K-Verband Command informed OKW that for the purpose of defending the Rhine crossings in the Wesel-Arnhem area, two *Linse*-groups with 24 remote-controlled boats and 100 spherical drifting mines together with an MEK of 80 men was at readiness to destroy the Rhine bridge pillars at Lohmannsheide. For the railway bridge at Remagen, 11 frogmen with 700 kg mines were at their disposal. The Command itself had been hit by fighter-bombers but was still operational. Around 17 March, Lt Wirth's squad of frogmen, who had made their way from Venice with two or three Italian remote-controlled SSB torpedoes, arrived.

Lt Schreiber led the operation, seven frogmen took part. The swimmers had to cover almost 17 kilometres of the Rhine in a temperature of only 7°C. They succeeded in damaging the Ludendorff Bridge so severely that it remained impassable for some time. The operation claimed four dead, two of whom died from hypothermia, and the others were made prisoner. Otto Skorzeny wrote:[6]

On 7 March 1945 a catastrophe occurred on the Western Front. The bridge over the Rhine at Remagen fell intact into the hands

171

of the Americans. One evening I was ordered to Führer HQ at the Reich Chancellery. Generaloberst Jodl gave me orders to send my frogmen to destroy the Rhine bridge at Remagen immediately … the water temperature of the Rhine at this time was only 6 to 8°C and the American bridgehead already extended almost 10 kilometres upstream. I therefore stated that I saw only a small chance of success. I would bring my best men to the locality and leave it to them to decide if we should take the risk. Untersturmführer Schreiber was leader of *Jagdkommando Donau*. He decided to go ahead with this almost hopeless endeavour. It was a few days before we brought the essential torpedo mines from the North Sea coast to the Rhine … when everything was ready, the bridgehead upstream was already 16 kilometres broad. The men swam off into the night: many of them went shivering with the cold. The Americans raked the water surface with searchlights. Soon the group came under fire from the river banks, and some were wounded. The disappointment of the frogmen must have been enormous when, not far short of the objective, they came up to several pontoon bridges which the US Army had erected. Despite that they brought up the explosive charges. Whether despite the cold they were still able to move their fingers only the survivors know, and they are not talking. Half-dead they hauled themselves to the river bank – and into captivity.

On 11 March 1945 FKpt Bartels took over command at Lower Rhine HQ *Lederstrumpf*. A second unit under Kptlt Uhde codenamed *Panther* was responsible for the Rhine-Moselle triangle. Oblt Dörpinghaus' unit received the codename *Puma*. To destroy the Rhine crossings in the Sauerland an additional frogman platoon (one officer, 15 men) and three *Linsen* groups from K-Flotilla 218 with 36 boats had been made available.

On 26 March 1945 Army Group H reported that K-operations had no point having regard to the way in which the situation was developing in the West. *Sonderkommando Puma* was transferred to Aschaffenburg: Dönitz agreed that K-Flotilla 218 should be moved from *Lederstrumpf* to reinforce the defence of the River Ems as far as Groningen. At the request of 12 Army, on 20 April 1945 two

Lederstrumpf groups were transferred to Magdeburg. The frogmen were to operate against the Elbe bridges at Barby using drifting mines and special explosives. Nothing further is known.

With regard to MEK 40 which operated in the West, the only information available is as follows: MEK 40 was 150-strong, trained at *Gelbkoppel* and had been formed for a special assignment at Mommark on the Danish island of Alsen. From August 1944 to March 1945 it was led by Kptlt Buschkämper, and from then until the war's end by Oblt Schulz. At the beginning of November 1944, MEK 40 was in the Scheldt area. From 8 to 12 December it perfomed espionage missions and during reconnaissance on the Drimmen peninsula, Holland Diep, north of Breda, took out a sentry and machine-gun nest. On the night of 22 January 1945, MEK 40 worked with Army units. With artillery support its saboteurs blew up a water tower and brought in prisoners after an operation at Anna Jakoba Polder east of Schouwen Island.

Operations in Hungary

By the end of 1944, Soviet troops in Hungary had reached the Danube. To prevent them crossing the river, Army Group South requested K-Verband for their support to destroy important bridges. As a result, the Kriegsmarine ordered *K-Einsatzstab Adria* to prepare the necessary explosive materials, and to plan and execute the operation. They were also to investigate the possibilities of operations by MEKs in the Apatin-Batina region.

On 1 December 1944, 1 and 3 Groups, MEK 71, reported to Army Group South in Hungary. At Paks, about 100 kilometres south of Buda, the MEK made its first reconnaissance sorties and set mines adrift in the Danube. On 2 December the Army Group made an urgent request for an operational unit with twelve *Linsen*. They were to go immediately to Gran on the Danube and report to *Brükostaffelstab 939*. The military situtation in that area then changed unfavourably with such abruptness that the Wehrmacht plan to operate the unit was cancelled.

Separate from these developments, on 10 December 1944 *Sonderkommando Glatze* led by Kptlt Friedrich Benthin, a *Linse* group for use on Lake Balaton, was set up. An Oblt commanded the Group, Lt Gerhard Weidlich commanded the remote-control team. The title

173

of the operation is not known. Commando operations were given cover-names which – for security reasons – were often changed in the preparation phase. As a rule in the MEKs they were never written down and were known only to those immediately involved. *Sonder-kommando Glatze* was ready to leave from Plön on 15 December 1944.

On 12 December *Einsatzstab Haun* informed SKL that the Army would welcome a *Linse* presence on Lake Balaton but only for its disruptive effect: the boats would find no worthwhile targets for their explosive cargo and were too light to mount artillery. Admiral Heye requested a decision from the Commander-in-Chief as to whether he should send his valuable *Linsen* under these circumstances. Dönitz decided in favour, but Lake Balaton then froze over, and the operation was called off.

A report dated 20 January 1945 states that a group from *Sonder-kommando Glatze* was sent to Dunaföldvar, 100 kilometres south of Budapest, to destroy a bridge in the sector controlled by 4 SS-Panzerkorps. After the Army had demolished a bridge in the vicinity, the Russians had put up an improvised crossing which was now required to be blown up by *Linsen*. What came of this intention is not recorded.

In February 1944 a *Linse* group was sent to Zagreb in Croatia to destroy a Soviet pontoon bridge about 30 to 40 kilometres south of the city. The attempt failed because boats and crews were diverted for other purposes. More successful was an operation in Hungary in which two Danube bridges were blown at Budapest, while on 29 March 1945 the Wehrmacht communique reported the sinking of four river-ships by *Linsen* at Neusatz on the Danube.

Operations in Southern France, Italy and the Adriatic
In the sectors of Wehrmacht C-in-C South and Admiralty Staff South the principal naval sabotage units operational were MEKs 20, 71 and 90. These were directed by the operational staff of KptzS Werner Hartmann whose HQ was at Levicio, about 100 kilometres north-west of Padua. On 7 October 1944 the boundaries of jurisdiction and German Naval Command Italy were changed, and KKpt Haun with Staff HQ at Opicina, a suburb of Trieste, became responsible for K-Verband in the Adriatic.

Despite Italy's capitulation in 1943, elements of the X-MAS Flotilla fought on the German side to the war's end. After Prince Borghese had relinquished command of the *Decima*, in 1944 his flotilla splintered into several independent groups, some of which sided with the partisans. K-Verband Command brought those remaining loyal to Germany into a special fighting unit under its K-Verband control. Because it had distinguished itself in anti-partisan warfare, Reichsführer-SS Heinrich Himmler wanted to equip the unit with radio and integrate it into the German network, but Naval Command Italy and Dönitz were both opposed to the idea.

K-Verband units in the Adriatic operated mainly from Pola against the British, New Zealanders and Tito-partisans occupying the Dalmatian islands. These were almost exclusively sabotage raids, either made independently or under the protection of German S-boats. About MEK 20, which originated from the Abwehr, very little is known. In the summer of 1944 it was at Cavallo in Italy, and in September at Sibenick and Split in Yugoslavia. Subsequently it was withdrawn from the Dalmatian islands. MEK 90 under Kptlt Jütz fought at Dubrovnic in Yugoslavia in September 1944 and escaped from the encirclement of the city. On 27 October it arrived at Metkovic with four dead, two wounded and no vehicles. Subsequently the unit left Trieste and made its way back via Zagreb and Vienna to Lübeck *Steinkoppel*.

MEK 71 was *en route* from Germany to Italy when it received orders to engage the Maquis in southern France. On 9–10 August 1944 MEK 71 captured two large French Resistance camps near Aix without loss to itself and made safe large quantities of materials. The unit then proceeded as planned to La Spezia, the most important naval base. After the Badoglio capitulation, the Italian Navy had scuttled there the submarines UIT-15 (ex-*Sparide*), UIT-16 (ex-*Murena*), UIT-20 (ex-*Grongo*) and some Type CB midget submarines. MEK considered that the boats could be raised and towed to Genoa. On 4 and 6 September all were destroyed in an RAF air raid. Whether CB midget submarines were ever used by the German side is not known.

On 1 October, MEK 71 was ordered to transfer to the Adriatic 75 men with full equipment and five *Linsen* for operations against the Dalmatian islands. Early in October 1944 groups of eight to ten men exercised at Monfalcone in the Adriatic. On 20 October MEK 71 moved up to Trieste, and on 24 October the Abwehr's 5 Marine-kommando from *Lehrkommando 700* frogman unit at Venice arrived at Haun's operations HQ Opicina to scout the islands of Clib, Silba and Premnuda to prepare reports for possible MEK operations. Fishing boats and canoes were to be used.

Leader of operations was Oblt Ross, the Group was headed by Feldwebel Mitschke. His first objectives were Komica Bay and Lissa on 17 October. A boat from 24 S-boat Flotilla was to carry the group from Pola to Sibenik from where on the second night they would attack the harbour. The men would enter in folding boats and attach explosives to destroyers, MTBs and freighters. They were to be brought out by S-boats, if this was not possible they were to paddle to Cape Plocca. The operation was called off because of winter storm Bora.

On 27 October Oblt Wolter arrived at Trieste with MEK 71. On the way he had tangled with partisans and had nine wounded plus two damaged *Linsen*. A section of his force left at once for Lussin, and Group Mitschke came under Wolter's command. On 31 October Mitschke began scouting with a platoon of five. On the night of 20 November at Sibenik he found no large ships or military targets of importance. After blowing up the Gruzzo light tower he returned to base.

On 9 January 1945 naval saboteurs of MEK 71 were taken by S-boats to the Dalmatian and east Italian coast. At Zadar they sank two freighters and on the Italian Adriatic coast demolished three bridges.[7]

At the beginning of December 1944 Kptlt Frenzel, a former U-boat commander, was appointed head of MEK Adriatic. Group commander Oblt Hering,[8] a German born in Italy, had 48 men at his disposal. On the night of 16 December MEK men blew up a light-house and harbour installations on the island of Metada. Between 8 and 10 January 1945 the men of *Kommando Hering* attacked bridges and roads in the Tenna estuary area on the Italian coast south of Ancona. S-33, S-58, S-60 and S-61 of 1 S-boat Division transported the men there.

The first group, Lt Kruse and Bootsmaat Sterzer, went ashore at Tenna from folding boats. They had orders to create havoc in the MTB base and blow up the bridge at the entrance to the Fermo ammunition factory. The other assault groups, each of four men, were to demolish the railway/road bridge over the Tenna and so halt Allied shipping along the Adriatic coast.

The second group (Obermaat Gericke) reached the railway bridge and goods yard at Porto San Elpidio. Oblt Hering and a midshipman, Stille, set the charges inside a bridge room. At 0245 all men were aboard S-boats for the return less two taken prisoner near Tolentino. Violent explosions were heard from the bridges, and an ammunition train erupted.

In another attack, 18 paired charges caused nine explosions on the base at Isto Island. Two tonnes of provisions were seized, a British officer and 20 men occupying the island were taken off by British MGB. In another raid at Zara, two coasters in the harbour were reported blown up. At Ruc Como, about 40 kilometres north-east of Milan, *Sonderkommando Zander* under Kptlt Nikolaus von Martiny was active, but active in what is unknown.

Operations on the Eastern Front

From November 1944 when the Red Army was already in East Prussia, naval sabotage units were used on the Eastern Front with increasing frequency. The swift Soviet advance was aided by numerous bridges and other facilities over and near inland waterways. These now became the target of K-Verband saboteurs. The MEKs could not halt the Soviets, but they could at least seriously disrupt their lines of supply. Frogmen and *Linsen* had been on the Eastern Front previously, at the Baranov bridgehead, on the Peipus and in the Baltic.

A few weeks before the capitulation, in March 1945 K-Verband Command fitted out a schooner as a Q-ship for Russian submarines operating between Windau and Memel and the tongue of land known as the Kurische Nehrung. For this purpose the schooner had explosives aboard with which the attacks were to be made. This interesting operation, *Steinbock*, was not proceeded with.

In early December 1944, Army Group A requested from SKL naval K-forces to destroy the bridges over the Vistula. The major Soviet breakout from the three Vistula bridgeheads was impending, speed was of the essence. K-Verband Command formed six operational groups with a total of 84 *Linsen* for Operation *Lucie,* but on 17 December when the Vistula froze over in a sudden cold snap, the planned operations became doubtful, and when the thickness of the ice was found to have increased on the 21st of the month *Sondergruppe Lucie* was stood down, the 84 *Linsen* were moved back to Fedderwardsiel and then onwards to help out in the west.

On 12 March 1945 MEK 85, formed in January that year under Oblt Wadenpfuhl with 90 men, was fully motorized and sent to Swinemünde to operate in the lower reaches of the Oder and Oderhaff. Suitable craft such as cutters, motor boats and canoes were pressed into service. In charge of the operation was Kptlt Meissner.

Besides MEK 85, *Sonderkommando Rübezahl* and *Kampfschwimmer-gruppe Ost* were stationed along the Oder. The latter frogman unit had been with *Lehrkommando 700* at Venice in the previous autumn and transferred to List on Sylt, moving to the Eastern front in February 1945 via Berlin at the request of the OKW and Reichsführer-SS. In February the 16-strong platoon led by Lt Fred Keller transferred to the Oder river near Fürstenberg. In the first operation on the 25th of the month the group towed two torpedo-mines to the Soviet supply bridge for the Vogelsang bridgehead near the small village about two kilometres north-east of modern Eisenhüttenstadt. The attempt failed because the strong current forced the torpedoes against the river bank. On 13 March 1945 the bridge was destroyed by two *Linsen*.

On 1 March 1945 Admiral Heye reported that explosive charges placed around the pillars of the Oder bridge at Aurith had failed to detonate. It was hoped that a back-up detonator on a 24-hour timer would work. The frogman team returned. The same day the attempt to demolish an Oder bridge at Küstrin also failed when the explosive charge, a so-called 'tree trunk packet' drifted away from the bridge and exploded at the bankside.[9]

On 5 March, OKW informed Admiral Heye that Hitler had given Luftwaffe Oberstleutnant Baumbacher orders to lead the attack on all Soviet crossing points over the Oder and Neisse rivers. All Wehrmacht arms of service were to place at his disposal all appropriate means to execute his assignment. It is assumed that he was to coordinate the Luftwaffe attacks.

On 7 March *Sondergruppe Rübezahl* attacked two Oder bridges. The bridge at Kalenzig was destroyed over fifty metres of its length, the ground supports and lower structure of the bridge at Rebus were ruined over thirty metres of its length so that the bridge was rendered unusable.

178

On the night of 13 March *Linsen* attacked the Oder bridge at Zellin. In order to cover the engine noise, four Ju 88s circled the operational zone. The air reconnaissance photographs taken later that day showed that the bridge had been demolished over 270 metres of its length. The Soviets then rebuilt it, together with a pontoon bridge. On 16 April Luftwaffe suicide pilots attacked the crossings at Zellin. Fähnrich Beichl dived his Fw190 filled with high explosive and carrying a 500 kg bomb into the bridge and destroyed it. The 40-strong Luftwaffe *Sondergruppe* destroyed in all seventeen Oder bridges between 16 and 17 April 1945.[10]

In the latter part of April 1945 the Soviet armies broke out of the Oder bridgeheads. On the evening of 24 April, Lt Keller reconnoitred the small island of Dievenow near Wollin which was still in German hands. After discussions with the island commandant the frogmen entered the water and drifted with their torpedo mines to the bridge linking the island to the Soviet-occupied mainland. Ashore they primed their charges. At 0417 hrs on 25 April 1945 the bridge was no more.

That same 24 April, Lt Albert Lindner (*Lehrkommando 700* and the Orne bridges attack) led his naval saboteurs and three frogmen to destroy the pontoon bridges at Nipperwiese and Fiddichow. Two men were to blow up four pontoons from under the bridge. For this purpose they were equipped with small 7.5 kg explosive packs called *Sprengfische*. They set out from the infantry trenches at Oderdamm, southeast of Schwedt. The frogmen were discovered by a sentry, a Russian grenade hit one of the *Sprengfische* which exploded at once leaving several dead and wounded. The operation was repeated the following evening and succeeded. At 0500 explosive charges ripped the pontoon bridge apart, but the four frogmen involved finished up as Soviet prisoners of war.

The last frogman operation on the Eastern Front was at Stettin. On the night of 25 April 1945 the last German troops evacuated the city. Only a section of the harbour remained in German hands. The Soviets held the high ground at Altdamm, on the far bank of the eastern arm of the Oder, and were firing into the city. They had infiltrated the harbour at a number of places. While setting a torpedo mine on a bridge pillar, Bootsmaat Künnicke was fired upon by a sentry. The mine drifted away and was lost. As it was already dawn, Künnicke hid in a barn and

179

rejoined his unit next day. Two other frogmen who were Stettiners laid low in a swampy meadow between the east and west arms of the Oder while the Red Army rolled past them. The hiding place was on the bank of the Möllnfahrt, the Stettin regatta course. The pair had obtained for themselves a fine motor boat, *Aristides*, in which they were proposing to transport their torpedo mines. In their hiding place on 8 May they heard explosions and shooting. On 11 May, after selecting an Oder bridge as their target, they met a German civilian who gave them the news that the war was over. The two frogmen hid their equipment and obtained civilian clothing, then joined local people clearing the streets of rubble. Unfortunately they did not escape the attention of the Russians, and a long and arduous captivity followed.

Notes

1 See Krätschmer, Ernst Günther: *Die Ritterkreuzträger der Waffen-SS*, Nation Europa Verlag, Coburg, 1999.

2 See particularly Kershaw, Robert J.: *Arnhem 1944*, Motorbuch, 2000.

3 Skorzeny, *op cit*, p. 55f. Hauptmann Friedrich Hummel alias Hellmer or Helmers (b. 8 February 1910, d. 1993) had a very varied life. Between 1929–1933 he sailed as an officer-apprentice aboard the full-rigger *Passat* to Chile, South Africa, Japan and China. Afterwards he studied law and entered the Hamburg Altona detective force in 1937. He rose to be Commissioner of Police at Detective HQ Hamburg and in 1942 was appointed to the SD in the rank of SS-Hauptsturmführer. Earlier, conscripted in the Army, he had served at the front in the Polish campaign and was promoted to Leutnant (R) on 1 November 1939, to Oberleutnant (R) on 1.2.1943 and to Major (R) in October 1944. His work as Group Leader of Abwehr Abt. II in Madrid (November 1942–August 1944) brought him to the frogman training facility in Italy where he was given a leading role as instructor and was later involved in operations. After the Allied landings in Normandy he led a frogman team at Caen. He was credited with sinking 50,000 tons of Allied shipping off southern Spain for which he was decorated with the Knight's Cross on 19 October 1944. It is also reported that he took part in commando operations against railway lines in Algeria disguised in local costume. Between 1 September 1944 and 7 May 1945 he commanded Front Reconnaissance II West. After the war he returned to the police, his last office being as senior court adviser on criminal law affairs at Flensburg.

4 Other sources state that the railway bridge was destroyed and a road bridge seriously damaged. Of the frogmen five were said to have returned safely, five were killed and two taken prisoner. Welham: *Kampfschwimmer*, p. 52.

5 Skorzeny, *op cit*, p. 57.

6 Skorzeny, *op cit*, p. 195f.

7 Hans Frank: *Die deutschen Schnellboote im Einsatz*, Mitler Verlag, 2006, p. 124.

8 For Hering's adventurous life see Lau, Manfred, *op cit*.

9 This bridge was destroyed by a Luftwaffe suicide pilot on 17 April 1945.

10 Saft, Ulrich: *Das bittere Ende der Luftwaffe*, Verlag Saft, Langenhagen, 1992.

Epilogue

In Admiral Canaris' military Abwehr, Amt Ausland/Abwehr, there existed diverse projects for overseas command operations which were coordinated with the *Küstenjäger* of Brandenburg Division and later with K-Verband Command. These were operations with something of the fantasy about them and therefore nothing came of them. One of the ideas was to transport frogmen by U-boat to New York where they would infiltrate the harbour and attach explosive charges to ships at anchor. Improbable? Agents were certainly landed along that coast by U-boat. Another idea was for saboteurs to blow up the overflow weir of the Panama Canal, thus putting it out of action for years.[1] Another idea was for *Biber* midget submarines to be taken by a BV flying boat to the Suez Canal to sink merchant shipping in the narrowest part and so block the access channel. In the footsteps of Günther Prien, commander of U-47, *Linse* explosive boats were to attack warships at Scapa Flow, a spectacular operation lacking strategic importance once capital ships had become less significant in the latter phase of the war. The *Linsen* would have been carried to the attack zone by Gotha 242 heavy gliders.

Following the Normandy Invasion, in collaboration with the Anglo-Iranian Oil Company, the Royal Navy and British steel industry had laid the so-called Pipeline under the Ocean (PLUTO) on the sea bed of the English Channel. Through two pipes 7.5 cms in diameter flowed 250 tonnes of fuel daily. The first preparations for this pipeline had been taken in hand in 1942. A multitude of technical problems caused by water pressure and the tides had had to be overcome. The pipeline,

183

90 kilometres long, was laid between the Isle of Wight and Cherbourg, and had been put down shortly after the landings of 6 June. K-Verband Command considered the possibility of using frogmen to destroy the pipeline using the underwater explosive *Nipolit*. A variation on the theme was to bore holes in the pipe to pump in chemical contaminants. Technical difficulties and fluid frontlines put an end to these schemes.

In 1943, the Abwehr planned Operation *Reisernte* to land agents and saboteurs on the coast of South America. They were looking for two two-masters of 150 to 200 gross tons each with good sailing qualities to mount an auxiliary motor of 100–150 hp. Crew would be the master and six hands. Passengers would be one officer and twelve men of a naval sabotage unit, presumably an MEK.

Two KFKs under construction at Burmester Werft Swinemünde were selected. After completion Bootswerft Eckmann of Hamburg Finkenwerder converted them to high seas sailing vessels with ketch rig. The boats were numbered KFK 203 and KFK 204 (thus duplicating the numbers of the escort KFKs of *Seehund-Lehrkommando 300* at Neustadt/Holstein).

The idea for the operation originated from LtzS (S) Christian Nissen, a merchant marine officer seconded to the Kriegsmarine and who held a master's certificate in sail. He had already made voyages to South Africa and South America to land Abwehr agents.[2]

In November 1944, Kptlt (S) Michael Opladen,[3] who had previously headed the MEK unit MAREI taken over by the K-Verband and incorporated into MEK 20, and instructed pilots in the one-man torpedo, received the plan and at the end of 1944 sent KFK 203 under LtzS (S) Nissen from Flensburg to Harstad in Norway. From this point onwards little more is known about the operation. On 13 February 1945, KFK 203 left Harstad under sail disguised as a Norwegian trawler. She carried provisions for a year.

If this voyage actually continued and to where KFK 203 was bound is unknown. Some weeks later a German naval station took down a short signal according to which the ketch was off West Africa and heading for the Persian Gulf and the Indian Ocean. This may have been disinformation. Nissen survived the war and rejoined the merchant marine as a master in sail. Whether he ever spoke out about this operation or left a memoir cannot be determined. The traces of KFK 203 are gone.

184

Notes

1 In 1942 the Luftwaffe had developed similar plans to destroy the Suez Canal locks using glider-borne troops and explosives. Lommel, Horst: *Geheimprojekte der DFS, 1935–1945*, Motorbuch, 2000.

2 See Chapters *Die Geistersegler der Abwehr* in Kurowski, Franz: *Deutsche Kommandotrupps 1939–1945 – Brandenburger und Abwehr im weltweiten Einsatz*, Motorbuch, 2003.

3 There is no trace of a Michael Opladen in Wehrmacht records.

Appendix

K-Verband Probationer and Operational Badges and Clasps

On 30 November 1944, the Commander-in Chief, Kriegsmarine, Grossadmiral Dönitz instituted the Probationer and Operational Badge for members of the K-Verband. Paragraph 1 of the introductory certificate states: 'In recognition of the skilful and successful attacks carried out by the K-Verband, I institute for the men of K-Verband Command probationer and operational service badges in the following form:

(a) Probationer's badge: swordfish within a circular border
(b) Service badges:

    1 Grade: swordfish inside decorative cordwork
    2 Grade: swordfish inside decorative cordwork with one sword
    3 Grade: swordfish inside decorative cordwork with two swords
    4 Grade: swordfish inside decorative cordwork with three swords
    5 Grade: Bronze clasp, swordfish inside decorative cordwork
    6 Grade: Silver clasp, swordfish inside decorative cordwork
    7 Grade: Gold clasp, swordfish inside decorative cordwork

Badges up to and including 4 Grade are to be worn on the right upper arm below the sleeve stitching on the shoulder, the clasps at the corresponding height above the medal ribbons.

Conditions Attaching to the Award (Para 11)

II Special Conditions

1   The Probationer's Badge (swordfish within circular border) is to be awarded to men of the K-Verband who volunteered for the unit, or were detached to the unit for special operations and who have completed training and probation in training ...

2   Service Badge
    (a) 1 Grade (swordfish in decorative cordwork) will be awarded to men who have proved themselves on operations, in the preparation therefor and in special trials ...
    (b) 2–4 Grade (swordfish in decorative cordwork with one, two or three swords) will be awarded after participation in an independent or command operation on land or at sea and have proven thereby ...
    (c) 5–7 Grade (bronze, silver or gold clasp). The bronze clasp will be awarded for the fourth major independent or commando operation on land or at sea, the silver clasp after the seventh such operation and the gold clasp after the tenth operation.

For especially outstanding achievements, but only for an independent operation, the clasp can be awarded earlier.'

It is known that Grades 1 to 4 were awarded, whether anybody received a clasp is not known.